THE ANATOMY OF LAUGHTER

LEGENDA

LEGENDA, founded in 1995 by the European Humanities Research Centre of the University of Oxford, is now a joint imprint of the Modern Humanities Research Association and Routledge. Titles range from medieval texts to contemporary cinema and form a widely comparative view of the modern humanities, including works on Arabic, Catalan, English, French, German, Greek, Italian, Portuguese, Russian, Spanish, and Yiddish literature. An Editorial Board of distinguished academic specialists works in collaboration with leading scholarly bodies such as the Society for French Studies and the British Comparative Literature Association.

MHRA

The Modern Humanities Research Association (MHRA) encourages and promotes advanced study and research in the field of the modern humanities, especially modern European languages and literature, including English, and also cinema. It also aims to break down the barriers between scholars working in different disciplines and to maintain the unity of humanistic scholarship in the face of increasing specialization. The Association fulfils this purpose primarily through the publication of journals, bibliographies, monographs and other aids to research.

Routledge
Taylor & Francis Group
LONDON AND NEW YORK

Routledge is a global publisher of academic books, journals and online resources in the humanities and social sciences. Founded in 1836, it has published many of the greatest thinkers and scholars of the last hundred years, including Adorno, Einstein, Russell, Popper, Wittgenstein, Jung, Bohm, Hayek, McLuhan, Marcuse and Sartre. Today Routledge is one of the world's leading academic publishers in the Humanities and Social Sciences. It publishes thousands of books and journals each year, serving scholars, instructors, and professional communities worldwide.

www.routledge.com

EDITH MCMORRAN (1936–2003)

The Anatomy of Laughter

❖

EDITED BY

TOBY GARFITT, EDITH MCMORRAN, AND JANE TAYLOR

Routledge
Taylor & Francis Group

LONDON AND NEW YORK

2005

First published 2005 by Modern Humanities Research Association and Routledge

2 Park Square, Milton Park, Abingdon, Oxfordshire OX14 4RN
52 Vanderbilt Avenue, New York, NY 10017

Routledge is an imprint of the Taylor & Francis Group, an informa business

First issued in paperback 2020

ISBN 13: 978-1-900755-72-6 (hbk)
ISBN 13: 978-0-367-60525-4 (pbk)

Copy-Editor: Michael Wood

CONTENTS

PREFACE

Il faut rire avant que d'être heureux,
de peur de mourir sans avoir ri.

LA BRUYÈRE, 'Du Cœur'

The present volume consists of a selection of the papers given at a major conference, *The Anatomy of Laughter/Traduire le Rire*, organized by Edith Franck McMorran at St Hugh's College, Oxford, in September 2001, under the auspices of TRIO (Translation Research in Oxford), the organization she had founded and nourished. Until 2001 TRIO had concentrated very largely on approaches to translation; this new venture was not only interdisciplinary, but highly ambitious, in that Edith wished to incorporate not just the humanities, but also the sciences, into the proceedings. So it was that physicists and psychoanalysts and philosophers and sociologists and translators spent a long weekend together in Oxford, invited by Edith and entertained by her, as ever, royally — and hilariously.

Edith did not live to see the publication of this volume, so very much the product of her energy and drive. But she would, we know, have wished to thank those who contributed to the success of the conference: Elizabeth Mansour who, as ever, made sure that the administrative side ran smoothly; the Organizing Committee — Jerome Fletcher (Dartington College of Arts), Anita Mehta (S. N. Bose National Centre for Basic Sciences, Calcutta), Jean-Michel Déprats (Paris X, Nanterre), Marie-Claire Pasquier (Paris X, Nanterre), and Aline Schulman (Paris III); Professor Malcolm Bowie, who welcomed the delegates to Oxford on behalf of the European Humanities Research Centre; the Maison Française in Oxford; the British Academy, who offered a generous subsidy towards the running of the conference; the Faculty of Medieval and Modern Languages in Oxford; the Crédit Agricole Indosuez, for their generous financial support. She would also, we know, have wanted to thank all those who attended the conference and who gave papers; we, as editors, would much have wished to publish all of them, but publication constrained us to make heart-rending choices.

The editors of the volume would also like to thank our delightfully prompt and cooperative contributors; Martin McLaughlin, Kareni Bannister, Graham Nelson, and Michael Wood, of Legenda, for all the work that has gone into the publication of this volume; and Linda Gowans, for her usual careful work in copy-editing it. We hope that the result is a volume that is worthy of Edith's own vision.

T.G.
J.H.M.T

EDITH FRANCK MCMORRAN (1936–2003)

No one who met Edith will forget her: that rather stylish, bird-like figure, that warmth and enthusiasm, that intelligent engagement with everything and everyone — art, music, literature, language, her students ... above all, her legion of friends and soon-to-be-friends. Edith's great gift, perhaps, was friendship, and if TRIO — 'Translation Research in Oxford', the organization she devised, worked for, and inspired — was such a success, it was because Edith, in pursuit of friendship and conversation, was irresistible.

Her passion was words. Her range was unusual: having gained the *Diplôme d'études supérieures* at the Sorbonne for a thesis on T. S. Eliot and Baudelaire, she was to be awarded an Oxford B.Litt. for a thesis on, of all people, Drieu la Rochelle. She had taught French everywhere, from the Lycée La Fontaine to Blackbird Leys Primary School, from Hong Kong to Kyoto to the Oxford where she was to make her home for nearly forty years. She translated everything, from tracts by an Under-Secretary-General of the United Nations, to the text for a volume on Chinese art. She taught her students, at St Hugh's especially but also at Pembroke, at St Anne's, at Worcester — all over Oxford, in fact — and devotedly, everything from Voltaire to Sartre to Baudelaire. And for Oxford, for St Hugh's, for the wider world of translators, she devised TRIO.

It stemmed from a very successful conference at the Maison Française in Oxford in 1992. Edith (and it is a considerable tribute to her determination, her charm and her range of contacts) had persuaded a group of very distinguished scholars, writers, and translators — David Bellos, Jean-Michel Déprats, John Wain, Barbara Wright, Theodore Zeldin — to come to Oxford to talk around the topic 'Traduire dans le temps, traduire dans l'espace'.[1] I remember a long conversation with Edith soon after that, when she raised the possibility of building on the conference by setting up a centre in Oxford that would be devoted to translation and would, as the conference had done, bring together professional translators and academics. I'm afraid I was a bit sceptical: good idea, I thought, but it's not going to work ... I was quite wrong. For the next ten years or so, Edith charmed and cajoled and programmed and inspired; and three times a year, in pursuit of all sorts of subjects — theatre and nonsense, psychoanalysis and dialects, Yves Bonnefoy and Mallarmé — translators and academics made their way to her Oxford colloquia, and spoke and translated ... and were royally, warmly entertained. For Edith regarded it as her role not merely to orchestrate, but to see to everyone's creature comforts, and nearly every meeting of TRIO saw her gather the speakers together at her house in Botley and feed them on good food and very nice wines. Those evenings were the essence of TRIO, and we shall undoubtedly remember Edith bustling around her kitchen, bringing out a huge dish of *pommes de terre dauphinoises*, or an excellent, ripe Brie, or a very French gâteau.

TRIO, surely, should survive Edith: it was, and is, an ornament to Oxford, something that the Faculty of Medieval and Modern Languages trumpeted to funding bodies, something that St Hugh's College was proud to house. Sadly, though, some of the heart will have gone out of it: Edith's commitment, the warmth she brought to it, are, we have to accept, irreplaceable.

Jane Taylor

1. Many of the contributions were later published in a volume edited by Edith and others: *Translation Here and There, Now and Then* (Exeter: Elm Bank Publications, 1996).

LIST OF CONTRIBUTORS

Laurent Bazin is in charge of 'action culturelle' at the Ministère de l'Education nationale, de l'enseignement supérieur et de la recherche, Paris.

Dominique Bertrand is Professor at the Université Blaise Pascal, Clermont Ferrand, France.

Sarah-Jayne Blakemore is a Royal Society Dorothy Hodgkin Research Fellow at the Institute of Cognitive Neuroscience at University College, London.

Sukanta Chaudhuri is Professor of English at Jadavpur University, Calcutta.

Ted Cohen is Professor in Philosophy at the University of Chicago.

Christie Davies is Professor of Sociology at the University of Reading.

Jean-Michel Déprats is Professor at the University of Paris X Nanterre, and a distinguished translator, notably of Shakespeare.

Iain Galbraith is a poet, translator, and prolific contributor to literary and cultural journals in the UK and abroad.

Toby Garfitt is Fellow in French at Magdalen College, Oxford.

Michael Holland is Fellow in French at St Hugh's College, Oxford.

Silke Kipper is a research fellow at the Institut für Biologie: Verhaltensbiologie, Freie Universität, Berlin.

Giselinde Kuipers is a research fellow in the Department of Arts and Culture at Erasmus University, Rotterdam.

Edith Franck McMorran, until her death in 2003, was Lecturer in French at St Hugh's College, Oxford.

Paul J. Memmi is a prolific translator/dubber for the cinema. He teaches on the specialized translation course at the University of Paris X Nanterre.

Adam Phillips is a psychoanalyst and author. He is General Editor of the new Penguin Modern Classics Freud translations.

Walter Redfern is Emeritus Professor of French at the University of Reading.

Georges Roque is Directeur de recherche at the Centre national de la recherche scientifique (CNRS), Paris. He is also attached to the Centre de recherches sur les arts et le langage (CRAL) at the Ecole des hautes études en sciences sociales, Paris.

Jane Taylor is Professor of Modern Languages at the University of Durham.

Natacha Thiéry teaches cinema at the University of Paris III Sorbonne Nouvelle.

Dietmar Todt is Professor at the Freie Universität, Berlin.

Gérard Toulouse is Professor at the Laboratoire de physique de l'Ecole normale supérieure, Paris.

INTRODUCTION

Jane Taylor

The great monastic library in Umberto Eco's *The Name of the Rose*[1] possesses, among a multiplicity of other treasures, a precious and extraordinary relic: the only surviving copy of Aristotle's treatise on comedy. But to Brother Jorge, the librarian, this is an inheritance no human hand should touch: laughter is dangerous, subversive, distracting, contemptible — unchristian. As a librarian, of course, he cannot bear to destroy the manuscript; but, lest anyone should read it and make it public, he has saturated each leaf in a deadly poison. When Eco's monk–detective hero, Brother William of Baskerville, finally understands what the librarian has been concealing, Jorge cannot tolerate the idea that anyone should read the manuscript and live; he tears it up leaf by leaf and stuffs the pages down his throat. He dies, ironically enough, laughing maniacally, and the great library, the work of centuries of humane scholarship, burns around him.

Aristotle's economical, confident declaration that 'no animal laughs save Man'[2] reverberates down the centuries through all that is written on laughter. But Aristotle himself is ambivalent on the subject: comedians, he says — and does not seem particularly to deprecate the fact — 'wandered from village to village ... being excluded contemptuously from the city'.[3] Following him, for moralists and theologians, writers of books of etiquette, sociologists, anthropologists, and psychoanalysts, laughter has remained a source of faint puzzlement and persistent disquiet. What are we to make of the curious facial contortions, the odd strangulated coughings and splutterings, the whoops and squeals that constitute 'laughter'? And of the fact that laughter is so alarmingly contagious? Ought we to be alarmed by displays that suggest such a disturbing lack of self-control, such surrender to the body? Or ought we to embrace the energy of laughter as therapeutic? Totalitarian states and authoritarian individuals have always, with good cause, been wary of laughter; arbiters of taste and social decorum have feared it may be vulgar and ill-bred.[4] And what about 'humour' as distinct from laughter proper? In the sense of 'comic', it is first attested, surprisingly, in 1682; previously, it had been used in the specifically medical sense to mean mental disposition.[5] The *Dictionnaire de l'Académie française* considers not merely the word but the phenomenon itself to be an English import,[6] as does Lessing in Germany.[7] But is humour really a culturally determined phenomenon? Or is it transhistorical? Transcultural? Can it be transposed? Translated? The French thinker Paul Valéry is pessimistic: 'Humour is untranslatable. If this was not the case, then the French would not use the word'.[8] But Shylock at least seems to think laughter an index of the humanity he shares with his Christian tormentors and which they refuse him: 'When you tickle us, do we not laugh?' Laughter, in other words, is, and remains, problematic: familiar and everyday, but dismayingly resistant to definitions.

It is no surprise, in these conditions, to find that for centuries scholars, scientists, and philosophers have engaged enthusiastically in the quixotic quest to define humour, and to pin down the spectacular irreverence of laughter. First, to try to understand the causes of laughter and what functions it might serve, biologically, psychologically, anthropologically, aesthetically, and so on. Secondly, quite simply to understand what happens physiologically to provoke the movements and sounds that define laughter — from Wyndham Lewis and his blithe contention that laughter is 'the mind sneezing',[9] to the painstakingly empirical René Descartes: 'Laughter consists in this: [1] blood coming from the right cavity of the heart through the arterial vein, suddenly and repeatedly swelling the lungs, compels the air they contain to come out forcefully through the windpipe, where it forms an inarticulate and explosive cry; and [2] the lungs as they swell and this air as it emerges each push against all the muscles of the diaphragm, chest, and throat, and thereby make the ones in the face that have some connection with them move. And what we call Laughter is only this action of the face, together with that inarticulate and explosive cry.'[10] It is, incidentally, this carefully anatomical approach that has characterized much meditation on laughter, starting in the sixteenth century with the careful observations of the physician Laurent Joubert (to whom Dominique Bertrand devotes a fascinating paper below), who, perhaps as early as 1560, wrote a long-neglected treatise on the causes and the anatomy of laughter. Joubert proposed that man can laugh, physiologically speaking, simply because, unlike that of animals, his 'pericardium is firmly attached to the diaphragm'; the cause of laughter is to be found in the emotional swing of contrary emotions acting on the diaphragm.

Very roughly put (and I acknowledge here a debt to those who have done wonders in systematizing a complex argument conducted over several centuries, and to John Morreall[11] in particular), three competing attitudes to laughter rule thought on the subject. The first, and probably still the one to which the greatest number of people will unthinkingly subscribe, can be called the 'superiority theory': that is, the belief that laughter is a form of derision and hence an instrument of domination. Proponents of this theory, notably Aristotle, Plato, or Hobbes, conceive of laughter as essentially derisive and self-congratulatory: we laugh because, as Hobbes puts it, of a '*sudden glory* arising from some conception of some eminency in ourselves, by comparison with the infirmity of others, or with our own formerly'.[12] The second is usually labelled the 'incongruity theory', according to which, because we believe that we live in an orderly world and expect certain patterns, we laugh in surprise or shock when we experience something that does not fit these patterns; there is, in other words, a mismatch between expectation and actuality. Those who subscribe to this theory — Henri Bergson, for example, or Arthur Koestler[13] — believe that laughter arises from the clash between two discrepant frames of reference: Bergson, for instance, considers that laughter arises from our perceiving 'something mechanical encrusted on the living' ('du mécanique plaqué sur du vivant'), as in the case of a human being behaving with absurd or robotic rigidity. Finally, there is what is often termed the 'relief theory', whereby laughter is thought to serve as a sort of social or psychological escape valve: here, according to theorists such as Freud,[14] laughter represents a release of surplus emotional energy. In jokes, we are able to address issues

— sexual or aggressive — that we would normally have to suppress; the ability to do so releases the energy that we would otherwise use in containing our emotions, and it is this energy, now no longer required, that finds expression in laughter.

What I say here is, of course, absurdly oversimplified, and it is with some trepidation (although I gratefully acknowledge that most of the more expert theorists and historians of laughter would, fortunately, agree) that I maintain that none of the theories seems sufficient, alone, to explain the phenomenon of laughter. The 'superiority theory', for instance, does not account for nonsense humour; the 'incongruity theory' cannot explain tickling; the 'relief theory' has difficulty with slapstick — Ken Dodd, famously, said that 'the trouble with Freud is that he never played the Glasgow Empire on a Saturday night'.[15] Even the innocuous phrase 'sense of humour' is awkwardly ambiguous. Does it, for example, mean 'shares my sense of humour'? Or does it mean 'laughs a lot, and is easily amused'? Or 'tells a lot of funny stories, is always the life and soul of the party'? It may be worth remembering that small ads in lonely hearts columns demanding a 'GSOH', or offering a 'VGSOH', because their writers are convinced that a sense of humour is essentially a positive and desirable personality characteristic,[16] could well risk throwing up someone whose inane giggles or relentless jokes are profoundly irritating. And anyway, as Frank Moore Colby notoriously said, 'Men will confess to treason, murder, arson, false teeth or a wig. How many will own up to a lack of humour?'[17]

These remarks go far towards explaining the surprising variety represented within the present volume. The conference that inspired these papers, organized by Edith McMorran in September 2001, arose with perfect logic from the activities of TRIO, the body of which she was the inspiration (see Preface). Over the years, TRIO had run conferences on the translation of humour of all sorts: the translation of nonsense; the translation of theatre — from Molière to *Trainspotting* to Shakespeare; the translation of puns; the translation of Lewis Carroll, or La Fontaine, or Brassens, or Breton, or T. S. Eliot's *Cats*. But it is impossible to talk about the translation or the transposition of the comic, from society to society, code to code, without asking questions about the triggers of laughter: is laughter universal, and if so, in what ways? What is specific to a particular society? Do certain societies endorse or condemn certain sorts of laughter? What provokes a belly-laugh in France, or America, or India, or Saudi Arabia? And what, indeed, *is* 'a belly-laugh'? Edith designed the present conference not, of course, to provide definitive answers to these questions — she recognized that that was an impossibility; rather, with her usual benign open-heartedness, she wanted to give the participants time to reflect on such questions, to create dialogues between speakers of all nationalities and all disciplines. The selection of papers included here attempts to echo that generous eclecticism.

And with Dominique Bertrand's essay on the 'anatomy' of laughter, the collection starts with the fact that laughter is a phenomenon expressed in and through the body — something that no doubt explains the distrust and distaste that made laughter so suspect to Umberto Eco's Brother Jorge, and indeed, in reality, to much of the medieval Church.[18] Silke Kipper and Dietmar Todt, two young biologists from Germany, then ask one of those deceptively simple questions that are so often unexpectedly fruitful: What *is* laughter? How can it be analysed in terms simply of sound, and in terms of the effect of laughter-as-sound on those who hear it? How do auditors recognize and understand laughter, and what are the minimum durations of sound necessary to provide the pleasure of laughter? What effects do such elements as rhythm, or pitch, or timing, have on the auditor? It would be easy for someone like myself, essentially literary, to dismiss their experiments as dismayingly mechanical; yet, in fact, without the building blocks that the physiology of laughter will provide, our understanding of laughter can only remain impressionistic. In the same way, I might be tempted to think of the tickling-machine devised by Sarah-Jayne Blakemore for her paper 'Why Can't You Tickle Yourself?' as just one of those experiments that make the *Daily Express* and the *Daily Mail* fume about 'taxpayers' money'. But the question is a fundamental one: this is laughter provoked not by any of the stimuli that constitute 'humour' or 'the comic', but simply by a physical sensation. And yet, to have its paradoxical effect, that physical sensation cannot be self-produced, cannot be solitary, must be produced by someone other than the subject; why? Blakemore, who presented her research with charm and humour at the conference, devised another of those wonderfully Heath-Robinson instruments with which to test tickling: a sort of tickling robot (we couldn't help but think of Ken Dodd's tickling-stick). What, we may ask, explains the constraints on tickling? The causes may, of course, be psychological[19] or sociological; Blakemore's research, however, like that in the previous paper, returns us, invaluably, to the body and its mechanisms, and thus, as it were, to the first principles of laughter.

The phrase *belly-laugh* is a useful one precisely because it reminds us of what we might call the bodiliness of laughter — as do other phrases like 'hearty laughter', or 'split one's sides', or 'fall about', or 'roll in the aisles'. But belly-laughs, as Michael Holland goes on to show, have a special place in the taxonomies of humour: like the fart at the funeral, they are the sort of bodily manifestation that cannot be controlled, that *escapes* us. Holland is not, here, thinking of that authorized transgression of power structures, the carnival;[20] not just humour as a means of attacking something formal or constraining; not, in other words, humour as a rational response to unbalance in society. Rather, he explores the laughter of disgust, the physicality of laughter: our shocked, uproarious reaction to Jarry's ferocious, terrifying world of greed and shit, Vitrac's mix of farts and sex and elegance. It is a betrayal of both of them to intellectualize; on the other hand, it is a betrayal not to take the '*belly*-laugh' seriously. What Holland brings out feeds, perhaps, in part into what I earlier called the 'relief theory' of laughter: an explosion of energy and vitality in what is otherwise a controlled and carefully rational mental universe.

The same might possibly be said of the two writers to whom Walter Redfern devotes his paper: Louis-Ferdinand Céline and Jules Vallès. We are not normally accustomed to thinking of Céline as comic: he is perceived as nihilistic, raw, ravaging literary decorums and ruthlessly exploding the comfortable nostrums on which we might base our existence — religion, law, politics, the parental instinct, and so on. To laugh seems dangerous; and yet, of course, Céline uses laughter precisely as a weapon. Tempting though it might be to look back to what I called the 'superiority theory', to do so would be wrong: Céline's is one of many test cases that pinpoint the uneasiness of taxonomies of laughter. He is not inviting us to recognize our own, or his, superiority — no sudden glories here; rather, we are to admit to our own complicities and accept his savage diagnosis of the comic, absurd pointlessness of our existence. In other words, this is laughter in which questions of 'taste' and 'decency' are irrelevancies, as they are in Jules Vallès's disturbing *L'Enfant* — I say 'disturbing', yet it may be that Vallès's novel is even more troubling now, in this era in which child abuse makes shocked headlines everywhere, than when it was published in 1878. Where can there be comedy in Jacques's brutal and brutalized existence, beaten by his monstrous mother? And yet Vallès's prose is disconcertingly awash with puns and wordplay and farcical incidents that defy convention and shock us all the more profoundly because they dehumanize Jacques's human dilemma. Do we return here to Bergsonian incongruities? Surely not. Vallès's brutalized Jacques, with his grimly ironic voice, and his appalling mother whose principles of parenthood stem from her own social unease, are not Bergsonian automata. Once again, laughter in this case can only escape neat classification.

What I have introduced here, of course, is the problem of decorum, or appropriateness, in laughter, a topic that preoccupies sociologists such as Giselinde Kuipers and Christie Davies, and, indirectly, the philosopher Ted Cohen. Kuipers tackles the awkward question of highbrow and lowbrow humour: 'awkward', because here too there are problems of definition and categorization. Her main focus is two Dutch comedians who, it seems, appeal to two different taste publics (a term I borrow from Herbert Gans),[21] the cultural preferences of which can be mapped onto class differences: one who wishes to be 'more than just funny', and who, therefore, may be regarded as highbrow; the other, more lowbrow, and having much in common with music hall and stand-up comedy. Kuipers examines what makes each of these comedians funny — is their humour primarily verbal? gestural? sharp and 'hard'? relevant? — and, by contrast, what makes the primary audience of each dislike the humour of the other. Her enquiry has implications not just for the study of humour, and not least because the cultures and publics she describes are not cohesive or bounded: humour here, in other words, is only one contributor, if an important one, to the group identity. Christie Davies, on the other hand, continuing researches he has pursued elsewhere,[22] focuses on humour and nationality, or, to be more precise, on universal jokes about those whom the joke tellers regard as stupid or absurd: the English of the Irish, the French of the Belgians, the Germans of the Frieslanders, and so on. Such jokes feed into stereotypes that seem self-evident to the joke teller but may well be perceived as offensive by the butt. Is this the Hobbesian laughter of superiority? As we respond to the story frame that goes 'There was an Englishman, an Irishman, and a Scotsman', are we marking our own belonging-ness to a culture that we regard as higher, or better, than that of our targets? Or are these simply what Ted Cohen calls 'meta-jokes',[23] that is, jokes which work only if you share certain cultural assumptions and which have no social thrust? Both Christie's paper and Cohen's open up one of those interesting dialogues mentioned earlier: the latter's Jewish jokes, which depend in part on our understanding what is meant by *shiva*, or implied by a skull-cap, are risky precisely because we may feel uneasy about laughing at seemingly racial jokes. But a conference on humour cannot simply confine itself to the comfortable: comedy, it might be said, ought to disturb.

As, indeed, does the humour of a play called *Sucking Dublin*, written in English and performed, largely in Iain Galbraith's translation, in Germany in 2000. Galbraith asks complex, important questions about the status of the translated play–text. The German production, it seems, was adapted — cut, rewritten, refocused — from the original text and from Galbraith's relatively faithful translation; and this challenges the integrity of what the author intended. But might this not be necessary? After all, what is acceptable humour varies greatly from society to society, as the anthropologist Mary Douglas has shown elsewhere;[24] and of all the arts, theatre, it might be argued, in its direct confrontation with its audience, has most need of taking those differences into account and of adapting its raw material, the play–text, accordingly. As Jean-Michel Déprats shows, for instance, to translate Shakespeare into French involves complex decisions, in particular in those brief passages where Shakespeare himself adopts French: in the fifth act of *Henry V*, say, where the French princess is attempting to learn English, and where the joke, for an English audience, is the mangling of the English — 'Oh what fools these foreigners be ...' (are we back to the superiority theory of laughter?) — and the occasional lucky double entendre. But what is the joke to be for a French audience? Déprats, rather than try to find some dubious equivalent effect (Old French? dog French? a handy French dialect?), trusts his actors: if the English is no longer comic, then it is they who will substitute business for verbal humour, they who will ensure that the author's pragmatic intention — laughter — is duly realized. Both Galbraith and Déprats, in other words, celebrate the performativity of the play–text: the collaboration that, for the stage, must be assumed between playwright, text, and translator.

But there is another variety of translation-for-performance, one that raises fearsome technical problems: the dubbed text. The prime source of the difficulty is, as Paul Memmi shows, the fact that dubbing demands, as far as is humanly possible, lip synchronization:[25] audiences prefer that when an actor is in shot, voice and syllable should, ideally, harmonize with gesture and play of expression. But there are other problems: the fact that humour may depend as much on phatic sound (*ums* and *ers*, hesitations, broken constructions, idiomatic fillers) as on the words spoken (and is the translator to transfer those?); the fact that it is notoriously difficult to weigh the impact of slang and taboo words in written as opposed to spoken form; the fact that all languages have idiosyncrasies that are conducive of humour but may be untranslatable (French *tu* and *vous*, for instance, which create register games that cannot be transposed into English); the fact that, in comedy in particular, timing creates comedy, and that timing, from one language to another, one code to another, is particularly difficult to coordinate. Memmi's process of reflection starts with these awkward technical problems, but rapidly moves on to ask broader questions about the very nature of laughter: How far is it simply instinctive? How far is it an intellectual response? And — to turn to Natacha Thiéry's paper — what about film? After all, here too, even the most verbally dexterous of films demands coordination of image and soundtrack. How do these two elements combine?

And what, we may well ask, about the butts of humour? Even ignoring the possibility that humour celebrates our own identity, or superiority, it is nevertheless difficult not to resent being laughed at. It is to this question that Adam Phillips's paper is devoted. His essay is a meditation on laughter as a cooperative, but essentially cruel, venture: the teaser and the teased. How, he asks, are we to understand the relationship? What is the pleasure that the laughter of teasing provides? Is the teaser succumbing to some sadistic impulse? And what might it be that makes us, as the teased, acquiesce in the process, if not positively welcome it? It is too simple, surely, to say, as Buckley does, that there is 'no butt without a message about a risible inferiority';[26] but to tease out the precise nature of the dependency between ourselves as teasers and our victims as teased requires, perhaps, some recognition of our own, not entirely laudable, lacks and needs.

Teasing, it is important to recognize, is only one facet of humour, and Sukanta Chaudhuri, among other things a distinguished translator of Bengali verse, and — of relevance in the present context — of nonsense, introduces us to a quite different aspect of the question. Like all those who translate nonsense,[27] Chaudhuri luxuriates in language: in the flamboyant coinages — *porcochard*, *storkoise* — that make us regret we have no Bengali. Rabindranath Tagore's nonsenses appeal to just that mechanism which governs our response to James Joyce and Lewis Carroll: the recognition that what seem like 'proper' sentences, with subjects, verbs and objects, are not quite sensible — urgently inviting us, of course, to try to 'make sense'. We, like Chaudhuri, savour the excitements of absurdity and linguistic transgression. Is there, perhaps, a sense in which we return to our childhood enjoyment of word invention?

But laughter is by no means always verbal, much as it may please linguists such as myself to imagine that it might be. Two of the contributors, Georges Roque and Laurent Bazin, ask one of those questions that, in retrospect, seem perfectly obvious: Why is it that in painting, and even more in sculpture, there are so few representations of laughter? I say obvious 'in retrospect', since most of us would probably feel intuitively that laughter must surely be the hallmark of paintings of carnivals or peasant games, such as those by Brueghel or Bosch. And yet, on close examination, we find that the celebrating voyagers in Bosch's *Ship of Fools* have barely a smile among them (indeed, the only laughter in Bosch's paintings comes from figures such as the leering and repulsive grotesques in his *Ecce Homo* who screech insults as Pilate leads Christ out before them); and that, for instance, the revellers in Brueghel's *Battle between Carnival and Lent*, or the children playing in his *Children's Games*, are surprisingly serious, even grim. Is it, perhaps, precisely because we like to imagine laughter in painting that we usually call Frans Hals's celebrated portrait *The 'Laughing' Cavalier*, even though he is, in fact, only smiling? Once we are attuned to this puzzling lack of laughter, we will find it something of a relief to come across such uncomplicatedly cheerful seventeenth-century Dutch portraits and genre paintings as Judith Leyster's children happily giggling and playing with a kitten, or her genial drinkers knocking back their Dutch gin with broad, open, celebratory grins.[28] But, as Laurent Bazin suggests, we shall continue to find it disturbing that laughter is so seldom depicted as being produced by the subjects of the paintings; rather, the laughter is ours, and at their expense — at their grotesqueries and ironies, their serene unawareness as a death's head jeers over their shoulders.[29]

And hence to what is perhaps the most startling of all the topics addressed during the conference: Gérard Toulouse's astonishingly wide-ranging paper on the physics and metaphysics of laughter. The programme he charts for the science of laughter is a very ambitious one, and richly documented: it is to investigate what, in evolutionary terms, is the function of laughter. He calls on some of the disciplines that this volume has explored: physiology, neuroscience, psychology. He takes evidence from sources of all sorts: anthropology, literature, music, ethics, philosophy, and so on. Laughter he sees as a challenge for science: what I earlier called the curious facial contortions, the odd strangulated coughings and splutterings, the whoops and squeals that constitute 'laughter' must surely have advanced human survival. And yet, what random mutations, what biological adaptations can it have been that produced effects so spectacular? Toulouse does not answer the question; he does no more than adumbrate some suggestions. And yet, in an era in which language must now be thought of as an evolutionary gain,[30] the question of the biological function of laughter is one that cannot be denied.

Humour, of course, is various: I can laugh at paradox ('Nostalgia isn't what it used to be'...), or at puns ('What do you get if you cross an elephant with a fish? Swimming trunks'...), or at the furtive pleasures of ignoring taboo. Sentences that are completely innocuous can, in English, be made into sexual innuendo simply by adding the phrase 'as the actress said to the bishop ...'. We are far, now, from the world in which a Cicero, severe as ever, could propose a tidy taxonomy of humour based on sheer acceptability in refined society: respectable humour, which is *elegans*, *urbanum*, *ingeniosum*, *facetum* ('witty'), as opposed to unacceptable humour, which is *inliberale* ('not suitable for a freeborn man'), *petulans* ('impudent'), *flagitiosum* ('disgraceful'), or even *obscenum*.[31] The sheer variety of the Oxford conference was one of its great pleasures, and the event illustrated by example the ways in which laughter is social, contagious, and, perhaps, therapeutic.

Notes to Introduction

1. 1980; trans. by William Weaver (San Diego, CA: Harcourt Brace Jovanovich, 1983).
2. *On the Parts of Animals*, x. 29. Not all modern authorities are quite as confident as Aristotle that laughter is specific to man: see, e.g., Mary Douglas, 'Do Dogs Laugh?', in her *Implicit Meanings: Essays in Anthropology* (London: Routledge, 1975), pp. 90–114. And Darwin certainly thought that laughter was shared with apes: see *The Expression of Emotion in Man and Animals* (1872; Chicago: University of Chicago Press, 1965), p. 196.
3. *Poetics*, 1448a; from the trans. by S. H. Butcher (London: Macmillan, 1902), p. 15.
4. Lord Chesterfield, for instance, considers that 'there is nothing so illiberal, and so ill-bred, as audible laughter': see his letter of 9 Mar. 1748 to his son, in *Letters*, ed. by David Roberts (Oxford: Oxford University Press, 1992), p. 72.
5. See *OED*, 'humour', 7.
6. 'Mot emprunté de l'anglais. Forme d'ironie à la fois plaisante et sérieuse, sentimentale et satirique, qui paraît appartenir particulièrement à l'esprit anglais.' This quotation is from the 8th edition (Paris: Hachette, 1935), but the contention already exists in the 1725 edition: see Walther von Wartburg, *Französisches etymologisches Wörterbuch*, IV (Tübingen: Mohr, 1956), 514.
7. *Sämmtliche Schriften*, ed. by Karl Lachmann, 13 vols. (Berlin: Botz, 1838–40), IV, 399.
8. 'Le mot humour est intraduisible. S'il ne l'était pas, les Français ne l'emploieraient pas': *Le Grand Robert de la langue française*, V, 288.
9. Wyndham Lewis, *The Complete Wild Body*, ed. by Bernard Lafourcade (Santa Barbara, CA: Black Sparrow Press, 1982). Thanks to Toby Garfitt for this reference.
10. *The Passions of the Soul [Les Passions de l'âme]*, trans. by Stephen Voss (Indianapolis and Cambridge: Hackett Publishing, 1989), article 124, 83–84. Descartes's treatise was first published in 1649. For

more recent descriptions of the physiology of laughter and smiling, see Mahadev L. Apte, *Humor and Laughter: An Anthropological Approach* (Ithaca, NY: Cornell University Press, 1985), pp. 239–60.

11. *Taking Laughter Seriously* (Albany, NY: State University of New York Press, 1983); I have found this the most helpful summary of available theories on the causes of laughter. I have also been much helped by George McFadden's discussions of Freud and Bergson in *Discovering the Comic* (Princeton, NJ: Princeton University Press, 1982), and by Simon Critchley's *On Humour* (London: Routledge, 2002).

12. *Human Nature*, in his *Works*, ed. by W. Molesworth (London: Bohn, 1839–45), IV, ch. 9. For a more recent account of the theory ('there is no laughter without a butt, and no butt without a message about a risible inferiority', p. xi), see F. H. Buckley, *The Morality of Laughter* (Ann Arbor, MI: University of Michigan Press, 2003).

13. Henri Bergson, *Le Rire. Essai sur la signification du comique* (Paris: Félix Alcan, 1900), and Arthur Koestler, *The Act of Creation* (London: Pan, 1966).

14. In *Jokes and their Relation to the Unconscious*, trans. by James Strachey (Harmondsworth: Penguin, 1976).

15. Quoted by Christopher P. Wilson, *Jokes: Form, Content, Use and Function* (London: Academic Press, 1979), p. 189.

16. No longer, it seems, as incontrovertible as one might once have thought. Nicholas A. Kuiper and Rod A. Martin conclude that 'uncritical endorsements of humor of whatever sort as contributing to psychological well-being are unwarranted': 'Is Sense of Humor a Positive Personality Characteristic?', in *The Sense of Humor: Explorations of a Personality Characteristic*, ed. by Willibald Ruch (Berlin and New York: Mouton de Gruyter, 1998), pp. 159–78 (p. 178).

17. Quoted by Edmund Bergler, *Laughter and the Sense of Humor* (New York: Holt, Rinehart, and Winston, 1956), p. 56.

18. Jacques Le Goff, 'Laughter in the Middle Ages', in *A Cultural History of Humour*, ed. by Jan Bremmer and Herman Roodenberg (Cambridge: Polity, 1997), pp. 96–110.

19. Those who have written on humour have been reluctant to address tickling: see, e.g., J. Y. T. Greig, *The Psychology of Laughter and Comedy* (New York: Dodd, Mead and Co., 1923), who says merely that 'one can tickle oneself only with difficulty, and, probably, only with the help of someone else' (p. 33). Freud is rather noncommittal on the subject: see Adam Phillips, 'On Tickling', in his *On Kissing, Tickling and Being Bored: Psychoanalytic Essays on the Unexamined Life* (Cambridge, MA: Harvard University Press, 1993), pp. 9–11.

20. On which, of course, see Mikhail Bakhtin, *L'Œuvre de François Rabelais et la culture populaire au Moyen Age et sous la Renaissance* (Paris: Gallimard, 1978); Eng. trans. from the Russian original by Helene Iswolsky (Bloomington: Indiana University Press; Cambridge, MA: MIT Press, 1968). Bakhtin's conception of laughter has been subjected, more recently, to some critical re-examination: see Bremmer and Roodenberg, pp. 54–60.

21. *Popular Culture and High Culture: An Analysis and Evaluation of Taste* (New York: Basic Books, 1974).

22. Christie Davies, *The Mirth of Nations* (New Brunswick, NJ: Transaction Publishers, 2002).

23. *Jokes: Philosophical Thoughts on Joking Matters* (Chicago: University of Chicago Press, 1999), p. 21. The example Cohen gives is the joke that goes: 'the thing about German food is that no matter how much you eat, an hour later you are hungry for power', which is comprehensible only if the hearer is familiar with stereotypes having to do both with Germans and with Chinese food. There are some interesting thoughts on jokes of the sort dealt with by Cohen and by Christie Davies, in Susan Purdie, *The Mastery of Discourse* (New York: Harvester Wheatsheaf, 1993), pp. 129–49.

24. *Natural Symbols: Explorations in Cosmology* (Harmondsworth: Penguin, 1978), p. 14.

25. Although it must be said that audiences vary as to how far they are disturbed by lack of synchronization: German audiences, for instance, tend to be less concerned than French. See Thomas Herbst, 'Dubbing and the Dubbed Text — Style and Cohesion: Textual Characteristics of a Special Form of Translation', in *Text Typology and Translation*, ed. by Anna Trosborg (Amsterdam: John Benjamins, 1997), pp. 291–308.

26. F. H. Buckley, *The Morality of Laughter* (Ann Arbor, MI: University of Michigan Press, 2003), p. xi.

27. I think of Guy Leclercq, for instance, in his adventurous translations of Lewis Carroll: *Les Aventures d'Alice au pays du merveilleux ailleurs* (Morlaix: Au bord des continents, 2000); and of the other,

impromptu translations, of Edward Lear and other 'difficult' writers, to which Leclercq so often treated TRIO workshops.

28. See James A. Welu and others, *Judith Leyster: Schilderes en een mannenwereld* [catalogue of an exhibition at the Frans Halsmuseum, Haarlem, 1993] (Zwolle: Waanders Uitgevers), pp. 131, 137. Dutch paintings, however, even of laughter, are rarely so uncomplicated: look, for instance, at Jan Steen's ribaldry and pointed use of gesture (see Mariët Westermann, 'How was Jan Steen Funny? Strategies and Functions of Comic Painting in the Seventeenth Century', in Bremmer and Roodenberg, pp. 134–78).

29. See, on this topic, Paul Barolsky, *Infinite Jest: Wit and Humor in Italian Renaissance Art* (Columbia: University of Missouri Press, 1978).

30. I am thinking of such recent books as Steven Pinker's *The Language Instinct* (Harmondsworth: Penguin, 1994), although Darwin himself, of course, was also, if reluctantly, persuaded that language ability is 'an instinctive tendency to acquire an art' (*The Expression of Emotion*, p. 20).

31. *De officiis*, I. 104; for a modern translation, see Cicero, *On Duties*, ed. by M. T. Griffin and E. M. Atkins (Cambridge: Cambridge University Press, 1991), p. 41.

CHAPTER 1

Anatomie et étymologie: ordre et désordre du rire selon Laurent Joubert

Dominique Bertrand

La Renaissance donne droit de cité au rire dans la littérature,[1] l'inscrivant plus largement dans des perspectives philosophiques, voire encyclopédiques. Des savants réputés s'intéressent à cette particularité désignée comme un privilège humain par les écrivains et les poètes.[2] Le souci de connaissance théorique de l'homme et de ses passions entraîne un intérêt particulier pour l'anatomie du rire autant que pour son éloquence. Médecine et rhétorique représentent alors les deux voies royales de la connaissance anthropologique.[3] La première, "par sa tendance encyclopédique, par son souci d'une connaissance totale de l'homme, corps et âme", se donne comme "la forme la plus achevée de la sagesse et la science la plus sûre du salut".[4] Quant à la rhétorique, elle est, selon Marc Fumaroli, "la nervure centrale d'une culture à la fois encyclopédique et religieuse qui définit l'homme comme sujet parlant".[5] Dans ce cadre, le rire est conçu comme un langage du corps qui pose un double problème de traduction: celui de sa transcription verbale (le codage vocalique des *ha ha ho ho*), celui de sa signification (joie, surprise, perception du ridicule). Nombre d'auteurs préoccupés de cerner les "mouvements de l'âme" s'attachent à décrypter le rire, ce qui revient à interroger son énigmatique interaction avec le corps.[6]

En publiant un important traité sur cette matière, *Traité du ris: contenant son essance, ses causes, et mervelheus effais*,[7] Laurent Joubert, médecin très célèbre en son temps,[8] consacre celui-ci en objet d'observation savante, récusant les erreurs populaires. Le médecin s'applique, dans un long prologue, à légitimer sa recherche. Pour lui, la connaissance des effets du rire fait partie des merveilles de nature accessibles à l'entendement humain, par opposition aux secrets qu'il serait vain ou dangereux de vouloir élucider.[9] Loin de relever d'une curiosité sacrilège, l'élucidation des causes du rire est une manière de célébrer la création divine:

> Les bons et beaus espris, craintifs, dociles, et deja bien institues, ne cesset de profonder et vouloir penetrer aus plus obscurs secres de nature: tant pour leur contantemant, que pour avoir mieus dequoy louër le Createur, montrant sa grandeur par mervelhe effets, qui nous retiret à contemplacion [par des spectacles merveilleux, qui entraînent notre admiration]. Il est bien vray, qu'il y ha des choses tant difficiles et cachees, que nous confessons libremant etre incogneuës à l'homme. (p. 3)

Ces précautions liminaires autorisent un optimisme scientifique apparemment inébranlable. Le médecin croit qu'il est possible de résoudre l'énigme du rire par une démarche analytique. Il invite à une compréhension naturelle du phénomène par le sujet qui en fait l'expérience: "pourquoy ne saurions-nous trouver les causes de ses effets, qui ont leur source et fondemant an nous? [...] j'estime qu'on peut antandre la condicion, force, et affeccion du Ris, puisqu'il nous est intrinseque, se manifestant au dehors" (p. 12–13). Cette transparence relative entre l'intérieur et l'extérieur fonde l'optimisme de notre médecin: "il n'y a chose an nous, qui, apres une sogneuse et bien fondee inquisicion, ne vienne an évidance" (p. 13).

Joubert se targue d'être le premier à entreprendre l'investigation systématique des causes du rire. Il prétend que ses prédécesseurs ont dédaigné de sonder les mécanismes cachés de cette passion, en raison de la trop grande proximité entre sa cause (le ridicule) et sa forme (p. 10). La démarche de Laurent Joubert articule étroitement l'analyse rhétorique du ridicule et l'exploration anatomique du corps ému par le rire: "je m'anquerray de la matiere, ou dequoy nous rions: puis de cet objet je cognoitray, qu'elles parties sont premieres à recevoir son effet" (p. 14). Que traduit le rire? Quels en sont les ressorts physiologiques? En corrélant ces deux questions, l'auteur espère dissiper les mystères du rire et décrire toutes ses "mutations particulières".

Si l'optimisme analytique triomphe au seuil du traité, le médecin se trouve cependant confronté à une série de difficultés cliniques qui l'obligent à emprunter une démarche analogique et à convoquer un savoir étymologique fondé sur l'autorité des auteurs anciens.

Rire et langage

Le médecin énonce un double principe de visibilité et de lisibilité des signes des passions. Il souligne la continuité entre les causes intérieures et les manifestations extérieures de la joie et de la tristesse: "Les effais de joye et de tristesse sont bien tant évidans, qu'ils n'ont besoin que d'être recités, sans autre preuve" (p. 83). S'écrivant directement sur le visage et le corps, ces affections simples ne posent aucune difficulté de déchiffrement. Les images qui sous-tendent cette corrélation entre visible et lisible sont précisées dans des notes marginales. Le visage est comparé à un tableau sur lequel sont représentés les caractères des passions ("signes de joye represantés au visage", note b, p. 74). Sur cette topique archaïque de la peinture des passions, Joubert greffe un imaginaire plus moderne de l'horloge, conférant à l'expression de la réjouissance l'automatisme d'un mécanisme: "La face est comme l'indice, ou le tableau d'un orloge, qui demontre le mouvemant interieur des roues" (note c, p. 75). Parmi les autres "accidans" corporels caractéristiques du rire, il relève l'agitation de la poitrine, la voix interrompue et le mouvement de la physionomie qui consiste à allonger les lèvres et élargir le menton.

Joubert déploie le tableau antithétique des signes visibles de la joie et de la tristesse. A la première correspond une dynamique de dilatation, à la seconde un mouvement de contraction. Mais après ce recensement des marques extérieures du rire, le traité laisse apparaître la difficulté réelle d'une anatomie morale et physique de la passion risifique.

Avant d'aborder la physiologie proprement dite, Joubert revient sur l'articulation du rire et du ridicule (chapitre 1). Il justifie le rappel de cette évidence, dans le cadre d'une observation qui procède des éléments les plus connus à ceux qui le sont moins. La matière ridicule est globalement rapportée, dans le droit-fil d'Aristote,[10] à "quelque chose laide, ou messeante, indigne toutefois de pitié et compassion" (p. 16). A l'appui de cette théorie, Joubert convoque des exemples nombreux et nuancés. Il insiste sur la spécificité de l'interprétation du ridicule, qui requiert le sentiment d'une inconvenance allié à une absence d'implication émotive. Ainsi le comique attendu de la chute inopinée d'un grand personnage qui s'étudiait à "marcher d'un pas fort grave et compassé" ne se vérifie-t-il pas lorsque cette personne nous touche de près: s'il s'agit de "notre parant, allié, ou grand amy [...] nous an aurions honte et compassion" (p. 19). La saisie du ridicule repose donc sur une représentation mentale et un processus cognitif complexes. En d'autres termes, la relation de cause à effet du ridicule au rire ne se vérifie jamais mécaniquement mais dépend d'un faisceau de circonstances subtiles autant que de leur juste interprétation.

L'herméneutique du ridicule est mise en rapport avec la compréhension linguistique. Joubert distingue de fait deux types de supports ridicules, ceux qui sont fondés sur une représentation visuelle et ceux qui sont de nature verbale. Si les premiers ne semblent pas poser problème, en vertu de leur immédiateté, la médiation du langage génère quant à elle des équivoques. L'importance spécifique des propos ridicules conduit Joubert à développer une réflexion sur le rôle déterminant de la compréhension verbale de la plaisanterie. Il compare les situations où le bon mot n'est pas compris à celles qui résultent de l'opacité d'une langue étrangère: "quand ils ne sont evidans, comme si on parle fort bas, ou an langage incognu" (p. 36). La question de la traduisibilité des mots d'esprit affleure à travers le constat des quiproquos générés par la barrière linguistique. Le rire n'est pas un langage universel, mais il requiert la compréhension de la langue dans laquelle le ridicule est mis en œuvre:[11]

> Si quelqu'un et antre Allemans, Basques, ou Bretons bretonans, ignorant leur langage, il les pourra ouïr jaser, et voir rire à gorge deployee, sans qu'il soit invité à faire de maime, parce qu'il n'antand pas le dequoy. (p. 36–37)

Joubert reprend l'exemple de l'obstacle linguistique pour montrer que le processus de contagion kinésique attesté dans certains cas n'est pas un rire véritable, dans la mesure où il est disjoint de la reconnaissance intellectuelle du ridicule:

> Tout ainsi qu'un Fransois qui et parmy des Alemans, n'antandant aucun mot de leur langage, neantmoins les oyt bien et les veid rire: mais s'il rid point avec eus [et pourtant il ne rit pas avec eux]: ou ce sera des laivres seulemant. (p. 295–96)

Le ridicule pose implicitement des problèmes de traduisibilité, d'une langue dans une autre, mais aussi à l'intérieur d'une même langue en raison du codage propre au mot d'esprit. Joubert note que la forme principale des propos ridicules est équivoque et qu'elle fait appel à des figures "communes aus Poëtes et Orateurs: comme d'amphibologie, enigme, comparaison, metaphore, ficcion, hyperbole, feintise, allegorie, emphase, beausemblant, dissimulation" (p. 31). Le décryptage des figures s'avère indispensable: la liste que nous propose Joubert trahit la complexité de ce langage crypté.

Il ressort de cette première étape de l'analyse que le rire traduit la reconnaissance du ridicule mais que la relation de l'un à l'autre n'a rien de nécessaire: "on peut bien rire, de ce qui n'et pas ridicule: et on ne rira pas toujours, quand la matiere se presente" (p. 38). L'importance de la médiation verbale se trouve largement mise en valeur par un médecin qui s'est aussi intéressé de près à des problèmes linguistiques. Rappelons qu'il est l'auteur d'un *Dialogue sur la cacographie française expliquant la cause de sa corruption*:[12] il y déplore le décalage entre l'orthographe et la prononciation du français, notant les difficultés d'apprentissage que cela pose aux apprenants étrangers. Joubert est aussi l'auteur d'un texte "déterminant pour la question de l'origine biologique du langage",[13] intitulé "Question vulgaire. Quel langage parleroit un enfant qui n'auroit jamais ouï parler". Il envisage dans cet opuscule publié à la suite de ses *Erreurs populaires* les fondements physiologiques, autant que psychologiques, de la différence entre langue humaine et cri animal. On va voir comment cette démarche d'anatomie comparée est reprise dans l'examen du rire.

L'anatomie du rire

Dans un second temps, Joubert tente de percer les mystères physiologiques du rire, et en particulier de résoudre une question épineuse, à savoir "quelle partie du cors ressoit premiere les ridicules" (chapitre V, p. 40). Il rencontre ici un important débat théorique, qui a divisé au Moyen-Age les tenants de deux visions du corps: "corps vertical ou linéaire avec à son sommet le cerveau [...] corps à organisation concentrique autour du cœur qui diffuse la vie à la périphérie".[14] La première vision suit Hippocrate, Platon, Galien, la seconde est d'obédience aristotélicienne. Les débats à la Renaissance pour déterminer le siège du rire[15] font intervenir un troisième lieu, la rate. Joubert élimine cette hypothèse, taxée de superstition populaire. Au terme de longues délibérations, il tranche en faveur "d'une affeccion du cœur, et nompas du cerveau" (titre du chapitre IX, p. 63).

Après avoir établi cette certitude anatomique, Joubert s'emploie à l'étayer en articulant étroitement l'argumentation physiologique et les considérations relatives à la cause morale du rire. Il prouve que le rire ne saurait se confondre avec l'expression de la joie pure, mais qu'il participe de deux mouvements contradictoires du cœur liés à la dualité intrinsèque des choses ridicules. Celles-ci causent en effet plaisir et tristesse dans la mesure où elles proviennent d'une laideur sans douleur, selon la conception aristotélicienne:

> Car la chose ridicule nous donne [...] plaisir, de ce qu'on la trouve indigne de pitié [...] Donc le cœur s'an rejouït, et s'elargit comme an la vraye joye. Il y ha aussi de la tristesse, pour ce que tout ridicule provient de laideur et messeance: le cœur marry de telle vilainie, comme santant douleur, s'etressit et resserre [...] Voila commant le Ris et fait, de la contrarieté ou debat de deux affeccions. (p. 87–88)

Le rire repose sur une contradiction morale et anatomique même si celle-ci peut échapper à l'observateur inattentif: le médecin note que de ces deux mouvements, la joie domine et que leur succession est si rapide qu'elle n'est pas repérable par les sens mais seulement accessible à une analyse rationnelle (p. 89). La complexité du rire vient donc perturber le principe de transparence physionomique allégué par Joubert: le bénéfice de ce désordre de la passion est de mettre en valeur l'habileté du déchiffreur de secrets finalement bien cachés au commun des mortels.

Si le propre de l'anatomie est de mettre au jour des ressorts invisibles, c'est à une investigation imaginaire que se livre Joubert. Procédant par conjecture et non par observation directe, le médecin invite son lecteur à se représenter l'ébranlement du cœur sous l'emprise de l'affection ridicule. Il donne à voir l'agitation de celui-ci à l'intérieur de la "boîtelette" que constitue le péricarde:

> Nous comprenons seulemant par raison et discours, que le cœur ha son pericarde assés ample, sans luy etre attaché, afin qu'il s'y remuë dedans an pleine liberté. Quand il et fort emu, comme an la baite à qui on ouvre la poitrine, tout et an branle. N'et-il pas raisonnable, qu'il an avienne autant d'une affeccion, qui trouble le mouvemant du cœur, d'une contrarieté que cause le Ris? (p. 93)

La mise au jour de ces ressorts corporels du rire se fonde sur des éléments fournis par des observations cliniques d'anatomie animale. C'est curieusement le modèle de la peur animale qui permet à Joubert de penser le trouble occasionné par le rire.

Joubert poursuit dans la voie de cette anatomie comparée de l'homme et de l'animal[16] pour mieux étayer une différence essentielle qui lui permet d'accréditer la topique aristotélicienne de la spécificité humaine du rire. Il note que le péricarde humain est attaché sur le diaphragme "d'une grande largeur aux hommes", à la différence des bêtes (p. 94), "comme on le voit par l'anatomie": ceci expliquerait que le cœur humain puisse commander au diaphragme et entraîner l'expiration violente qui caractérise le rire. Dépourvus de cette particularité anatomique, les animaux sont incapables de rire au sens plein du terme. Joubert revient sur cette question essentielle "à savoir si le seul homme rit". La solution de ce problème représente un enjeu majeur, confortant l'éloge du rire comme attribut divin. Le médecin souligne la convergence de l'observation anatomique avec les données premières de l'expérience: "[elle] verifie cela, car outre l'homme, nul animal rit, sinon paravanture d'un ris batard, simulé ou contrefait, tel que nous appellons canins et sardonic" (p. 231). Joubert étaye son argumentation sur la spécificité humaine du rire par des considérations morales liées à la sociabilité et à l'activité intellectuelle: ces autres caractéristiques majeures de l'homme expliqueraient son besoin de récréation:

> Or la vertu et puissance de rire, et à bon droit peculieremant concedee à l'homme, afin qu'il eut moyen de recreer [détendre] quelquefois son esprit, travalhé et lassé d'occupacions serieuses, comme de l'etude, contamplacions, composicions, traité[s] d'affaires, administracions publiques, et semblables propres à l'homme. Car de tous les animaus, le seul homme et né apte à l'etude, contamplacion, negociacion, et toute sorte d'affaires: laiquelles occupacions le randet un peu rude, severe, chagrin, difficile, brusque, facheus et melancholique. Et d'autant qu'il convenoit à l'homme d'etre animal sociable, politic et gracieus, afin que l'un vequit et conversat avecques l'autre plaisammant et beninemant, Dieu luy ha ordonné le Ris, pour recreacion parmy ses deportemans: afin de lacher quelque fois commodemant les reines de son esprit. (p. 231–32)

Le *topos* du "propre de l'homme"[17] permet à Joubert de démontrer la cohérence d'un ordre, l'organisation anatomique servant les desseins d'une Nature identifiée à la raison divine:

> Et d'autant que nature n'antreprand rien temerairemant, et aussi qu'il n'appert pas qu'elle ayt onques [jamais] voulu chose qui ne fut consonante à raison, il ha fallu

qu'elle ayt accommodé la forme de l'homme, à etre bien ancline au Ris, et ayt fabriqué industrieusemant au cors humain, des instrumans convenables à produire le Ris. Car elle n'ha pas fassonné tous les animaus d'une maime sorte, et puis donné à cettuy-cy la puissance de rire, la deniant aus autres [...]

Elle donques ha fassonné, baty et composé le cors humain, de telle fasson, qu'il obeyt facilemant aussi tôt que l'esprit et emu de l'objet risifique, et soudain le represante d'un ris extérieur. Nous avons ansegné au premier livre, que le cœur et le diaphragme an sont les premiers instrumans: y ajoutant an outre, que ez [chez les] hommes le pericarde et attaché au diaphragme [...] d'une grande largeur, fort differammant des baites: dequoy aussi nous colligeons [reconnaissons], que l'homme seul peut rire. (p. 234–36)

La boucle est bouclée et l'entreprise d'élucidation du rire apparemment triomphante.

Le rire et ses mots: une parfaite cohérence?

La démonstration à laquelle se livre Joubert à partir du "propre de l'homme" n'est qu'un miroir grossissant de sa démarche, mettant en lumière son souci de retrouver une cohérence parfaite, un ordre naturel.

Une grande partie de l'effort explicatif du traité tend à expliciter les corrélations anatomiques entre le principe interne du rire et ses manifestations extérieures: le chapitre XVIII montre le lien entre la dilatation du diaphragme et le double processus d'agitation de la poitrine et d'interruption de la voix: "le diaphragme [...] forcé du cœur, violante de maime la poitrine, qui luy obeït" (p. 101). La succession des chapitres physiologiques du traité de Joubert sert à prouver la cohérence d'une organisation corporelle qui ne laisse rien au hasard: le diaphragme "fait accorder à son branle plusieurs autres muscles, qui ont amitié ou intelligeance avec luy" (p. 111), y compris ceux de la bouche. L'enchaînement naturel est le tremblement de la voix: "comme le Ris n'et jamais sans agitacion de poitrine, aussi ne peut-il etre qu'on n'oye sortir de la bouche (ou pour le moins du nez) l'air faisant un bruit decoupé" (p. 102).

Ces accidents ordonnés renvoient à la conception d'un ordonnancement supérieur, d'origine divine. L'exploration anatomique n'est que la mise en évidence de cette mécanique parfaite:

L'anatomie nous anseigne, que les parties ampruntet les unes des autres, et celles qui sont antretenües ou conjointes de commune liaison, ont mutuël consantemant. Car toutes les parties de nottre cors se ressantet du bien et du mal qui et au foye, par le moyen des veines, arteres et ners, qui an procedet (p. 112)

Aux bouleversements du visage correspondent de fait ceux de tout le corps dans le rire véhément:

Il et donq aisé d'antandre, commant la poitrine etant ebranlee par le Ris dissolu, on voit branler de maimes bras et epaules: voire branler de sorte, qu'on ne les peut retenir. Et quoy? les cuisses an anduret bien secousse, les piés an trepignet, et le cors s'amoncelle tout, par le consantemant des muscles de toutes pars forcés et retirés. Car aussi tout s'antretient, et et lié ansamble par ners, ligamans, et tandons. (p. 124)

L'ordre que dévoile Joubert ne saurait être parfait s'il ne reposait *in fine* sur une harmonie entre les mouvements du corps et de l'âme, principe sous-jacent à l'étude successive de la rhétorique du rire et de ses fondements physiologiques. Le second livre du rire fait état d'une hiérarchie ordonnée du corps et de l'âme:

> Nous usons du commandemant de l'esprit, et service du cors. [...] Or donc, eu egard à l'excelance de l'ame celeste et divine, il falloit bien que son receptacle fut assés mou et delicat, à fin qu'elle n'an fut rien ampechee, ains an usa facillemant, comme d'un instrumant ployable. (p. 157)

La preuve ultime de cet ordre divin du rire semble fournie par sa consignation dans la sagesse proverbiale et les locutions stéréotypées. Ce n'est pas le moindre paradoxe de la démarche de Joubert, ennemi des superstitions populaires, que de le voir alléguer des formules figées à l'appui de ses analyses savantes. La vérité du rire est déposée dans le langage, l'anatomie ne faisant que confirmer par des preuves savantes la justesse des métaphores courantes: "on dit vulgairemant, il rit de bon cœur, et nompas de bon cerveau, denotant le lieu d'où procede l'affection risoire" (p. 64–65); "l'epithete de tramblant" apparaît aussi "tresconvenable à sa naturelle condition", à savoir les secousses de la poitrine accompagnées d'une "voix dechiquetée" (p. 102). De l'anatomie du rire à sa traduction verbale, il n'existe apparemment pas de hiatus. Joubert est un homme de la Renaissance pour qui la connaissance des mots du rire recouvre une connaissance de la chose.[18] Pourtant ce cratylisme qui semble caractéristique d'un âge des signatures, ne servirait-il pas à masquer certaines apories de l'analyse?

Celles-ci sont inhérentes à un *distinguo* qui obsède Joubert, celui du vrai rire et de ses contrefaçons. Il suffit apparemment d'introduire une précision d'épithète pour différencier le rire authentique de ses formes dénaturées. Joubert oppose ainsi le vrai rire "naturel" et ses déviations "contre nature": rire maniaque, rire canin ou rictus accompagnant les fièvres, la morsure par la tarentule ou l'empoisonnement par une herbe propre à la Sardaigne (cause du rire dit "sardonien"). La question du rire sardonien soulève celle de la discordance entre l'expression du visage et le sentiment intérieur: "celuy rit d'un Ris Sardonien, qui ne fait qu'elargir les laivres, et au reste il et interieuremant travalhé de colere ou de tristesse" (p. 216). Ce faux rire n'est pas une exception: dans le même registre de dissonance émotionnelle, Joubert cite le "Ris canin, lequel et ainsi dit, de ce que le rieur decouvre seulemant les dans". Ces rictus contredisent le principe anatomique et moral du vrai rire: "tel et le Ris de ceus qui ne riet du cœur" (ibid.).

En traitant des formes factices du rire, Joubert prétend cependant toujours vérifier la cohérence de son modèle explicatif. Les rires faux pèchent par défaut des critères rhétoriques et physiologiques qui fondent la définition du rire vrai. Ces formes de rire "malsain et batard" provoquent une "convulsion" qui dénature en somme le tremblement propre au rire. Le médecin distingue des degrés différents de dénaturation du rire: les formes convulsives sont plus fausses que celui qui provient du diaphragme blessé (p. 183–89). Celui-ci présente de fait toutes les caractéristiques anatomiques du rire, hormis sa cause morale essentielle, la reconnaissance de l'objet ridicule.

Dans la même perspective, la mimique des nouveaux-nés fournit à Joubert une preuve *a contrario* de sa double définition rhétorique et anatomique du rire (reconnaissance du ridicule — ébranlement du cœur). En effet les enfants

> ne font que retirer la bouche, tout ainsi que au Ris canin (ou si vous aimés mieus, comme on fait au Sou-ris, qui et de mignardise, caresse et attrait amoureus) sans aucune agitacion du diaphragme et de la poitrine, sans aucune secousse des poumons, et finalement sans aucun son de vois antre-coupee. (p. 296)

La facticité de ce rire tient à son absence de motivation ridicule qui fonde un jeu anatomique incomplet.[19] Il ressort que le sourire rituel d'accueil et de séduction est pour Joubert bien distinct du rire, dont il diverge par sa signification morale autant que par son mécanisme anatomique.

De la transparence à l'opacité des signes: retour aux origines ou le salut par l'épithète de nature

Le moins que l'on puisse dire, c'est que la lisibilité des signes du visage apparaît bien compromise au terme de cet inventaire des rires factices. Le traité de Joubert n'échappe pas à cette loi générale, formulée par Daniel Ménager: "Un discours sur le rire est toujours un discours sur l'opacité des signes".[20] Des fausses notes un peu trop nombreuses viennent brouiller le *credo* initial du médecin en faveur d'une transparence rhétorique des passions. Au sein même de la démonstration d'une cohérence physiologique, s'insinue le soupçon que les signes de la douleur et du plaisir sont équivoques: "Voyés deux hommes an peinture, desquels l'un rie si fort, qu'il se defassonne tout: l'autre se debate etrangemant, se plaigne, et pleure à grosses larmes", ce qui conduit Joubert à constater que "la grieve douleur et la tristesse font retirer le diaphragme, etraissir la poitrine, anfoncer le vantre, et suspandre la respiracion", à l'instar du rire (p. 111). Les conséquences du diaphragme blessé brouillent aussi la rhétorique des passions: ce désordre pathologique communique au corps le spasme du rire, mais ce n'est qu'un "faus semblant [...] qu'on appelle Canin" (p. 112). Joubert semble prendre en défaut le langage lui-même, qui ne dispose pas d'une épithète spécifique pour désigner précisément le rire provoqué par la blessure du diaphragme.

Qu'en est-il dès lors de cette prétendue authentification étymologique à laquelle se livre le médecin, lorsqu'il déploie et commente une liste d'épithètes du ris, en s'abritant derrière l'autorité des auteurs et en particulier des poètes antiques? On peut y voir un processus compensatoire, une manière de circonscrire le désordre latent des symptômes mensongers ou pathologiques du rire en s'abritant derrière les certitudes d'un ordre verbal dûment accrédité.

Joubert procède de manière accumulative, se bornant à inventorier les épithètes qui se rapportent au rire naturel et à ses déformations pathologiques. Il commence par celle qui corrobore le mieux les principes anatomiques qu'il a dégagés: à savoir celui de "ris tremblant". Il oppose ensuite les modulations variables du rire: le *modeste* et le *cachin*. Celui-ci serait synonyme de celui que les Grecs appellent "syncrousien, de ce qu'il crole [tremble] et ebranle fort" (p. 213). Mais Joubert conteste un autre équivalent proposé par certains pour ce rire à gorge déployée, celui de *sardonien*.

Cette épithète donne lieu à un abondant débat étymologique, pour lequel Joubert renvoie à l'autorité des *Adages* d'Erasme.[21] Il est significatif que Joubert mentionne l'autorité du philosophe sans entrer dans le détail d'une étymologie trouble. L'origine de ce rire ne serait pas la Sardaigne, mais plutôt l'île de Sardon au large de Carthage où un rire rituel accompagnait le sacrifice des vieillards avec leurs enfants: Erasme se réfère à d'autres exemples de cette rencontre du rire et de la mort, cas-limite de dégradation du rire en rictus inquiétant.[22] Le rire sardonien, cette "limite du rire",[23] perturbe les classifications de Joubert, obligé de distinguer deux rires sardoniens: l'un de convulsion, l'autre de simple simulation, qui renvoie à l'usage métaphorique de l'expression (p. 217–18).

Se découvre une infinie complexité de l'émotion, dont la littérature grecque rend compte. Joubert en vient à citer le fameux rire d'Ajax dans l'Iliade, rire "de rage, felonie". Ce rire agressif est aussi un rire paradoxal qui naîtrait de l'appréhension soudaine d'un danger par une personne qui "se rit et se jouë, plongé[e] an voluptés ou malefices" (p. 217).

Ces épithètes signalent une discordance entre l'expression extérieure — apparence de rire — et la signification intérieure — qui ne se confond pas toujours avec le plaisir provoqué par une pure et simple reconnaissance du ridicule. Leur infinie variété, due à l'imagination des auteurs,[24] induit un déplacement de l'analyse vers des formes de glose anecdotique et légendaire. Joubert propose aux lecteurs curieux de prolonger cette recherche dont il suggère la dimension infinie.[25]

De l'analyse anatomique au déploiement analogique

Ce renoncement à l'exhaustivité est lourd d'implications. C'est en somme reconnaître que le système anatomique et rhétorique très cohérent mis au jour dans le premier livre du *Traité du ris* ne saurait épuiser la richesse d'une matière, sur laquelle l'auteur juge essentiel de revenir dans un second livre contenant "sa definicion, ses especes, differances, et divers epithetes". L'*incipit* de ce second livre se place sous le signe des prodiges de la nature et de leur diversité irréductible à l'ordre du discours.[26] Le corps humain est désigné comme un assemblage de singularités dignes d'admiration "lequelles si on vouloit expliquer et poursuivre curieusemant, à peine an viendroit on a-bout" (p. 140). Autant dire que la possibilité de généraliser, condition d'un discours scientifique, tend à se dissoudre au profit d'une déclinaison de la variété des phénomènes observables. Le début de ce second livre, discrètement sceptique, contraste avec l'optimisme analytique qui fondait la préface et la démarche du premier livre.

Joubert ne s'avoue toutefois pas vaincu par ces difficultés et il ne cesse de se poser en déchiffreur des signes d'une passion dont il célèbre l'extraordinaire éloquence. C'est selon lui celle qui imprime le plus de marque "non seulement au visage, ains aussi an tout le cors" (p. 160). Il décline avec un plaisir évident les marques physiologiques de cette pléthore expressive:

> [C]ecy accompagne le Ris, grand fante de bouche, retiremant insigne des laivres, la vois ou son antrerompu et chancelant: la rougeur du visage, et la sueur qui aucunefois an sort par tout le cors: l'etincellemant des yeus, avec effusion de larmes: l'anfleure des veines au front et au cou: la tous, la rejeccion de ce qu'on ha dans la bouche et au nez: l'ebranlemant de la poitrine, des epaules, bras, cuisses, jambes, et de tout le cors, comme un trepignemant: la grand douleur des coutés, des flancs, et du vantre: le vuidange des boyaus et de la vessie: la defalhance de cœur à faute d'haleine, et quelques autres accidans. Ce qui augmante plus la mervelhe et, qu'une chose de-neant, du tout vaine et legiere, emeuve l'esprit de si grand agitacion. (p. 160–61)

On peut s'interroger sur un tel inventaire, redondant par rapport au livre I et qui énonce un principe d'ouverture infinie des caractères de la passion risifique. Ce principe de liste ouverte gouverne aussi le réseau de correspondances entre le microcosme et le macrocosme que Joubert suggère à partir de considérations sur l'extrême variété des expressions du rire et de ses vocalises:

> An l'espece des hommes il y ha autant de visages differans, qu'il y ha de figures au monde: autant de diversités, tant au parler, que à la vois, et [...] autant de divers Ris. Il y an ha que vous diriés quand ils riet, que ce sont oyes qui sifflet: et d'autres que ce sont des oysons gromelans. Il y an ha qui rapportet au gemir des pigeons ramiers, ou des tourtorelles an leur vidüité: les autres au chat-huant, et qui au coq d'Inde, qui au paon. Les autres resonnet un piou piou, à mode de poulets. Des autres on diroit que c'et un cheval qui hanit, ou un ane qui brait, ou un porc qui grunit, ou un chien qui jappe ou qui s'etrangle. Il y an ha qui retiret [ressemblent] au son des charettes mal ointes, les autres aus calhous qu'on remuë dans un seau, les autres à une potee de chous qui bout: les autres ont un' autre raisonnance, outre le minois et la grimace du visage, qui et an divers si diverse que rien plus. Parquoy de poursuyvre toutes ses differances particulieremant, comme il seroit impossible, aussi seroit-il inutile. (p. 210–11)

Le rire retrouve place et sens dans un rayonnement de similitudes qui évoque l'espace universel des ressemblances propre à l'épistémé de la Renaissance telle que la décrit Michel Foucault.[27] Au-delà des analogies entre l'homme et l'animal, domaine traditionnel de la lecture physiognomonique, Joubert se plaît à varier sur les correspondances sonores entre la voix du rire et les bruits du monde.

Reste que cette infinie diversité annule en partie la cohérence analytique visée par le médecin dans son premier livre. La comparaison poétique a succédé à l'investigation savante, dans une tentative ultime de conjurer un désordre phénoménologique qui confirme la dimension "prodigieuse" du rire et le légitime comme sujet d'investigation livresque.

Conclusion

De l'anatomie du rire à sa traduction dans le langage corporel et à ses représentations langagières, la quête d'une cohérence oriente la démarche de Joubert. L'anatomie rejoint les données d'une sagesse proverbiale. Pour cet esprit encyclopédique de la Renaissance, l'ordre physiologique du rire, objet d'une patiente élucidation anatomique, devrait se retrouver inscrit dans les mots. Mais ce bel édifice cratylien semble fragile. Le recours aux épithètes du rire compense en partie les apories de l'analyse dans sa confrontation aux manifestations mensongères de la passion risifique. L'herméneutique analogique traditionnelle se trouve également convoquée pour pallier le constat d'une infinie diversité de la prose du rire, fascinante mais déroutante au regard du projet initial de résoudre tous les mystères du "proprium hominis".

Entre ordre et désordre, l'écriture du rire que nous propose Joubert est orientée par un constant souci d'élucidation et de mise au jour d'une cohérence. La confiance qui domine chez le médecin humaniste dans l'analyse rationnelle de la passion s'effritera nettement dans les traités ou parties de traités que le siècle suivant consacrera au rire.[28] Cureau de la Chambre ne nourrit plus d'illusions sur la possibilité de parvenir à une connaissance complète du rire: "on peut facilement croire que le ris est un mot équivoque qui marque des effets de différente nature...".[29] Sa position épistémologique apparaît ambiguë, oscillant entre le désir de dépasser cette aporie et celui d'apporter un démenti aux illusions de connaissance totale de prédécesseurs naïfs. Cureau se borne à enregistrer la diversité des rires et des visages, soulignant la vanité de toute description et renonçant à déployer les correspondances du microcosme et du macrocosme.[30] Récusant la cohérence du système anatomique de Joubert, le médecin de Louis XIV souligne la contradiction entre l'action de l'âme et celle du corps: pour lui, seule la contraction des muscles se fait "par le commandement de l'âme, tout le reste se faisant par nécessité et sans dessein":[31] l'articulation entre anatomie et sémiologie se défait, le propre des passions selon Cureau étant l'anarchie des signes qu'elles génèrent, par suite de l'agitation des esprits.[32] La lisibilité des caractères des passions évolue chez Descartes vers une analyse strictement différentielle et restreinte, par suite du déclin de l'interprétation analogique.[33]

Les gassendistes rejettent l'analyse mécaniste pour mieux souligner l'illisibilité des passions et contester l'ordre anthropocentrique qui prévalait dans le traité de Joubert. Une dérision de la vanité humaine transparaît sous la plume de Cureau, qui tend à faire du ridicule, et non du rire, le propre de l'homme, en se fondant précisément sur cette obscurité de son rapport au rire: "il n'y a rien qui soit plus ridicule que de voir celui qui se mêle de contrôler toute la nature [...] ignorer la chose qui lui est la plus propre et la plus familière".[34] Gassendi pourfend quant à lui avec une très grande virulence le syllogisme scolastique du "risus proprium hominis",[35] insistant sur l'opacité des signes des passions et l'irréductibilité des langages humain et animal.[36] Alors que pour Laurent Joubert, le privilège incontesté d'un rire humain n'excluait pas un jeu de correspondances entre les signes humains et les manifestations animales, le siècle suivant fait entrer le "propre de l'homme" dans une ère du soupçon généralisé, préparant la voie au scepticisme désabusé de Voltaire, qui récusera toute prétention à l'analyse métaphysique autant qu'anatomique du rire: "Ceux qui cherchent des causes métaphysiques au rire ne sont pas gais. Ceux qui savent pourquoi cette espèce de joie retire vers les oreilles le muscle zygomatique, l'un des treize muscles de la bouche, sont bien savants".[37]

Notes

1. George Minois, *Histoire du rire et de la dérision* (Paris: Fayard, 2000), p. 266.
2. On connaît la célèbre exergue du *Gargantua*: "Mieux est de ris que de larmes escrire,/ Pour ce que rire est le propre de l'homme" (Rabelais, *Œuvres complètes*, éd. par Guy Demerson, Paris: Le Seuil, 1973). Ronsard écrit aussi, dans un poème dédié *A monsieur de Belot*:

   > Dieu qui soubz l'homme le monde a soumis
   > A l'homme seul, le seul rire a permis
   > Pour s'esgayer et non pas à la beste,
   > Qui n'a raison ny esprit en la teste.

   ("L'Ombre du cheval", in *Le Sixième Livre des poèmes*, in *Œuvres complètes*, éd. par Paul Laumonier, xv; Paris: Société des textes français modernes, 1953 v 95–99, p. 143).
3. Voir les études fondamentales de Marc Fumaroli, *L'Age de l'éloquence* (Genève: Droz, 1980; Paris: Albin Michel, 1994), et de Louis Van Delft, *Littérature et anthropologie* (Paris: Presses universitaires de France, 1993).

4. Roland Antonioli, *Rabelais et la médecine*, Etudes rabelaisiennes, XII (Genève: Droz, 1976), p. 6.

5. Marc Fumaroli, "Rhétorique et littérature de la Renaissance et de l'époque classique", in *Actes du XIe Congrès de l'Association Guillaume-Budé* (Paris: Belles-Lettres, 1985), I, p. 135.

6. Voir Dominique Bertrand, *Dire le rire à l'âge classique* (Aix-en-Provence: Presses de l'Université de Provence, 1995).

7. Je m'appuierai sur l'édition de 1579 (Paris: Chesneau; Genève: Slatkine, 1973). Certains spécialistes font remonter la première édition de l'œuvre à 1560.

8. Il est médecin du roi et chancelier de l'Université de Montpellier où il a succédé à Rondelet.

9. Au nombre de ces éléments insondables, Joubert compte le foudre, mais aussi des effets plus familiers et néanmoins étranges (les dents qui grincent lorsqu'on entend déchirer un drap, la contagion des bâillements...).

10. La *Poétique* fait découler le rire d'un "défaut ou d'une laideur qui n'entraînent ni douleur ni dommage" (1449b).

11. Le médecin reviendra sur ce lien du rire et de la compréhension verbale pour trancher le problème de savoir si l'enfant avant le quarantième jour rit.

12. Opuscule que l'on trouve à la suite du *Traité du ris* dans la réédition Slatkine.

13. Selon la formule de Marie-Luce Demonet, in *Les Voix du signe. Nature et origine du langage à la Renaissance (1480–1580)* (Paris: Champion, 1992), p. 494.

14. Jean-Marie Fritz, *Le Discours du fou au Moyen-Age* (Paris: Presses universitaires de France, 1992), p. 129.

15. Voir Daniel Ménager, *La Renaissance et le rire* (Paris: Presses universitaires de France, 1995), p. 20.

16. Cette anatomie comparée remonte à la plus haute antiquité, comme le rappelle Van Delft (p. 239). Elle a été pratiquée à la Renaissance par Vésale, qui entendait dénoncer les erreurs de Galien.

17. Sur ce lieu commun, voir mon étude "Le Propre de l'homme: évolutions d'un cliché apologétique, ironique et ludique", in *La Comédie sociale*, dir. par Nelly Feuerhahn et Françoise Sylvos (Vincennes: Presses universitaires de Vincennes, 1997), p. 31–42.

18. On ne saurait toutefois postuler que la Renaissance dans son ensemble ait adhéré à la doctrine de Cratyle. Pour un état de la réflexion sur la langue à cette époque, on se reportera à la thèse de Demonet (*Les Voix du signe*).

19. Le médecin explique par la mollesse et l'humidité de l'esprit des enfants leur inclination à imiter les mouvements du rire qu'ils voient imprimés sur les lèvres de leurs proches.

20. *La Renaissance et le rire*, p. 44.

21. *Opera omnia* (Amsterdam and Oxford: North-Holland, 1981), II, 5, p. 289–97.

22. Sur cette question du rire sardonique, on se reportera notamment aux deux articles suivants: Michel Delon, "Le Rire sardonique", *Dix-huitième siècle*, 32 (2000), 255–64; et Alain Ballabriga, "Le Rire et la mort: du rire sardonique au rire funéraire", *Humoresques*, 14 (juin 2001), 21–31.

23. Selon la formule de Delon, "Le Rire sardonique".

24. Voir en particulier le "ris catonien", qui désigne le rire excessif de Caton dont la sévérité habituelle ne résista pas au spectacle d'un âne mangeant des chardons (p. 218).

25. "Je panse qu'il y ha plusieurs autres nuncupacions, et epithetes du ris, que je lairray chercher aus curieus" (p. 219)

26. Sur le rapport de la Renaissance aux singularités de la nature, voir l'étude de Jean Céard, *La Nature et les prodiges* (Genève: Droz, 1977; 1996).

27. *Les Mots et les choses* (Paris: Gallimard, 1966), p. 210–12.

28. Cureau de la Chambre se démarque ostensiblement de l'analyse de Joubert dans le chapitre qu'il consacre au rire, au sein de son volume consacré aux *Charactères des passions* (Paris: Pierre Rocolet, 1640).

29. (Paris: Jacques d'Allin, 1658), p. 218.

30. "de vouloir décrire toute cette diversité de mouvements, d'air, de contenance qu'il donne à chacun, ce seroit autant que si l'on voloit depeindre les hommes ensemble, puisqu'il n'y en a pas un qui ne fasse en riant quelque grimasse particuliere " (p. 221).

31. p. 265.

32. "Combien de pas perdus, de postures ridicules et de paroles ridicules dans les passions?" (p. 22).

33. Voir Bertrand, *Dire le rire*; on se reportera aussi à l'étude plus précise intitulée "Rire et sémiotique corporelle de la Renaissance à l'âge classique: une nouvelle lisibilité", in *La Peinture des passions de*

la *Renaissance à l'Age classique* (Saint-Etienne : Publications de l'Université de Saint-Etienne, 1995), p. 281–92.

34. *Les Charactères des passions*, p. 218.

35. Voir *Exercitationum paradoxicarum adversus Aristoteleos* (Amsterdam: 1649; Paris: Adrianum Ulacq, 1659), Exercitatio quinta; voir la traduction de Bernard Rochot (Paris: Vrin, 1962).

36. Sur ce point, Bertrand, *Dire le rire*, p. 25–27, et "Le propre de l'homme".

37. Voltaire, *Œuvres complètes*, éd. par Louis Moland (Paris: Garnier, 1877–85), xx, 374.

CHAPTER 2

The Sound of Laughter:
Recent Concepts and Findings in
Research into Laughter Vocalizations

Silke Kipper and Dietmar Todt

The various effects and functions of human laughter and the striking impact of laughter on social relationships have been the object of inquiry from time immemorial. Since Darwin's *The Expression of the Emotions in Man and Animals* (London, 1872) at least, human laughter has also been the object of research in natural and social sciences, investigated by scholars from such diverse disciplines as anthropology, biology, linguistics, literature studies, philosophy, physiology, psychology, and sociology. For the behavioural biologist, laughter is seen as a species-specific, non-verbal signal behaviour that is almost always used in a social context.[1] Laughter can have contagious effects,[2] and it can facilitate positive emotional and behavioural responses.[3] What we attempt here is to understand these effects and functions of laughter by investigating the rules governing its perception and production.

We propose to outline some of the specific contributions that behavioural biology makes to our understanding of laughter. These include, in the first place, detailed observations of the situations in which laughter is expressed: Who is laughing with whom, and when, and about what or whom?[4] A second important aspect concerns the sounds, facial expressions, and gestures of laughter, and deals with the following questions: How does laughter cause its specific effects? How do we actually distinguish laughter from several other signalling behaviours? In this paper we focus on this latter aspect, and above all stress the acoustic features of laughter.

Characteristics of Human Laughter

As already indicated, laughter, like many other human signal behaviours, is a multimodal display composed of visual and auditory signal components. The visual display of laughter includes a number of specific facial and postural expressions; the components typically involved have been described as follows:

> The upper lip is raised in smiling, it partially uncovers the teeth and also brings down a downward curving of the furrows, which extend from the wings of both nostrils to the corners of the mouth. This in turn, produces a puffing, or rounding out of the cheeks on the outer side of the furrows; creases also occur momentarily

under the eye sockets, the eyes themselves undergo a general change which can best be described as becoming bright and sparkling.[5]

An excellent review of current knowledge on the 'anatomy of laughter', focusing on facial muscles involved and other visible facial and postural expressions, is provided by Ruch and Ekman.[6] Whether the visible or the audible signal components should be treated as the 'evolutionarily older' parts of laughter is still a matter of controversy.[7] In the current state of our knowledge, visual as well as acoustic displays of laughter seem to be promising candidates for representing the biological roots of laughter.

The Structure of Laughter Vocalizations

Although laughter includes both visual and auditory signal components, typical responses to laughter, such as its contagious effect, or positive emotional reactions in the recipient, can be elicited by the acoustic components alone.[8] The canned laughter in television 'sitcoms' or commercial 'laugh-boxes' are examples of this effect in everyday life.

The first quantitative studies on the acoustic characteristics of laughter described it as a simply structured and stereotyped human act.[9] This might well be true if one compares laughter to human speech.[10] However, more recent studies have pointed to a high variability in laughter sounds.[11] In the following discussion we elaborate on the way in which even 'simple' structures can be seen to involve complex behaviour patterns.

In order to understand the mechanisms of the production and perception of laughter, we need to start with a detailed observation and description of this mode of behaviour. Several studies of the acoustics of laughter have shown that laughter consists of sound patterns interrupted by short segments of silence.[12] What is probably the most striking feature of laughter is that these sound patterns are almost always organized in a rhythmical manner: in other words, laughter rarely consists of one single sound alone.[13]

We have developed a hierarchical model to describe the sound patterns of laughter in more detail (see fig. 1).[14] Each discrete sound pattern of laughter, interrupted by short pauses, we call 'laughter elements' (for example, *ha*). Laughter elements can

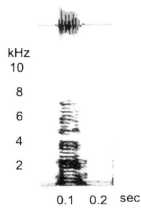

kHz
10

8

6

4

2

0.1   0.2   sec

FIG. 1. The hierarchical organization of laughter vocalizations: amplitude envelope curves and spectrograms.
(a) Laughter element, with specific acoustic characteristics

sample frequency = 22 kHz, resolution = 16-bit
Program Avisoft-SASLab Pro software (R. Specht, Berlin)

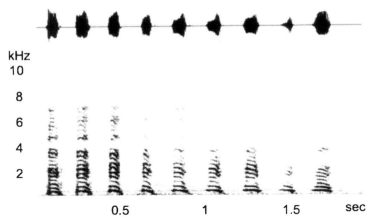

FIG. I. (b) Laughter series (similar laughter elements with slight parameter variations)

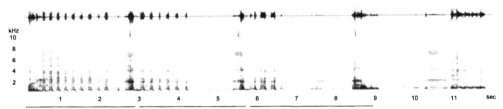

FIG. I. (c) Laughter phrases (one or more laughter phrases form a bout of laughter)
i = sound elements produced during inspiration

show a large variability of acoustic characteristics: they can be voiced or unvoiced, including vowel-like, snort- and grunt-like properties.[15] Successive elements are typically organized as follows: when someone starts to laugh, an isolated, often more pronounced, element is produced, followed by several elements and — sometimes after a prolonged silent interval — one or more final inspiratory sounds. Such a succession of elements forms a 'phrase of laughter' (fig. I(c)). If someone is laughing heartily in a specific context, this 'bout of laughter' will often consist of more than one laughter phrase. Within a phrase, we often find rhythmical element sequences having similar acoustic properties — the 'laughter series' (fig. I (b)). Laughter series consist on average of four or five laughter elements,[16] and are almost always produced during expiration. Such series have often been characterized as 'stereotype structured'.[17] However, within such series of laughter, successive elements almost always show slight changes of acoustic parameters (for example, in the duration, frequency or amplitude of elements). This results in dynamic changes of particular parameters within a phrase, thereby forming gradients. Elements might, for instance, get shorter and shorter towards the end of a laughter series, or the pitch might decrease from element to element. Therefore, we would suggest replacing the term 'stereotyped', and calling these series 'homotype' instead (that is, series consisting of similar, but not identical, elements). Homotype series are important components of communicative systems in non-human primates and other vertebrates,[18] and they can be treated as a source of cryptic but biologically significant information.[19]

This hierarchical organization of laughter sounds seems to be crucial for the listener's detection and evaluation of a laughter episode. There is strong experimental evidence that a recipient, while listening to a laughter-episode, is decoding more than just the information that 'somebody is laughing' (see below). This is no doubt also corroborated by the sheer variety of words in the language describing the sound of laughter. We can, for example, chortle, chuckle, giggle, guffaw, howl, roar, scream, shriek, snigger, snort, or titter. Most of these words not only describe a distinct quality of laughter sounds, they also imply different things about the laughter's intention or disposition. Such information is meaningful for communicative purposes — it might, in other words, affect the level of information conveyed and influence the state of listeners — and it can be conveyed on each of the hierarchical levels of laughter sounds, for example by the quality of the laughter elements, or by parameter changes within a laughter series.

The Evaluation of Laughter by Human Listeners: Experimental Approaches

Bachorowski and Owren's study on the evaluation of voiced and unvoiced laughter was the first to show that listeners differ in their evaluation of laughter depending on the acoustic quality of the laughter elements.[20] In our research group we focused on another hierarchy level, namely the phrases and series of laughter, with changes of acoustic parameters within the succession of the elements of a series. Our central questions were the following: What makes a sequence of successive *ha*-elements sound like laughter? Which acoustic features are used to extract additional information out of a laughter utterance? And which features within a series or phrase evoke particular positive responses?

Like any other acoustic signal, laughter can be characterized by three physical domains: duration, frequency characteristics, including the fundamental frequency perceived as pitch, and energy distribution over the signal. To determine in more detail the role of parameter variation within series of laughter, we adopted a 'reductionistic' approach, in which we investigated the complex structure of laughter by examining each of its properties separately.

We extracted single laughter elements from recordings of natural laughter, digitized them, and changed their duration, frequency, or amplitude. Using this 'construction-kit', we composed artificial laughter series comprising several elements with well-defined parameter changes. Sound analyses of naturally occurring laughter,[21] and typical laughter-sounds as described in other studies[22] guided us in the design of test series with varying rhythms and/or pitch contours. These modified series were broadcast to our participants (more than 400 students took part in the studies), and, immediately after being heard, were rated by means of questionnaires containing, for example, bipolar adjective-pairs such as 'pleasant vs. unpleasant' or 'happy vs. sad', and by scales with statements such as ' ... sounds like laughter' or '... makes me laugh'. With the help of statistical procedures (principal component analyses), answers were subsequently correlated, resulting in a 'Laugh-like' value for each tested series

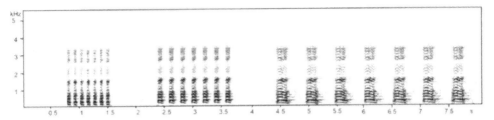

FIG. 2. (a) Examples of artificially modified laughter phrases

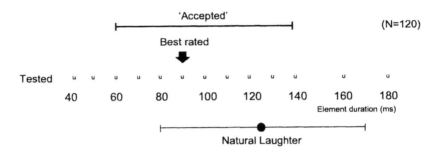

FIG. 2. (b) Results of playback experiments

'Accepted' refers to series that were rated as laughter by at least 80% of participants. Below the time axis is given the mean and S.D. for the element duration measured in natural laughter series (424 laugh-elements in 50 phrases performed by 14 persons).

of artificial laughter. A detailed description of our approach and of the methods we applied is given in our previously published papers.[23]

In an initial experiment we examined whether the duration of laughter elements would affect the rating of subjects (fig. 2). Listeners rated series within a wide range of element durations as laughter. However, there were clear differences in the evaluation of the quality of these series. Laughter series with an element duration of about 90 milliseconds were highest rated. These results were well within the range of durations measured in naturally occurring laughter elements.[24]

Since laughter is often characterized as a 'stereotype sounding', we investigated whether series with a very regular temporal structure (that is, no variation in the duration of successive elements) would get better ratings than series with varied timings or rhythms. To examine this issue, we created phrases that differed in their temporal structure (see fig. 3 for design and results). Phrases with irregular variation in element duration received better ratings than a control not displaying any variation in timing. And a quite similar result was obtained for series with constantly decreasing or increasing element duration. Significantly better ratings were obtained for phrases that differed in a more complex and probably 'surprising' manner: long–short or long–short–short (sounding *Haaa-ha* or *Haaaa-ha-ha*). Thus, adding a specific rhythmic pattern to temporal variability seems to be crucial for a positive evaluation of laughter.[25]

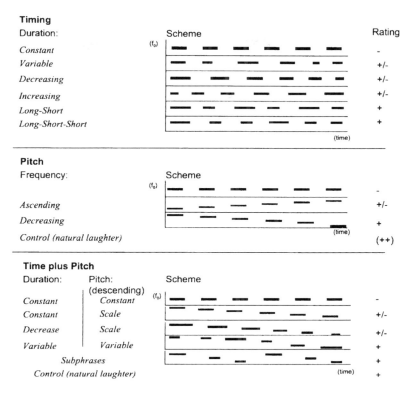

FIG. 3. Rationale and results of playback experiments with artificially modified laughter phrases. Bars in the schemes illustrate the duration and pitch of each laughter element.

- significant worse rated, +/- intermediate rated, + significant better rated

N (Timing) = 61, N (Pitch) = 79, N (Time plus Pitch) = 120 participants

Next, we investigated whether deviating results would be obtained when, instead of temporal features, another parameter, namely the fundamental frequency of laughter elements (here referred to as pitch), was varied. Out of a number of possible patterns we chose three categories of stimuli: constant pitch, and elements regularly rising or falling in pitch (fig. 3, middle). Regularity here refers to a whole-tone scale, that is, where the pitch of successive elements differs by a whole step. The best-rated phrases were those with a descending pitch contour. Subjects characterized these series as 'friendly, familiar and contagious'.[26]

Finally, the outcomes of these studies led us to plan a more integrative experiment, where both element pitch and element timing varied in a specific manner (fig. 3, bottom). Here, we combined the results obtained up to that point and developed test series with specific pitch courses and rhythmical temporal variations. Series with no changes in element duration and constantly declining pitch were low rated, whereas series with changes in both parameters were better rated. Series with descending pitch coupled with 'pronounced elements' (in the timing and the pitch) led to the best results and were rated as being as good as 'natural', not modified, laughter. Referring to the preceding experiments, these series combined the best-rated rhythm with the best-rated pitch-course.[27]

A Model for the Evaluation of Laughter by Human Listeners

So far, most studies have investigated the performance, evaluation and functions of laughter in general, but have devoted little attention to the different qualities of laughter. Our experiments on the evaluation of laughter provide evidence that listeners use the sound of laughter not only to recognize this behaviour in a given situation, but also, via the specific performance of this behaviour, to determine the quality of the laughter. This process leads to a judgement on, or evaluation of, the laughter by listeners. As our experiments demonstrated, such evaluation depends on the performance of parameter changes within laughter series. The acoustic properties characterizing an individual voice do not, by contrast, have that crucial impact on the evaluation of laughter.[28]

Summarizing the results of our playback experiments, we would suggest the following three-part model for intrinsic data-processing by a person listening to a laughter episode (fig. 4). First, a 'recognition mechanism' decides whether or not a given utterance should be perceived as laughter; the serial organization and rhythmic appearance of a vocalization seems to be crucial here. Secondly, the trajectories of intra-serial parameter changes are used to evaluate the quality of laughter; in this fashion, a listener can extract information about intentions and dispositions of the person laughing. Thirdly, accentuated elements or unexpected parameter shifts between successive elements within laughter phrases (and probably also between successive phrases) could account for the contagious effect of laughter. Future research should investigate further the value of this model for our understanding of the mechanisms and functions of human laughter. The suggested mechanisms are in line with proven models of perceptual accomplishments in humans and in non-human primates,[29] and have now been tested in terms of laughter processing.

The second and third parts of this model lead to an additional consideration: if we do indeed extrapolate vectors or rules of parameter variation when we hear a laughter-phrase, and if a violation of these rules (in terms of accentuated elements) leads to contagious reactions, then this process has astonishing similarities to the mental processes underlying our sense of humour. According to the widely accepted theory of humour elicitation,[30] such mental processes are likewise characterized by a reinterpretation of expectations about a situation after an unexpected turn. Although it is far too early to speculate further on this similarity between contagious effects of laughter sounds and humour-eliciting situations, future research should bear this correspondence in mind.

Another interesting aspect of our results are the implications for the so-called 'vector hypothesis'. Originally, this hypothesis was put forward to explain results on the communicative use of vocalizations produced in series of similar sounds, but later it was found to have a more general relevance.[31] The hypothesis predicts that a succession of sound elements can signal a ritualized distance variation of particular

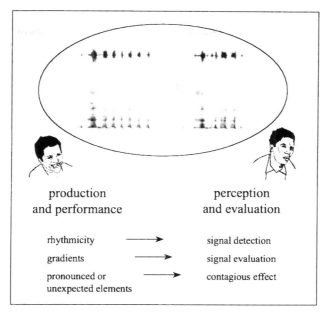

FIG. 4. A preliminary model describing the use of acoustic features of
laughter for its evaluation.

vocal parameters: for instance, an increase in pitch or loudness could symbolize a
signaller's approach, and encode a message that would repel or would suggest risk or
danger. An opposite vector of parameter changes would then stand for messages with
a contrary meaning and which are meant to be decoded as an invitation to closer
contact. With this as a reference, we hypothesized that laughter phrases with negative
vectors of parameter changes — that is, decreasing pitch or duration — would be
evaluated as a particularly friendly message, or a vector of conciliation. Most of our
results confirmed this assumption. The applicability of the 'vector hypothesis' to other
laughter hierarchy levels will be the object of ongoing research. One should expect
characteristic trajectories of parameter changes not only within phrases, but also in
successive phrases, that is, within a bout of laughter.

Outlook

Laughter is produced and perceived in a number of different situations in daily life,[32]
and most of our decisions in social interactions are affected by the perception and
evaluation of non-verbal behaviours.[33] Future research should focus on how those
decisions are achieved and on the role that different qualities of a mode of behaviour
such as laughter play within this process. The present experiments are a first step in
that direction. Investigations of the serial and hierarchical organization of naturally
occurring laughter, and of the way in which it is perceived and evaluated should
further improve our understanding of this non-verbal human signal behaviour.

Notes to Chapter 2

We thank J. Vettin and H. Hultsch for commenting on earlier drafts of this manuscript. A. Ceric kindly provided illustrations. The experiments were funded in part by a grant from the research commission (FNK) of the Freie Universität Berlin.

1. Reviewed in R. R. Provine, *Laughter: A Scientific Investigation* (London: Faber, 2000).
2. See A. J. Chapman, 'Funniness of Jokes, Canned Laughter and Recall Performance', *Sociometry*, 36 (1973), 569–78; and R. R. Provine, 'Contagious Laughter: Laughter is a Sufficient Stimulus for Laughs and Smiles', *Bulletin of the Psychonomic Society*, 30 (1992), 1–4.
3. Reviewed in Provine, *Laughter: A Scientific Investigation*.
4. See K. Grammer, 'Strangers Meet: Laughter and Non-Verbal Signs of Interest in Opposite-Sex Encounters', *Journal of Nonverbal Behavior*, 14 (1990), 209–36; and D. Keltner and G. A. Bonanno, 'A Study of Laughter and Dissociation: Distinct Correlates of Laughter and Smiling during Bereavement', *Journal of Personality and Social Psychology*, 73 (1997), 687–702.
5. See J. J. M. Askenasy, 'The Functions and Dysfunctions of Laughter', *Journal of General Psychology*, 114 (1987), 317–34.
6. W. Ruch and P. Ekman, 'The Expressive Pattern of Laughter', in *Emotion, Qualia and Consciousness*, ed. by A. W. Kaszniak (Tokyo: World Scientific Publisher, 2001), pp. 426–43.
7. See J. Vettin and D. Todt, 'Human Laughter, Social Play and Play Vocalizations of Non-Human Primates: An Evolutionary Approach', *Behaviour*, 142 (2005), pp. 217–40.
8. See Provine, 'Contagious Laughter'; G. N. Martin and C. D. Gray, 'The Effect of Audience Laughter on Men's and Women's Responses to Humor', *Journal of Social Psychology*, 136 (1996), 221–31; T. J. Lawson, B. Downing, and H. Cetola, 'An Attributional Explanation for the Effect of Audience Laughter on Perceived Funniness', *Basic and Applied Social Psychology*, 20 (1998), 243–49; S. Kipper and D. Todt, 'The Role of Rhythm and Pitch in the Evaluation of Human Laughter', *Journal of Nonverbal Behavior*, 25 (2003), 255–72.
9. R. R. Provine and Y. L. Yong, 'Laughter: A Stereotyped Human Vocalization', *Ethology*, 89 (1991), 115–24.
10. D. E. Mowrer, L. L. LaPointe, and J. Case, 'Analysis of Five Acoustic Correlates of Laughter', *Journal of Nonverbal Behavior*, 11 (1987), 191–99; H. Rothgänger and others, 'Analysis of Laughter and Speech Sounds in Italian and German Students', *Naturwissenschaften*, 85 (1998), 394–402.
11. J.-A. Bachorowski, M. J. Smoski, and M. J. Owren, 'The Acoustic Features of Human Laughter', *Journal of the Acoustic Society of America*, 110 (2001), 1581–97.
12. G. S. Hall and A. Allin, 'The Psychology of Tickling, Laughing, and the Comic', *American Journal of Psychology*, 9 (1897), 1–41; L. L. Lapointe, D. M. Mowrer, and J. L. Case, 'A Comparative Acoustic Analysis of the Laugh Responses of 20- and 70-Year-Old Males', *International Journal of Aging and Human Development*, 31 (1990), 1–9.
13. E. E. Nwokah and others, 'The Integration of Laughter and Speech in Vocal Communication: A Dynamic Systems Perspective', *Journal of Speech, Language, and Hearing Research*, 42 (1999), 880–94; S. Kipper and D. Todt, 'Variation of Sound Parameters Affects the Evaluation of Human Laughter', *Behaviour*, 138 (2001), 1161–78.
14. Kipper and Todt, 'Variation of Sound Parameters'; and S. Kipper and D. Todt 'Dynamic-Acoustic Variation Causes Differences in Evaluations of Laughter', *Perceptual and Motor Skills*, 96 (2003), 799–809.
15. Bachorowski, Smoski, and Owren, 'The Acoustic Features '.
16. Mowrer, LaPointe, and Case, 'Analysis of Five Acoustic Correlates'; Rothgänger and others, 'Analysis of Laughter and Speech Sounds'; Bachorowski, Smoski, and Owren, 'The Acoustic Features'.
17. Provine and Yong, 'Laughter: A Stereotyped Human Vocalization'.
18. D. Todt, 'Hinweis-Charakter und Mittlerfunktion von Verhalten', *Zeitschrift für Semiotik*, 8 (1986), 183–232; D. Todt, 'Serial Calling as a Mediator of Interaction Processes: Crying in Primates', in *Primate Vocal Communication*, ed. by D. Todt, P. Goedeking, and D. Symmes (Berlin: Springer, 1988), pp. 88–103; K. R. Scherer and A. Kappas, 'Primate Vocal Expression of Affective State', in *Primate Vocal Communication*, pp. 171–94; P. Marler, C. S. Evans, and M. D. Hauser, 'Animal Signals: Motivational, Referential, or Both?', in *Nonverbal Vocal Communication*, ed. by H. Papousek, U. Jürgens, and M. Papousek (Cambridge: Cambridge University Press: 1992), pp. 66–86; H. Hultsch and D. Todt, 'Rules

of Parameter Variation in Homotype Series of Birdsong can Indicate a "Sollwert" Significance', *Behavioural Processes*, 38 (1996), 175–82.

19. D. Todt and H. Hultsch, 'Variation that Follows Rules', *Behavioral and Brain Sciences*, 15 (1992), 289–90.

20. J.-A. Bachorowski and M. J. Owren, 'Not All Laughs are Alike: Voiced but not Unvoiced Laughter Readily Elicits Positive Affect', *Psychological Science*, 12 (2001), 252–57.

21. Kipper and Todt, 'Dynamic-Acoustic Variation Causes Differences'.

22. M. S. Edmonson, 'Notes on Laughter', *Anthropological Linguistics*, 29 (1987), 23–33; Rothgänger and others, 'Analysis of Laughter and Speech Sounds'; Provine, *Laughter: A Scientific Investigation*.

23. Kipper and Todt, 'Variation of Sound Parameters', 'The Role of Rhythm and Pitch'.

24. Kipper and Todt, 'Dynamic-Acoustic Variation Differences'.

25. Kipper and Todt, 'The Role of Rhythm and Pitch'.

26. Kipper and Todt, 'Variation of Sound Parameters'.

27. Kipper and Todt, 'The Role of Rhythm and Pitch'.

28. Kipper and Todt, 'The Role of Rhythm and Pitch', 'Dynamic-Acoustic Variation Differences'.

29. Reviewed in J. Pittam and K. R. Scherer, 'Vocal Expression and Communication of Emotion', in *Handbook of Emotions*, ed. by M. Lewis and J. M. Haviland (New York: Guildford, 1993), pp. 185–97.

30. R. S. Wyer, Jr and J. E. Collins II, 'A Theory of Humor Elicitation', *Psychological Review*, 99 (1992), 663–88.

31. Todt, 'Hinweis-Charakter und Mittlerfunktion'.

32. R. A. Martin and N. A. Kuiper, 'Daily Occurrence of Laughter: Relationships with Age, Gender and Type A Personality', *HUMOR: International Journal of Humor Research*, 12 (1999), 355–84.

33. P. Ekman and others, 'Relative Importance of Face, Body, and Speech in Judgements of Personality and Affect', *Journal of Personality and Social Psychology*, 38 (1980), 270–77; Grammer, 'Strangers Meet'; J. P. W. Scharlemann and others, 'The Value of a Smile: Game Theory with a Human Face', *Journal of Economic Psychology*, 22 (2001), 617–40.

CHAPTER 3

Why Can't You Tickle Yourself?

Sarah-Jayne Blakemore

Tickling: a Universal Phenomenon

Tickling is a common, perhaps universal, experience. Depictions of people engaged in some kind of tickling activity, whether it be between siblings, parents and children, or lovers, can be found in the art of many countries and cultures. Tickling someone often causes people to smile and laugh in a way that is indistinguishable from the laughter caused by being highly amused. However, tickling is a curious, paradoxical phenomenon. A ticklish person will often wriggle and writhe in agony as well as laugh hysterically when being tickled. Francis Bacon in the seventeenth century commented that: '[when tickled] men even in a grieved state of mind ... cannot sometimes forbear laughing' (Bacon 1677).

Tickling usually occurs only between people who know each other well: children are likely to be tickled by their parents and siblings, adults are likely only to be tickled by their lovers. Normally the tickler is someone who desires to express emotion and affection through their tickle; the source of the tickle is a friendly one. Although there is often an inequality of power during tickling — ticklishness increases if the ticklee feels that they cannot escape from the tickler — ticklishness normally occurs in situations that are entirely non-threatening. Charles Darwin (1872) suggested that if a stranger tried to tickle a child the child would scream with fear rather than squeal with laughter. Darwin proposed that tickling is an important aspect of social and sexual bonding, and prominent in the development of communication between mothers and babies. Tickle-induced laughter, he argued, is socially-induced and results from close physical contact with another person. An alternative claim is that tickle-induced laughter is purely reflexive, something that happens without our voluntary control, similar to the reflex induced when a doctor taps one's knee.

Even animals seem to be ticklish. When you tickle the great apes, they react with what is believed to be an analog of laughter — a panting sound. Recent research shows that even rats squeal with pleasure when tickled, although you need a bat detector to hear the sounds because they are at frequencies too high for human ears to detect. But as sounds they are interpreted as joy because they differ markedly from distress calls, and instead are similar to the sounds made by a male while courting females. The suggestion that tickling behaviour appears to be universal among mammals suggests it may lie at the root of the complex social behaviour of our species.

You Can't Tickle Yourself

Tickling is a pleasure that 'cannot be reproduced in the absence of another', wrote Adam Phillips (1994). The distinction between self sensations and external sensations seems to be physiologically hard-wired. Humans can readily distinguish between sensations that are produced by one's own movements and sensations that are caused by a change in the environment. This ability is important because it enables us to pick out stimuli that correspond to potentially biologically significant external events from stimuli that arise simply as a consequence of our own motor actions. It has been proposed that information about motor commands is used to distinguish the sensory consequences of our own actions from externally produced sensory stimuli (Wolpert & others 1995; Jeannerod 1997; Wolpert 1997).

This kind of mechanism can be used to maintain perceptual stability in the presence of self-produced movement. Helmholtz (1867) noted that when making eye movements, the percept of the world remains stable despite the movement of the retinal image. He suggested that the *effort of will* involved in making eye movements contains information about the sensory consequences of the eye movement, which is sent to the visual areas in order for perceptual compensation to occur. Holst (1954) investigated this hypothesis and suggested that when sending motor commands to move the eyes, the motor areas of the brain send a parallel *efference copy* to the visual areas. This is used to predict the sensory consequences (*corollary discharge*) of the movement, and this prediction is the signal used to compensate for retinal displacement during eye movements (Sperry 1950).

Although these mechanisms have mainly been studied with reference to eye movements, it appears that sensory predictions produced in conjunction with motor commands are not restricted to eye movements, but also provide perceptual stability in the context of all self-produced actions. Our ability to monitor, and recognize as our own, self-generated limb movements, touch, speech and thoughts suggests the existence of a more general 'self-monitoring' mechanism (Feinberg 1978; Frith 1992).

Forward Models Predict the Consequences of Action

It has recently been suggested that this self-monitoring mechanism involves an internal representation of the motor system (Frith & others 2000). Internal 'forward models' mimic aspects of the external world and the motor system in order to capture the forward or causal relationship between actions and their outcomes (Ito 1970; Wolpert & others 1995). Forward models make predictions about the sensory consequences of self-generated movements on the basis of the efference copy generated in parallel with the motor command. Here, efference copy is an exact replica of the motor command. An analogy might be e-mail: if the motor command is the e-mail itself, efference copy is the carbon copy of the e-mail. It contains the same information as the e-mail but is sent somewhere else.

The predicted sensory consequences are then compared with the actual sensory feedback from the movement. Self-produced sensations can be correctly predicted on the basis of motor commands, and there will therefore be little or no sensory discrepancy resulting from the comparison between the predicted and actual sensory feedback. In contrast, externally generated sensations are not associated with any efference copy and therefore cannot be predicted by the model and will produce a higher level of sensory discrepancy. By using such a system, it is possible to cancel out sensations induced by self-generated movement and thereby distinguish sensory events due to self-produced motion from sensory feedback caused by the environment, such as contact with objects.

Forward Models in Schizophrenia

Frith (1992) proposed that a defect in this kind of central self-monitoring mechanism might underlie auditory hallucinations and passivity phenomena, which are 'first rank' features in schizophrenia (Schneider 1959). Auditory hallucinations normally consist of hearing spoken voices (Hoffman 1986; Johnstone 1991). The essence of passivity experiences (or delusions of control) is that the subject experiences his or her will as replaced by that of some other force or agency (Wing & others 1974): 'My fingers pick up the pen, but I don't control them. What they do is nothing to do with me ... The force moved my lips. I began to speak. The words were made for me' (Mellors 1970).

Frith has suggested that these abnormal experiences arise through a lack of awareness of intended actions. Such an impairment might cause thoughts or actions to become isolated from the sense of will normally associated with them. This would result in the interpretation of internally generated voices or thoughts as external voices (auditory hallucinations and thought insertion) and of one's own movements and speech as externally caused (passivity experiences). It has been suggested that the experience of passivity arises from a lack of awareness of the predicted limb position based on the forward model (Frith & others 2000). Thus the patient is aware of the intention to move and of the movement having occurred, but is not aware of having initiated the movement. It is as if the movement, though intended, has been initiated by some external force.

The Perception of the Sensory Consequences of Actions

Evidence suggests that the sensory consequences of some self-generated movements are perceived differently from identical sensory input when it is externally generated. An example of such differential perception is the phenomenon that people cannot tickle themselves (Weiskrantz & others 1971). It has been argued that efference copy underlies this phenomenon. In Weiskrantz, Elliot and Darlington's study, a tactile stimulus that transversed the sole of the subject's foot was administered either by the experimenter or by the subject. Subjects rated the self-administered tactile stimulus as less tickly than the externally administered tactile stimulus. The authors attributed the differences in response to the mode of delivery: self-administered tactile stimulation produces efference copy whereas externally administered tactile stimulation does not. The authors concluded that the attenuation signal is based mainly on the efference copy signal produced in concordance with a self-generated movement.

We designed an experiment to test whether the perceptual attenuation of self-produced tactile stimulation is due to precise sensory predictions of the forward model. Subjects were asked to rate the sensation of a tactile stimulus on the palm of their hand when the correspondence between self-generated movement and its sensory consequences was altered. This was achieved by introducing parametrically varied degrees of delay or trajectory rotation between the subject's movement and the resultant tactile stimulation. The result of increasing the delay or trajectory rotation is that the sensory stimulus no longer corresponds to what would normally be expected based on the efference copy produced in parallel with the motor command. Therefore, as the delay or trajectory rotation increases, the sensory prediction becomes less accurate. A robotic interface was employed to produce the delays and trajectory rotations. Subjects moved a robotic arm with their left hand and this movement caused a second foam-tipped robotic arm to move across their right palm. Thus, motion of the left hand determined the tactile stimulus on the right palm. By using this robotic interface so that the tactile stimulus could be delivered under remote control by the subject, *delays* of 100, 200 and 300 milliseconds (ms) were introduced between the movement of the left hand and the tactile stimulus on the right palm. In a further condition, *trajectory rotations* of 30°, 60° and 90° were introduced between the direction of the left hand movement and the direction of the tactile stimulus on the right palm.

The results showed that subjects rated the self-produced tactile sensation as being significantly less tickly, intense, and pleasant than an identical stimulus produced by the robot (Blakemore & others 1999). Furthermore, subjects reported a progressive increase in the tickly rating as the delay was increased between 0 ms and 200 ms and as the trajectory rotation was increased between 0° and 90°. These results support the hypothesis that the perceptual attenuation of self-produced tactile stimulation is due to precise sensory predictions. When there is no delay or trajectory rotation, the model correctly predicts the sensory consequences of the movement; so no sensory discrepancy ensues between the predicted and actual sensory information, and the motor command to the left hand can be used to attenuate the sensation on the right palm. As the sensory feedback deviates from the prediction of the model (by increasing the delay or trajectory rotation), the sensory discrepancy between the predicted and actual sensory feedback increases, which leads to a decrease in the amount of sensory attenuation.

The Physiological Basis of the Perceptual Modulation of Self-produced Sensory Stimuli

Neuronal responses in the somatosensory cortex (the area of the brain that processes touch) are attenuated by self-generated movement (Chapin & Woodward 1982; Chapman 1994). There is less response from somatosensory neurons when an animal actively moves its skin over a surface than when the surface is moved over the animal's skin. It is possible that this movement-induced somatosensory gating is the physiological correlate of the decreased sensation associated with self-produced tactile stimuli in humans. In order for somatosensory cortex activity to be attenuated to self-produced sensory stimuli, these stimuli need to be predicted accurately. The cerebellum is a possible site for a forward model of the motor apparatus that provides predictions of the sensory consequences of motor commands (for example: Ito 1970; Miall & others 1993; Wolpert & others 1998; Imamizu & others 2000).

In a second study, we used a brain-imaging technique called functional Magnetic Resonance Imaging (fMRI) to examine the neural basis of self-produced versus externally produced tactile stimuli in humans (Blakemore & others 1998). Subjects were scanned while a tactile stimulation device was used to apply a tactile stimulus (a piece of soft foam) to the subject's left palm. This stimulus was produced either by the subject's right hand or by the experimenter. The results showed an increase in activity of the secondary somatosensory cortex (SII) and the anterior cingulate gyrus (ACG) when subjects experienced an externally produced tactile stimulus relative to a self-produced tactile stimulus. The reduction in activity in these areas to self-produced tactile stimulation might be the physiological correlate of the reduced perception associated with this type of stimulation. The activity in the ACG in particular may have been related to the increased tickliness and pleasantness of externally produced compared to self-produced tactile stimuli. Previous studies have implicated this area in affective behaviour and positive reinforcement (Vogt & Gabriel 1993).

While the decrease in activity in SII and ACG might underlie the reduced perception of self-produced tactile stimuli, the pattern of brain activity in the cerebellum suggests that this area is the source of the SII and ACG modulation. In SII and ACG, activity was attenuated by all movement: these areas were equally activated by movement that did and movement that did not result in tactile stimulation. In contrast, the right anterior cerebellar cortex was selectively deactivated by self-produced movement when that resulted in a tactile stimulus, but not by movement alone, and significantly activated by externally produced tactile stimulation. This pattern suggests that the cerebellum differentiates between movements depending on their specific sensory consequences. Our data suggest that the cerebellum is involved in predicting the specific sensory consequences of movements, and in providing the signal that is used to attenuate the somatosensory response to self-produced tactile stimulation.

A second brain imaging experiment supported the proposal that the cerebellum distinguishes between movements depending on their specific sensory consequences (Blakemore & others 2001). In this experiment participants were scanned using positron emission tomography (PET) while generating a tactile stimulus on the palm of their hand, as before. This time, however, the tactile stimulation was produced under remote control via a robotic interface. Participants moved a robotic arm with their left hand and this movement caused a second foam-tipped robotic arm to move across their right palm. By using this robotic interface so that the tactile stimulus could be delivered under remote control by the participant, delays of 0, 100, 200 and 300 ms were introduced between the movement of the left hand and the tactile stimulus on the right palm. Under all delays the left hand made the same movements and the right hand experienced the tactile stimulus. Only the temporal correspondence between the movement of the left hand and the sensory effect on the right palm was altered. The assumption behind this design was that as the delay increases, the forward model prediction becomes less accurate, and the sensory discrepancy between the predicted and actual sensory feedback from movement increases. Blood flow in the right cerebellar cortex significantly correlated with delay. This suggests that activity in this region increases as the actual feedback from movement deviates from the predicted sensory feedback. On the basis of these results, we proposed that the cerebellum is involved in signalling discrepancies between the predicted and actual consequences of action.

The Perception of the Sensory Consequences of Actions in Patients with Auditory Hallucinations and/or Passivity Experiences

To test the hypothesis that certain symptomatology associated with schizophrenia is due to a defect in self-monitoring, we investigated whether patients with auditory hallucinations and/or passivity experiences are abnormally aware of the sensory consequences of their own movements. Patients with a diagnosis of schizophrenia, bipolar affective disorder, or depression were divided into two groups on the basis of the presence or absence of auditory hallucinations and/or passivity experiences. These patient groups and a group of age-matched normal control subjects were asked to rate the perception of a tactile sensation on the palm of their left hand. The tactile stimulation was either self-produced by movement of the subject's right hand or externally produced by the experimenter.

The results demonstrated that normal control subjects, and patients with neither auditory hallucinations nor passivity experiences, experienced self-produced stimuli as less intense, tickly, and pleasant than identical, externally produced tactile stimuli. In contrast, patients with these symptoms did not show a decrease in their perceptual ratings for tactile stimuli produced by themselves as compared to those produced by the experimenter (Blakemore & others 2000). These results support the proposal that auditory hallucinations and passivity experiences are associated with an abnormality in the forward model mechanism that normally allows us to distinguish self-produced from externally produced sensations. It is possible that the neural system associated with this mechanism, or part of it, operates abnormally in people with such symptoms.

Conclusion

This research supports the proposal that the attenuation of self-produced tactile stimulation is due to the sensory predictions made by an internal forward model of the motor system. Brain-imaging studies have demonstrated that this sensory attenuation might be mediated by the somatosensory cortex and anterior cingulate cortex: these areas are activated less by a self-produced tactile stimulus than by the same stimulus when it is externally produced. Furthermore, evidence suggests that the cerebellum might be involved in generating the prediction of the sensory consequences of movement. Thus, it seems that the mechanism that distinguishes self-stimulation and external tactile stimulation is hard-wired in the human brain. This mechanism is useful because it allows biologically important information (such as external sensations) to be picked out from the less important sensory information, such as that which is self-produced, that constantly bombards the brain. A possibly accidental consequence of this filtering system is that a self-produced tickle does not feel as intense as an external tickle.

Acknowledgement

The work discussed in this article was funded by the Wellcome Trust.

References

BACON, FRANCIS. 1677. *Sylva Sylvarum, or A Natural History* (London: S. G. and B. Griffin for T. Lee), VII, 721–66

BLAKEMORE, S.-J., D. M. WOLPERT & C. D. FRITH. 1998. 'Central Cancellation of Self-Produced Tickle Sensation', *Nature Neuroscience*, 1: 635–40

—— C. D. FRITH & D. M. WOLPERT. 1999. 'Spatiotemporal Prediction Modulates the Perception of Self-Produced Stimuli', *Journal of Cognitive Neuroscience*, 11: 551–59

—— —— —— 2001. 'The Cerebellum is Involved in Predicting the Sensory Consequences of Action', *NeuroReport*, 12: 1879–85

—— & others. 2000. 'The Perception of Self-produced Sensory Stimuli in Patients with Auditory Hallucinations and Passivity Experiences: Evidence for a Breakdown in Self-monitoring', *Psychological Medicine*, 30: 1131–39

CHAPIN, J. K. & D. J. WOODWARD. 1982. 'Somatic Sensory Transmission to the Cortex during Movement: Gating of Single Cell Responses to Touch', *Experimental Neurology*, 78: 654–69

CHAPMAN, C. E. 1994. 'Active versus Passive Touch: Factors Influencing the Transmission of Somatosensory Signals to Primary Somatosensory Cortex', *Canadian Journal of Physiology and Pharmacology*, 72: 558–70

DARWIN, C. 1872. *The Expression of the Emotions in Man and Animals* (London: John Murray)

FEINBERG, I. 1978. 'Efference Copy and Corollary Discharge: Implications for Thinking and its Disorders', *Schizophrenia Bulletin*, 4: 636–40

FRITH, C. D. 1992. *The Cognitive Neuropsychology of Schizophrenia* (Hove: L. Erlbaum)

—— S.-J. BLAKEMORE & D. M. WOLPERT. 2000. 'Abnormalities in the Awareness and Control of Action', *Philosophical Transactions of the Royal Society of London: Biological Sciences*, 355: 1771–88

HELMHOLTZ, H. 1867. *Handbuch der Physiologischen Optik* (Hamburg: Voss)

HOFFMAN, R. E. 1986. 'Verbal Hallucinations and Language Production Processes in Schizophrenia', *Behavioral and Brain Sciences*, 9: 503–17

HOLST, E. VON. 1954. 'Relations between the Central Nervous System and the Peripheral Organs', *British Journal of Animal Behaviour*, 2: 89–94

IMAMIZU, I. & others. 2000. 'Human Cerebellar Activity Reflecting an Acquired Internal Model of a New Tool', *Nature*, 403: 192–95

ITO, M. 1970. 'Neurophysiological Aspects of the Cerebellar Motor Control System', *International Journal of Neurology*, 7: 162–76

JEANNEROD, M. 1997. *The Cognitive Neuropsychology of Action* (Oxford and Cambridge, MA: Blackwell)

JOHNSTONE, E. C. 1991. 'Defining Characteristics of Schizophrenia', *British Journal of Psychiatry Supplement*, 13: 5–6

MELLORS, C. S. 1970. 'First-Rank Symptoms of Schizophrenia', *British Journal of Psychiatry*, 117: 15–23

MIALL, R. C. & others. 1993. 'Is the Cerebellum a Smith Predictor?', *Journal of Motor Behaviour*, 25: 203–16

PHILLIPS, A. 1994. *On Kissing, Tickling, and Being Bored: Psychoanalytic Essays on the Unexamined Life* (Cambridge, MA: Harvard University Press)

SCHNEIDER, K. 1959. *Clinical Psychopathology* (New York: Grune & Stratton)

SPERRY, R. W. 1950. 'Neural Basis of Spontaneous Optokinetic Responses Produced by Visual Inversion', *Journal of Comparative Physiological Psychology*, 43: 482–89

VOGT, B. A. & M. GABRIEL (eds.). 1993. *Neurobiology of Cingulate Cortex and Limbic Thalamus* (Boston: Birkauser)

WEISKRANTZ, L., J. ELLIOT & C. DARLINGTON. 1971. 'Preliminary Observations of Tickling Oneself', *Nature*, 230: 598–99

WING, J. K., J. E. COOPER & N. SARTORIUS. 1974. *Description and Classification of Psychiatric Symptoms* (London: Cambridge University Press)

WOLPERT, D. M. 1997. 'Computational Approaches to Motor Control', *Trends in Cognitive Sciences*, 1: 209–16

—— Z. GHAHRAMANI & M. I. JORDAN. 1995. 'An Internal Model for Sensorimotor Integration', *Science*, 269: 1880–82

—— R. C. MIALL & M. KAWATO. 1998. 'Internal Models in the Cerebellum', *Trends in Cognitive Sciences*, 2: 338–47

CHAPTER 4

Belly Laughs

Michael Holland

On l'a échappé belle!
RAYMOND DEVOS[1]

According to Bergson, laughter 'poses a challenge to philosophical speculation'.[2] And of all laughter, I would suggest, it is what we call the *belly laugh* that poses the greatest challenge of all. It is a common experience, as common as a yawn or a sigh, and what all these common experiences have in common is the fact that they *escape* us. And they escape us in so far as they briefly challenge the supremacy of our rational minds, momentarily giving our bodies the lead in responding to what it is that we are experiencing. It is because they escape us in this way that they pose a challenge to philosophical speculation, and to rational analysis in general. When a yawn, a sigh, or a belly laugh escapes me, I temporarily lose my rational oversight of the border line *between* the subjective and the objective. My mind and my body are no longer as distinct from each other as reason would dictate. If what escapes me escapes philosophical analysis, therefore, it is because it cannot be reduced, neatly and obligingly, to the status of an *object* of speculation or analysis.

But the belly laugh goes further than that. It does not just escape analysis by refusing to be an object for an analysis: in so doing, it deprives analysis of its rational subject. In other words, its escape interferes with my ability to engage in rational analysis. The challenge it poses is not confined to philosophy, therefore: it extends to the entire field of rational sociability that we call the human world. You may say that a yawn does that too, and indeed that all laughter can do the same thing. Yawning and laughing are a sort of declaration of independence in the face of rational argument, a refusal to go along with what someone is saying (indeed they may well be happening as I speak!).

Still, the belly laugh is different. Yawning and laughter base their challenge to rational analysis on a continuing awareness of what it is they are challenging: to continue to mount a challenge, they require me to go on paying attention to what it is they challenge. But when a laugh becomes a belly laugh, it completely extinguishes my attention to what someone is saying. My laughter ceases to accompany rational analysis (critically or approvingly), and as it escapes it takes me with it, leaving rational analysis behind — eclipsed, or rather, somewhere beneath the horizon, its function entirely usurped. In short, it is of the essence of the belly laugh that it escapes rational analysis by substituting itself entirely for rational analysis.

An illustration of this: in a science class, the teacher may liven up a presentation of, say, heat conduction in metals, by recalling an age when men of science explained the phenomenon by saying that little red demons ran from the fire into the metal and made it glow. The laughter that will no doubt arise in response to such a preposterous belief will in no way obscure the scientific knowledge that the teacher is seeking to impart, and will in fact probably assist in the learning process. But imagine the teacher has some peculiar, idiosyncratic speech habit; for example, separating the 'n' of the indefinite article 'an' from the 'a' and attaching it to the opening vowel of the noun the article qualifies, thus creating a sort of private vocabulary consisting of words such as a *nacid*, a *nalkali*, a *natom,* a *nexperiment*, a *nobstacle* etc. Add to that a habit of saying 'eeer, eeer' a lot while addressing the class, so that, very occasionally, he will come out with sentences such as: 'eeer...if you mix...eeer...a...eeer...nacid...and a... eeer...nalkali etc.'. It is most unlikely that such a teacher will ever elicit from a class the sort of laughter that accompanies analytical thought and, as it were, oils its works, for the simple reason that the class, as a body, will be predisposed to laugh only at occurrences of the teacher's verbal idiosyncrasy, making it as a consequence acutely attentive to the teacher, whilst paying no attention at all to what the teacher is trying to get it to understand.

It is this rogue — and roguish — attention that defines the belly laugh and dist- inguishes it from other forms of laughter, as well as from yawning or sighing. With this sort of uncontrollable laughter, we defy the rules and discipline that reason dictates. It is hugely liberating. It gives us instant access to absolute freedom from all current constraints upon us. And it would be reasonable to assume that that is why we rate it so positively. But things are not so straightforward. The freedom we achieve in the belly laugh does not transfer control to us. It is a freedom over which we have no control. Indeed, if enjoyed unchecked, it causes us gradually to *lose* that control which is essential to our existence as rational and moral social beings: control over our bodily functions. The belly laugh does not just come *from* the belly: it results in an escape of bodily fluids that rapidly extends *to* the belly, as we cry with laughing, wet ourselves, and eventually even lose control of our bowels. As we dissolve into the uncontrollable laughter we call the belly laugh, the process described metaphorically can thus leave behind an embarrassing physical trace. In a sense, we die laughing: actors call the helpless laughter that sometimes overtakes them on stage *corpsing*, and our loss of composure prefigures our ultimate physical decomposition.

The attention we pay in every circumstance of our lives, from the most crucial to the most banal, and which is constitutive of our rational and moral self (the one we approve of and seek approval for), is thus shadowed in us by what may be called an attention in waiting, an attention that bides its time. This attention exists in an uneasy truce with the attention to which we owe what empowers us as rational beings. Furthermore, not only is it as powerful as that attention: it is in fact *more* powerful than rational attention. For most of the time, its superior power displays itself as self–abnegation, which it graciously allows our rational attention to claim the credit for as a sign of *its* superior power, until, unpredictably almost always (at least from the standpoint of our rational self), it is awakened. The attention in waiting, which was silently shadowing the unbroken activity of our rational attention, suddenly and overwhelmingly *gives* attention to something that, from the rational standpoint, is at best of no *particular* significance, and is usually quite meaningless, distracting the person in whom it has awakened from rational sociability, sweeping them away on its waves into the solitude of their own bodies, and ultimately exposing them, in full bodily *un*control, to acute embarrassment: first that of others, then, as they regain their rational attention to things, their own.

From that perspective, the astonishing thing is how much we value the experience of such laughter, and how little we fear it (although we all know the *dread* of going into a situation where rational attention is required, and above all the composure that is its outer sign, knowing that we, alone or in connivance with others, are likely to get the giggles). This raises two issues, which I can only leave hanging:

1. Does the glance exchanged with another person or persons, or else their physical proximity, each of which can provide the trigger for uncontrollable laughter, make the belly laugh a mode of communication or even communion? Or is it always ultimately a solitary experience?

2. In what relation does that experience stand to the sexual relation, as expressed by the glance or by physical proximity? Is it possible to imagine a parallel universe in which procreation is dealt with swiftly and efficiently, while desire, from seduction to orgasm, is satisfied by means of paroxysms of laughter, in a physical relation for which the other is indispensable, but where no one actually touches anyone? Which leads to one of those impossible questions (such as, would you rather be blind or deaf?): which would you give up, the orgasm or the belly laugh?

Simply to illustrate the enigma to which all of that points, I recall a lecture given by a renowned anthropologist in the 1970s. To illustrate what he meant by taboo words, the anthropologist said that if he pronounced the word VIRGIN in front of the audience, sooner or later someone would begin to laugh uncontrollably. This idea produced a ripple of laughter from the audience in response. Then there was silence. He said VIRGIN. After a pause, a poor, unfortunate individual began to laugh uncontrollably, to the amusement, but also the unease, of the audience; to the acute embarrassment of the laugher; and, one assumes, to the immense satisfaction of the anthropologist! No loss of bodily control of the sort I have referred to (at least, none that I was aware of). Nevertheless, an intriguing confrontation, somewhere in the body, between loss of composure through laughter and the absolute sexual composure of virginity.

Culturally speaking, none of what I have been saying about the belly laugh is particularly original. In the knowledge that we have this well-spring of total and uncontrollable freedom in us, our culture has long provided us with a time and a place for belly laughs: music halls, cabarets, working men's clubs, comedy stores, and, more generally, theatre, radio, and TV shows all provide outlets for belly laughs to escape; a variety of venues where, for a time, we can abandon ourselves to the absolute freedom of this 'primitive' activity, without regard for correctness of any sort (although usually, it must be said, without abandoning control of our bodies entirely). And the primary role of such institutionalization, I would suggest, is to offer a model of containment to people for when they cannot contain themselves. British culture, so deficient in many of the areas where European culture has flourished over the last century, leaves other nations standing in the domain of comedy — which is to say: the belly laugh. From Fringe to Flying Circus, from Goons to League of Gentlemen, from ITMA to AbFab, from Hilda Baker to Victoria Wood, the British are brutish to perfection.

But what I want to focus on here is a form of belly laugh that is not corralled, contained, and turned into a form of controlled escapism — that being the only *cultural* form of it we know; but which is not just on the loose either, *out* of control, disruptive and ultimately destructive — which is the only *social* form of it we know. It is a form that, in both social and cultural terms, is very new, even though it first appeared over one hundred years ago. And it arises from allowing belly laughs to escape, and escape us, within a situation where their presence is unexpected and incongruous, a situation that is therefore forced to contain what it is not designed to contain.

This takes us to France at the very end of the nineteenth century, where a major institution, the theatre — serious theatre — became the site of a radical experiment. A truly bizarre individual named Alfred Jarry persuaded the director of one of the major Paris theatres to let him put on a play he had written. The play's title was *Ubu roi*.[3] It was originally conceived by a group of schoolboys as a satire on their science master. It ran for all of one night, on 10 December 1896, yet it is widely seen as *the* seminal work for the entire avant-garde tradition in twentieth-century theatre. And all of the originality of Jarry's play is reflected in the role it gives to the belly laugh. This is, first and foremost, because of the role played by the belly in *Ubu roi*. Ubu is a grotesque glutton. He has his literary forebears in Shakespeare, in Rabelais, and that is not without significance, as we shall see. Yet his *effect* on the audience that night, but also on audiences ever since, had nothing whatsoever to do with literature and the socio-cultural community which that presupposes in an audience: Ubu is simply gross, both verbally and physically. His opening word is 'Merdre!' ('Shittr' in Barbara Wright's translation);[4] his gut is the bulging focus of his attention and his activity; he feeds, and feeds his guests, on dishes made of shit, and wields a toilet-brush as an offensive weapon, forcing his enemies at one point to lick it, whereupon they fall down dead.

I hope I am disgusting you. I hope some of my readers at least are laughing while feeling disgusted. Because among those who didn't simply walk out in 1896 (and a good number did), that mix of laughter and disgust, which made up their response to the figure of Ubu, was what allowed them to recognize Jarry's play as something new and original. And it did so by confronting them with something that everyone has always *fleetingly* known to be true, but been unable to *focus* upon: the fact that belly laughs happen in the belly, that they shift the locus of our experience firmly into our bellies, and, as I have indicated, if allowed to take hold, everything that both the term 'the belly' and the belly itself conceal from our perceptions starts to escape ever more uncontrollably. Ubu's effect upon us is thus first and foremost *physical*. Although he may recall figures from the literature of earlier times (Gargantua, Falstaff), or customs of low comedy from across the ages, he disgusts and amuses by his presence on stage and by that presence alone, making us forcibly aware of the fullest implications of our belly laugh in a way that, for the modern age, is quite unique. But that is only half of what makes Ubu such an original figure. If all Jarry did with his character was make his audience simultaneously laugh from the gut and be disgusted at the gut, he would certainly have made the belly laugh into a more complex psychological experience; nevertheless, he would still have kept it sealed off from the world of rational sociability. Seeing *Ubu* might allow the audience to 'get in touch' more effectively with its belly laughter than, say, going to see the Pétomane, who was active around the same time: the experience would have been just as much of a closet *divertissement*. But Ubu is not just a grotesque and infantile being by whom we are simultaneously disgusted and amused. Jarry also makes him the former King of Aragon, and the key conspirator in a plot to kill the rightful king of Poland, Wenceslas, and seize his throne. In other words, *Ubu roi* has a discernible and recognizable historical subject.

As a result, Jarry's play elicits a response from us on what normally are two mutually exclusive levels: hilarity and disgust (our belly laugh) on the one hand, and, on the other, rational engagement with a coherent plot. Moreover, this is not just the plot of one particular play: it is laden with references to other plots from within the literary tradition I referred to earlier (the most obvious one being *Macbeth*). Consequently, in its cumbersome yet hugely simplified development, *Ubu roi* may be seen as an abstract of the central plot around which the rational — that is to say, Western — social world is constructed, and which much of its drama enacts: the struggle for power, the seizing and holding of power, the losing of power, with all of the brutality and violence attendant on that cycle, which the rational world veils from view in order, precisely, to appear rational to itself. In short, Jarry does not just expose the nature of our belly laugh to us, he situates what he exposes to us — the all-powerful nature of our gut, its irrepressible urge to ingest and excrete — at the very heart of human power relations. By doing so, he obliges us to break down the institutionalized isolation of our belly laughter from our participation in the world of rational sociability; to laugh right down into our bellies while simultaneously reflecting on the fundamentals of the world we know; and in the process, to gain a radical, even revolutionary insight into the true source of the values with which power surrounds itself.

Ubu roi was a one-night stand, and was not put on again, except by puppets, until after Jarry's death in 1907. But as well as exercising a general influence over all of the avant-garde or experimental theatre of the twentieth century, Jarry's spirit and his name were revived thirty years after his death by Antonin Artaud and Roger Vitrac, who founded the short-lived but very influential Théâtre Alfred Jarry in Paris in 1926. This period in twentieth-century theatre is best known for Artaud's doctrine of a Theatre of Cruelty; but I wish to focus here on one of the plays put on by the Théâtre Alfred Jarry — Roger Vitrac's *Victor, ou les enfants au pouvoir* (*Victor, or Children in Power*), which was written and performed in 1928.[5]

Although *Victor* is a very different play from *Ubu roi*, it brings about the same forced and uncomfortable juxtaposition or interference between our belly laughter and our rational activity as *Ubu* does. Superficially, it is a typical bourgeois drawing-room drama of the time. A couple invite another couple and their daughter Esther to a birthday party for their son, Victor, who is nine. Typically in such drama, there is a sexual sub-plot: Victor's father and Esther's mother are lovers. Esther's father is barking mad, and unaware of their affair, while Victor, though only nine, is precociously intelligent and *very* observant! Rather like a complex mechanism, all of whose cogs have been eccentrically mounted and equipped with their own drive, once the action of the play begins, the familiar dramatic plot goes increasingly out of control (something Ionesco will exploit a quarter of a century later). Esther's father hangs himself from a flagpole, Esther starts to have fits, Victor's father beats him brutally, and a pitch of frenzy is inexorably reached, exposing the violence that inhabits the very heart of the ruling class, the bourgeoisie, but doing so directly, rather than indirectly as *Ubu* did.

So far, however, there has been no sign, in what I have described, of anything in the play corresponding to the disgusting presence of Ubu. There is a link, and it lies in the fact that, recalling the schoolboy origins of *Ubu roi*, Victor is a child. Initially, however, the link appears to be broken. For whereas Ubu is powerfully without a sexual libido, which recalls my question as to whether the belly laugh bears any relation to sexuality, Victor's opening words to his nursemaid, as the curtain goes up, appear to point in the opposite direction. They are in fact a play on words that isn't directly translatable. Where the English 'Hail Mary' says 'blessed is the fruit of thy womb', the French says 'le fruit de vos *entrailles* est béni' — literally, 'blessed is the fruit of your *entrails*' (a curious intrusion of the belly into the domain of the sacred!). Victor's pun, designed to annoy his nurse, is to say 'et le fruit de votre *entaille* est béni', which is to say, not the fruit of your womb, or even your belly, but the fruit of your *cleft* (*entaille* meaning a cleft or deep cut), a clear reference not to the organ of child-bearing but to the female genitalia.

At this opening moment, the play thus seems to be anticipating the sexual sub-plot by presenting its nine-year-old hero as sexually precocious (by 1920s' standards anyway), precociousness and adultery being two forms of sexuality that threaten the bourgeois social order. But then, about half-way through the play, when the social situation is reaching a peak of frenzy, a character suddenly appears who will first intensify the play's focus on sexuality, then brutally overturn it in a manner that rivals Ubu's deeds for disgustingness, and in the process reinstate the belly laugh as the focus of the theatre which Jarry invented. The character's name is Ida Mortemart, whom the stage direction describes as a woman of great beauty, and she enters the drawing room wearing full evening dress (II, iv). She is, it turns out, a childhood friend of Victor's mother. However, her presence in the play is incongruous[6] and not quite real. She is an apparition, the ideal of woman incarnate, and as such, it should be noted, she is as far removed from the sexual as Ubu is, except that, in our culture, ideal beauty is a transcendence of desire — a sublimation — whereas gut fixation is the opposite — a sublation or superseding, what might even be called a *transdescendence* of desire.

A conversation between Ida and the other characters develops, during which a Colonel, there on a visit and who talks about nothing but war, says to Ida: 'And would you believe it, Madame, they asked for a canon' (II, v). 'A canon?' Ida replies, and then farts. The incarnation of feminine beauty *farts*. Transcendence and transdescendence become momentarily indistinguishable. The stage direction reads: *There is a moment of stupor and embarrassment.* Ida hides her head in her hands. But then she farts again and keeps on farting, all the while begging for forgiveness, even threatening suicide. Soon, stupor on the part of the other characters is replaced by uncontrollable laughter, which she encourages: 'Go on,' she says, 'laugh. That way there'll be no embarrassment on my side or yours. It'll calm us down. There's only one remedy, and that's laughter.' Gradually, the characters' laughter subsides, though not her farting. And crucially, the stage direction indicates that the characters *must wait till the audience's laughter also subsides before continuing the scene.*

At this point in the play, in other words, actors and characters enter into a relationship that briefly interrupts the progress of the play. The actors in effect place themselves at an *equal distance* from what is going on in the play to that of the audience, leaving the drama concentrated, momentarily, in the enigmatic and troubling presence of Ida alone, while they briefly abandon their own parts in the play and act the part of the audience: acting (perhaps really experiencing) the belly laughter that is really that of the audience, and mirroring it in its rise and fall. As in *Ubu roi*, therefore, but more radically and decisively, from within the heart of the overt and highly conventional drama something erupts on to the scene from somewhere on another scene entirely, something *ob*scene which the rational social order must of necessity repress, but which the theatre of Jarry then Vitrac brings into stark confrontation with the rational order by offering a play set on *two* scenes: one calling forth a response from our minds, the other triggering a response from our bellies.

Having provided an interpretation of this momentary situation — namely, only laughter can make the belly acceptable — Ida makes to go. But at this moment the greater complexity of Vitrac's play becomes fully apparent, as the tension set up by Victor between belly and sex, *entrailles* and *entaille*, comes to a head. Esther having run off, with all the adults in pursuit, Victor sits on Ida's lap — or her thighs as he lasciviously calls them — and begins to kiss her neck (II, vi). He tells her that he is in love, and although he can't do anything about it, being only nine, he asks Ida to tell him what goes on between men and women. As she obliges, whispering in Victor's ear, we hear the cries of the adults in the garden, where Esther is having a fit. As they begin to return to the stage, Victor slides off Ida's lap. It would appear that desire has prevailed, that the belly has become libidinal. But Victor turns the tables: as Ida leaves, he shouts after her that she is a liar, then asks her a favour: 'Go on, fart, just for me'. Ida screams and rushes off, calling Victor a monster. At that point, Esther is carried on, unconscious, her dress torn, her arms scratched, foaming at the mouth. Far from appearing stronger than the belly, sex is eclipsed by the frenzied farting of Ida Mortemart, while our belly laugh, as in the case of Ubu, coexists painfully with our contemplation of the violence at the heart of human social relations.

There is no simpler, no surer mark of our common humanity than the belly laugh. Uniquely, it puts our bodies on an equal footing with the loftiest activities of our minds. And as Jarry and Vitrac have shown, given the right medium, belly laughs can carry us to the threshold of a new and constructive relationship between the two modes on which we have our being: a non-dualistic interaction between our bodies and our minds.

Notes to Chapter 4

1. 'Le Rire primitif', in *A plus d'un titre. Sketches inédits* (Paris: Olivier Orban, 1989), pp. 48–51. The sketch can also be found on both the CD and the video recording entitled *Olympia 99*. Devos, a Belgian, is one of the rare stand-up comedians in the French-speaking world, where his work is accorded the status of serious art. This sketch starts out from the idea that laughter is a form of

energy that expends itself by causing the most fragile and vulnerable muscles in our bodies to vibrate. In reality, these are the facial muscles. But what if, instead, they were the muscles in the buttocks? With words and actions, Devos pursues the implications of this hypothesis, to hilarious effect, coming back to the observation 'On l'a échappé belle': we had a narrow escape. I began my paper at the TRIO conference on laughter by playing a recording of the sketch.

2. Henri Bergson, *Le Rire. Essai sur la signification du comique* (1889; Paris: Presses universitaires de France, 1940), p. 1.

3. Alfred Jarry, *Ubu roi*, in *Tout Ubu* (Paris: Livre de Poche, 1962).

4. Alfred Jarry, *Ubu roi*, trans. by Barbara Wright (1951; London: Gabberbocchus Press, 1961), p. 9.

5. Roger Vitrac, *Victor, ou les Enfants au pouvoir* in *Théâtre* (1946; Paris: Gallimard, 1973), pp. 7–90.

6. In an extended exchange, she explains that she has come to see someone with the same name as Victor's mother, living in the same street, but who is not Victor's mother. This labouring of coincidence clearly anticipates the recognition scene between Mr and Mrs Martin in scene IV of Ionesco's *Bald Primadonna* (1950). It prompts the following observation from Victor's father, Charles: 'if a dramatist had used this stratagem, so as to have you turn up here, at this precise moment, he'd have been attacked for being implausible' (my translation).

CHAPTER 5

Upping the Ante/i:
Exaggeration in Céline and Vallès

Walter Redfern

In the small world, it is by way of a critical commonplace (and the *common place* is where, by definition, we all live) to say that Céline's *Mort à crédit* takes off in various ways from Vallès's *L'Enfant*. At the very least they are validly comparable. For his part, Céline remains today an outsize bone of contention in French culture, because of his alleged, and real, collaboration during the Second World War. I am principally drawn to his comic practice. The latter does not justify the former; neither does it need to be excused, only analysed. I do not claim that Céline's humour saves him. Humour does not take itself for the saviour. Rag-picker, perhaps.

Sartre once wrote that a communist could not write a novel proper, because, believing in the inevitability of the historical process, he could only underplay the freedom, of character and of narrative, essential to the novel (that is, of course, the novel bourgeois-ly conceived).[1] Along comparable lines, it has often been assumed that fascism and humour make unhappy bedfellows. Dictators do appear to lack a sense of humour (a sense of proportion) — except of the most gloatingly sadistic variety.

The title *Mort à crédit* picks up on the old *image d'Epinal* (popular edifying print) entitled 'Crédit est mort' — a motto very popular with small shopkeepers. The title, especially in its American translation, *Death on the Instalment Plan*, also introduces the chief theme: dragged-out decay and demise. On publication, *Mort à crédit* was almost universally panned, on both Right and Left, first for doing the dirty on humankind (the would-be humanist reaction), and secondly for its gutter-level language. The family at its chaotic heart — the father who never rises above the rank of subsidiary clerk in an insurance firm, and the mother who struggles endlessly to sell lace-wear — are excluded, or sidelined, from the French economic system of their day, based upon credit and the gold standard. (Céline's actual family life was considerably more comfortable than, and different from, that depicted in *Mort à crédit*.) In a vain effort to keep up with the times, the father, Auguste, buys a typewriter which — with black irony — will later be the very weapon with which his verbally brutalized son half-kills him. The name Auguste refers both to the autocratic emperor Augustus and to the archetypal French circus-clown, 'l'Auguste'. The father is dictatorial, comic and manic. *Mort à crédit* as a whole imposes a spasmic view of life as inherently conflictual, violent, and unstable. Bodies, projects, alike decay and fail. The desperate parents will put up with anything for the sake of a sale. For instance, dogs foul the pavement in the passage where the parents and their pathetic business just about live. Passers-by take the hint and ape the canines. There is no point in complaining: 'Souvent ça devenait des clients, les pisseurs, avec ou sans chien'.[2] This circumscribed home territory is the old central Paris of covered passages, but it is far from the bullfight phenomenon, *la querencia*, the place in the arena where the bull feels safe. In *Mort à crédit*, nobody feels safe.

The son, Ferdinand, is sickly, loose-bowelled, and given to frenzied, superlative onanism. He lives as if everybody and everything were out to get him, and maintains a vigilant mistrust of all. Throughout, Céline keeps his finger firmly placed upon the panic-button. The father, like the teacher-parent in Vallès's *L'Enfant*, is pitifully proud of his classical education, his *humanités*; he often resorts to Latin quotes when declaiming anti-son anathemas, which are presented as virtuoso performances. In everyday experience, anger can lead to and be fuelled by overblown repetition. It is largely self-igniting. It overstates the case. Auguste is too big for the claustrophobically tiny family flat. But his largely one-way discourse is constantly let down by physical fiascos, as when he drops a bar of soap, and all three hurl themselves to the floor, poking with a broom-handle under the piano and hitting each other on the head in the cack-handed process. In all this mayhem, does the targeted son try to understand, forgive, justify his parents, as does Vallès's young hero, Jacques Vingtras? As narrator, the son certainly gives them their head and, overall, is himself embroiled undetachably in the seething family mess. The child, Ferdinand, says: 'Je lui demandais pardon d'avoir été insolent. Pour la comédie, puisque c'était pas vrai du tout' (p. 560). This contrasts with Jacques Vingtras's more complex efforts to take on board his mother's brutal 'logic', the 'système' of her child-rearing. Both authors, however, exploit the difference between what is expressed and what is communicated, but it is a difference that depends on the recipient having eyes to see. Ferdinand's crippled mother, somewhat kindlier than her spouse, receives this Beckettian testimonial from her son: 'Elle a tout fait pour que je vive, c'est naître qu'il aurait pas fallu!' (p. 552). That first noble sentiment is undermined by the disabused tack-on (a common dodge also in Vallès). Despite his attempt to murder his father, any talk of Oedipal triangles, although Céline had wind of Freudian theory, seems reductive in this context.

The parents fatalistically view Ferdinand as incorrigible, whereas the Vingtras genitors always strive to reshape their lad. Ferdinand's parents are supported by a Parisian Greek chorus of neighbours who chime in to indict the boy. After a particularly vicious verbal onslaught from Auguste, Ferdinand, maddened uncontrollably, knocks him down with that precious typewriter, and then tries to throttle him (pp. 823–24). He has to be hauled away by neighbours, who proceed to beat him up. As happens repeatedly in other traumatic scenes, Ferdinand collapses into diarrhoea and vomiting. Later, after voicing some pity for the multiple woes of his crumbling parents, Ferdinand switches to moaning about their lack of compassion for *him*: 'Martyrs! Il fallait pas comparer!' (p. 989).

For a long spell, *Mort à crédit* moves cross-Channel to Kent. The boy longs to get to England alone, so as to disappear, to stop being the dead centre of adult critical attention, indeed to blot out talk altogether. To this end, at the sardonically named

Meanwell College, he becomes a kind of elective mute, refusing to learn English, while acquiring a Martian perspective on its phonology: 'Je détestais pas l'intonation anglaise. C'est agréable, c'est élégant, c'est flexible. C'est une espèce de musique, ça vient comme d'une autre planète' (p. 738). As with Jacques Vingtras, Ferdinand's obsession with boats, the sea, 'partir!' shows how ready he is to 'se dépayser', to go foreign if not to go native. In practice, however, he resembles the literal-minded homing pigeons late in the novel, who only ever embark on short, sad flights (pp. 858–59). On his arrival, he loses himself in a Saturday-night crowd in Chatham, where he achieves the anonymity he pines for, as he moves across a social spectrum going from the Salvation Army to the Kentucky Minstrels. At the school, after fighting to establish himself as king rat, he befriends a mentally subnormal boy, who drinks from drainpipes, tries to eat door-knobs and the headmaster's false teeth. Do we always know for sure what *is* exaggeration? Aren't we often too small-minded? The term 'adynaton', since way back, has denoted impossibility, which has thus always been conceivable.

Back in Paris, Ferdinand spends more time and energy avoiding work than finding it or doing it. He is stretching his credit. Eventually he teams up with the would-be encyclopedist and inveterate inventor Courtial des Pereires, reminiscent of some *fous littéraires* or literary cranks of the nineteenth century, who is one of nature's hyperbolists: 'Il magnifiait, écrasait, imprévisiblement d'ailleurs, par la parole, la plume, le manifeste' (p. 836). He is even capable of *reverse* amplification, miniaturization. Courtial's greatest work is 'l'œuvre complète d'Auguste Comte, ramenée au strict format d'une "prière positive" en vingt-deux versets acrostiches' (p. 840). Trying to give this prayer 'un petit goût entraînant bien français, il l'avait déduite en "rébus", retournée comme une camisole [...] rendue revancharde ... cornélienne ... agressive et puis péteuse' (p. 840). He varnishes his detachable collar, then wears it for two years.

What purpose does exaggeration serve? It seizes on one, or a minor, aspect of an idea, a spectacle, a phrasing, and underlines it, divorces it from its context, and bloats it. As with caricature: all head and little body, so as to make the viewer concentrate on the head in near-isolation; and also, naturally, so as to convey an element of big-headedness, pretention.

Courtial is a creature of violent seesaws: larger than life, then petty in the extreme. His inventions range from balloons (inflation) to submarines (blowing tanks), the empyrean to Hades. Fleeing the city, he takes up agriculture and runs a 'Phalanstery of the New Race', which sounds like a Nazi eugenics programme, although on the ground the young pupils in fact gain a counter-education, as they are allowed to run wild criminally and to ransack the neighbourhood. This programme turns out to be another of the many business failures of *Mort à crédit*. Finally, Courtial blows himself to pieces. A trowel and a wheelbarrow are drafted in to scoop up and transport his *disjecta membra* (pp. 1043–44). A mad cleric plunges his hands ecstatically into these gory remains.

Exaggeration can also reduce the value of something, be*little* it, mock it. So, not 'intelligenti pauca' (a word to the wise), but 'intelligenti multa' (a plethora to the percipient). Céline not only makes the big bigger, he makes the small loom larger. When Ferdinand contemplates running away from Meanwell College, he immediately thinks that this desertion would sink the failing establishment for good: it would not have enough pupils for a football team (p. 737). Céline is highly conscious of his own hyperbolism:

> Je les surpassais tous de beaucoup question virulence par l'intensité de ma révolte, l'enthousiasme destructeur! La Transe ... l'Hyperbole ... le gigotage anathématique ... c'était vraiment pas concevable à quel prodigieux paroxysme je parvenais à me hausser dans la colère absolue ... je tenais tout ça de mon papa. (p. 875)

In a different context, I am reminded of Jacques Vingtras saying when he gets a windfall of sweets: 'Je les aime quand j'en ai trop'.[3] Nobody sounds prouder than Céline on the sheer pleasure of verbally swollen wrath. The constant bellyaching is at times lyrical, as with the archetypal French concierge. No wonder that the French place him in their long tradition of 'les grands exaspérés'. It is not a case of William Blake's piously hopeful 'the road of excess leads to the palace of wisdom'.[4] It is more in line with Léon Bloy's 'On ne voit le mal de ce monde qu'à la condition de l'exagérer'.[5] It is Thoreau who puts the case persuasively for justified hyperbolism:

> I fear chiefly lest my expression may not be *extravagant* enough, may not wander far enough beyond the narrow limits of my daily experience, so as to be adequate to the truth of which I have been convinced. Extra vagance! It depends on how you are yarded [...] I desire to speed somewhere *without* bounds [...] for I am convinced that I cannot exaggerate enough even to lay the foundation of a true expression.[6]

In other words, exaggeration, traditionally associated with falsity, can in fact be redeployed so as to serve the cause of some sort of truth. Fontanier makes the same point more abstractly and soberly:

> L'hyperbole augmente ou diminue les choses avec excès, et les présente bien au-dessus ou bien au-dessous de ce qu'elles sont, dans la vue, non de tromper, mais d'amener à la vérité même, et de fixer, par ce qu'elle dit d'incroyable, ce qu'il faut réellement croire.[7]

By definition, an author (*auctor*) is an *augmenter* (Latin *augere*). 'To improve upon' means to increase.

In *Mort à crédit*, a cross-Channel ferry in rough seas begets an epic mass vomiting, in which virtually the entire boatload literally feeds the fishes, shoots cats, barfs, upchucks, spews, and exhibits a technicolour yawn (pp. 622–25). In Céline, heaving with laughter and eructating because of excess intake or traumatic anxiety are coterminous. His comedy, and this *is* a richly comic scene, is never a relief but an exacerbation. There are in *Mort à crédit* fevered sections (literal or metaphorical), and the narrative is consistently febrile in structure and tone. Even if much of the narrative is static, it is frenetically so. And it is varied by the hero's instinct for vagrancy — the picaresque as permanent digression. The famous three full stops separating phrases or sentences embody fragmentation, hiccuping, anger, laughter, retching. Such syncopation is of the Jazz Age. Yet despite everything, the atomizing Céline is very attached to linkages. In a letter he spoke of his ambition to 'tenir cette espèce de délire en élan'.[8] Of the climactic duel scene in Vallès's *Le Bachelier*, Céline says: ' L'une des rares scènes de délire que l'on trouve dans la littérature française [...] Cela n'a jamais été égalé ni chez les Russes ni chez les Américains — la littérature française ne délire presque jamais'.[9] Can exaggeration be controlled, like skids by expert drivers? It is a key element in much humour: many jokes are wilfully excessive, highlighting inordinately stupid ideas or behaviour, or exceptional finesse.

The effect of much of Céline's dialogue (or more accurately monologue) is that of reading aloud a French version of Roget's *Thesaurus*: variations on themes, proliferating synonyms (for example, 'Tu t'en balances! ... Tu restes hermétique n'est-ce pas? Calfaté ... Bien sanglé au fond de ta substance ... Tu ne communiques avec rien' (p. 865)). Comparably, in Vallès, the physical variations on beating the child anticipate the maddening rhythms of Ravel's *Bolero*. Virtually the only relief for Céline's agonist from verbal diarrhoea, diarrhetoric, is elective mutism. Discourse here *is* exchange, but only in the military sense of broadsides, sniping, parting shots, not in the sense of dialogue. The frequent *engueulades* (slanging-matches, bawlings-out) are largely inconclusive; nobody persuades anyone. The total impact of such full-frontal attack on the reader is very often, of course, punch-drunkenness. Céline is such a natural escalater that he grants virtuoso powers of vituperation even to the enemies of the hero.

Céline raises the poser: can laughter ever be totally nihilistic, iconoclastic? Surely, however tenuously, it still keeps some kind of faith with what we can agree to call life. Laughter, in Céline, is always *le rire jaune*, laughing the other side of your face. Julia Kristeva describes Céline as 'libérateur d'un rire sans complaisance mais néanmoins complice'. This formula captures both the ruthlessness and the appeal of Céline. In general, Kristeva sees in him 'un rire horrifié: le comique de l'abjection [...] Devant l'apocalypse, il s'exclame d'une horreur voisine de l'extase'. She likens this laughter to that of the Hebrew prophets (Céline himself counted St John in *Revelation* as a master).[10] In his corner of existence, like a trapped rat, Céline's hero, despite his creator's entrenched anti-Semitism, takes refuge in Jewish humour: the wailing-wall of lamentations, putting God on trial, and querying the point and the equity of creation. If not overtly fascist, except in some of the father's outbursts, *Mort à crédit* constructs a fictional world ripe for a fascist take-over: economic crisis, class hatred, dirt and decay and disorder everywhere, and a largely irrelevant republican government. Céline's humour is anti-humanist. It is anti-*bonhomie*, anti-charm. He makes few efforts, à la Gide, to *disarm* readers, but many to browbeat and suffocate us.

According to Walter Benjamin,

> the seeds of the 'culte de la blague', which reappears in George Sorel and has become an integral part of fascist propaganda, are first found in Baudelaire. The spirit in which Céline wrote his *Bagatelles pour un massacre*, and its very title, go back directly to a diary entry by Baudelaire: 'A fine conspiracy could be organised for the purpose of exterminating the Jewish race.'[11]

We Anglo-Saxons borrowed the term *blague* from the French. (It is strange how *loan*-words are the only area where we can borrow without having to pay back. What, however, about plagiarism?) *Blague* is the telling of tall stories, with a subtext of lying, but the major thrust is provocation via exaggeration. In France, the *blague* was long held to be quintessentially Parisian, although that stereotype may have been merely metropolitan umbilicism. *Blague* has been called 'a multifaceted term', 'a microsystem'.[12] One stream could be called 'amplificatio ad absurdum', going to ridiculous lengths. The *blagueur* often adopts the tone of world-weariness, blaséness. Such a tactic can pull the wool; it can also unmask. The *blague* is not confined to would-be aristocratic jokers; it is often the only thing that the have-nots have.

For Jules Vallès, the *blague* was an existential strategy, an artifice of self-preservation. Although in his writings he milks suffering for all it is worth, he shows discretion over real-life experiences, whereas Céline is decidedly indiscreet about mainly invented ones. Vallès's *L'Enfant* is no joke, *and* richly, complexly funny. Its hero Jacques Vingtras *gags* (that is, jokes and retches) against parental *gags* (vetoes). In a typical example of pointed hyperbole, he finds the local jail gayer in atmosphere than his grim home or authoritarian school. Frequently, Vallès exploits Romantic irony, in which the second part of a sentence militates against the spirit of the first part, and thereby hints that second thoughts were first ones all along. Here is the mother lining up the child for a beating: 'Elle me battait pour mon bien, voyez-vous. Sa main hésita plus d'une fois; elle dut prendre son pied' (p. 202). The mother hesitates, but only to make the swing of her arms more accurate. If we readers fail to see this special irony, we are as stupid as she who cannot manage irony, but only sarcasm. She is a one-woman band and her son the drum: 'Elle m'a travaillé dans tous les sens, pincé, balafré, tamponné, bourré, souffleté, frotté, cardé et tanné' (p. 258). When Jacques claims to relish being beaten unmercifully by his mother or father, for it will toughen his hide for the sailor's life he longs to escape to, it is ambiguous how much this rhetorical ploy is overloaded irony, how much a defence-tactic (to save face if not bottom), or how much *galéjade*, exuberant blarney (a safety-valve). Although Vallès generally presses the loud pedal, I am reminded of the 'whisper-jokes' of Nazi Germany. (The blackest irony of all in Vallès's life was that others were mistakenly murdered in his place in the Paris Commune of 1871, in which he played an important political role: an atrocious *quiproquo*.)

Jacques, like his mother in her own sweet way, is governed by a perverse but dogged logic. How is he to find good, or a less gratuitous evil, in parents to all appearances monstrous? This child, wanting to be loved or at least to lead a less denatured life, assumes the thought processes of his intra-family foes, while retaining an instinctive sense that theirs is not the way that people should live together. Against the proverb, he knows that to understand is not to forgive, but it is to mitigate resentment and to try to fellow-feel. Thus Vallès makes the boy seemingly internalize his mother's force-feeding (of onion hash, precepts, or leatherings). He allows for the well-documented fact that battered children often do blame themselves for their suffering, and protect their abusive parents by all manner of subterfuges. Besides, the mother's tyranny proves that her son is indeed a rebel, which is his choice of being. In all, he is striving to understand the enemy, an invaluable lesson that he will go on extending in militant adult life. As a child, he already instinctively loosens or breaks corsets, in order to go over the top. Vallès once responded to a caricature of himself as a big-headed man attached to a mongrel by saying: 'Chargez: allez-y, forcez la dose!'.[13] In both senses, Vallès was a great *barker*.

Mother and son fight a running battle: his desire to be expansive versus her private ideological constipation. There remain, as in Ferdinand's family, ineradicable bonds. At school, too, Jacques fights a rearguard action against the pedagogical rhetoric of his day. As a well-drilled rhetorician, Vallès knows how to subvert enemy rhetoric. To the rhetorical question 'What could take a mother's place?', Jacques replies: 'A shillelagh' (p. 212). The mother is herself a composite rhetorical figure: a living paradox (solicitous/ brutal), and so an oxymoron, a mixed metaphor (a peasant petty bourgeoise), a chiasmus (her ambition to cross class-boundaries), a pun (grating, atrocious). All of these figures suggest tugs and tensions, layered or conflicting meanings. *L'Enfant* is propelled, via its insistent graphic present, between rapidly shifting moods and tones. This family drama is shown to have wider social implications. Citizens, too, are in the position of children: spoken for, talked down to, kept violently in their place, which is to be seen and not heard.

As in *Mort à crédit*, exaggeration is rife. A rare kiss from the mother projects Jacques against the wall, where his head knocks in a protruding nail (p. 273). Overall, the mother piles it on thick in her treatment of her son. The father, for his part, harps on the need to kowtow to superiors. And Jacques competes with this pair of inflaters by upping the ante in his narration. In his own right, Jacques, clumsy in all things except jumping over gates, has a saving gracelessness, what I would call 'maladroiture'. *L'Enfant* houses much knockabout farce, silent comedy, as when Jacques's jagged shoe eviscerates his headmaster's carpet while he tries to advance in reverential fashion. Mother and son are natural, habitual, reciprocal overreachers. It is a kind of Yiddish mother-and-son double-act, although we should remember the Jewish proverb: 'Crooked parents can produce straight children'. At school, Jacques practises overkill when, writing Latin verses as an exercise, he parrots an existing pastiche about parrots: psittacism squared or cubed, but also a splendidly targeted joke against educationally enforced plagiarism. In Vallès, as against Céline, laughter is a sign of life, a style of commitment, a dampener of stereotypical exclamation (that recurrent vice of French literature and life).

Why compare Céline and Vallès? In both, the context is petty bourgeois; the hero is an only child. Both sets of parents struggle unavailingly to hoist themselves above the lower echelons. The two fathers are inordinately proud of their formal education, yet essentially failures in their professional lives. Both sons want to do violence to the paterfamilias (Céline's succeeds), and work to reject their schooling. On the other hand, sex is natural and healthy in Vallès, and unhealthy in Céline (voyeurism, much misogyny, as well as a capacity for adoration of selected women: Ferdinand desires to literally eat the headmaster's ravishing wife; p. 742). Both authors love *fêtes foraines*, especially their shooting-galleries.[14] Céline several times declared a strong affinity with Vallès, who also knew bitter exile. 'Je me vois plutôt très Vallès'.[15] In many ways, they were enemy brothers, terrible twins. In both, childhood is seen as crucial, and excruciated. In Céline, the body is disgusting but veracious; in Vallès clumsy but truth-telling, and the source of our most intense pleasures. Unusually in the French tradition, both are very corporeal writers. In political terms, Céline is obviously far more negatively apocalyptic, and he does not in any way share Vallès's vaguish faith in 'le peuple'. Céline, above all, warms to the iconoclastic verve of Vallès's prose.

These two magnifiers help us to see more clearly, or at least more interestingly and intricately. Both Vallès and Céline were rebels, in their non-conformist ideas, in their destabilized structures, and in their humour. What Barthes said, pretty pompously, in his more firebrand youth goes very well towards describing the breath of fresh, or in Céline's case often stinking, air that the pair let into French literature: 'L'écriture révolutionnaire fut ce geste emphatique [...] Ce qui paraît aujourd'hui de l'enflure, n'était alors que la taille de la réalité. [...] Jamais langage ne fut plus invraisemblable et moins imposteur.'[16]

In March 1992 I read in a newspaper that in India 10,000 peasants had resolved to transform all their militant activism against the regional government into collective laughter directed at every official pronouncement. After all, in democracy we find *mock*. This venture would be mass-exaggeration in action, and proves, if this were really necessary, that hyperbole can be a political act, and, at its best, is not to be sniffed at, to put it mildly. The grassroots can grow into a threatening forest.

Exaggeration, we have seen, can inflate or minimize. It can generate comedy. Laughter, in return, can reinforce rebelliousness: 'upping the *anti*', so to speak. Hyperbole is a serious joke.

Notes to Chapter 5

1. Jean-Paul Sartre, '*La Conspiration* par Paul Nizan', *Situations* I (Paris: Gallimard, 1947), p. 29.
2. All references to *Mort à crédit* are to the Pléiade edition, I (Paris: Gallimard, 1981), here p. 572. Henceforth they appear in parentheses, in most instances after my own translation of the quotations.
3. Jules Vallès, *L'Enfant*, in *Œuvres*, II, ed. by Roger Bellet (Paris: Gallimard, c. 1990), p. 183. All further references to the text are in parentheses after quotations (or translations).
4. William Blake, 'Proverbs of Hell', in *The Marriage of Heaven and Hell*. In *Complete Works*, ed. by Geoffrey Keynes (Oxford: Oxford University Press, 1984), p. 150.
5. Léon Bloy, *Journal*, III (Paris: Mercure de France, 1963), p. 314.
6. Henry Thoreau, *Walden* (New York: New American Library, 1960), p. 215. 'Yard' is a long-attested word for the penis. *Walden* is full of punning. Thoreau's contemporary, P. J. Barnum, similarly lauded his own notorious ballyhoo.
7. Pierre Fontanier, *Les Figures du discours* (1821–27; Paris: Flammarion, 1977), p. 123. His English opposite number, George Puttenham, on the other hand, talks (tautologously) of 'too much surplusage' as a rhetorical vice. See *The Art of English Poesie*, ed. by Edward Arber (London: Alexander Murray, 1869), p. 264.
8. Céline, letter to N★★★ of 30 Sept. 1932, in *Cahiers Céline*, 5 (1979), 73.
9. Céline, letter to Milton Hindus of 12 June 1947, in 'Céline', *Cahiers de l'Herne*, 2 (1965), 80.
10. Julia Kristeva, *Pouvoirs de l'horreur: essai sur l'abjection* (Paris: Seuil, 1980), pp. 157, 240, 240–41.
11. Walter Benjamin, *Charles Baudelaire: A Lyric Poet in the Era of High Capitalism*. trans. by Harry Zohn (London: NLB, 1973), p. 14.
12. Jean René Klein, *Le Vocabulaire des mœurs de la 'vie parisienne' sous le Second Empire: introduction à l'étude du langage boulevardier* (Louvain: Nauwelaerts, 1976), p. 174.
13. Quoted in Gaston Gille, *Jules Vallès*, I (Paris: Flammarion, 1941), pp. v–vi.
14. Cf. Céline's dedication to *Bagatelles pour un massacre* (Paris: Denoël, 1937): 'A mes potes du théâtre en toile'.
15. Céline, in a letter to Pierre Monnier. See Pierre Monnier, *Ferdinand furieux* (Lausanne: L'Age d'homme, 1979), p. 113.
16. Roland Barthes, *Le Degré zéro de l'écriture* (Paris: Seuil, 1972), p. 20.

CHAPTER 6

Humour Styles and Class Cultures: Highbrow Humour and Lowbrow Humour in the Netherlands

Giselinde Kuipers

Even among people speaking the same language, the sharing of humour can be impeded by cultural differences. Take, for example, the difference between American and British humour: although Britons and Americans speak (mostly) the same language, the use of humour in these countries differs in many ways. This difference has been described as the distinction between American overstatement and British understatement (as is usually the case with clichés, this is a sweeping generalization with a convincing note to it). Between Americans and Britons, there is a difference in cultural style that shows in many aspects of their cultures. It shows particularly prominently in their sense of humour.

Different cultures have different humour styles — different notions of what humour is, and what good humour should be. Such humour styles provide people with criteria for distinguishing between good and bad comedy; they influence the way people use humour in daily life, and they guide the interpretation of other people's attempts at being funny. Such differences in humour styles exist within countries, as well as across countries: they may vary between regions, ages, occupations, and, very importantly, between social classes. One of the most distinctive differences in humour styles in most western countries is the difference between popular humour and intellectual humour.

In virtually every domain of culture, there is a distinction between highbrow and lowbrow tastes: in art and literature, as well as in clothing, interior decoration, hairstyles, and television entertainment.[1] These taste differences are related to cultural differences between social classes.[2] In this article I present some materials from a study of highbrow and lowbrow humour in the Netherlands, which I analyse using the notion of humour style. This concept, I argue, is very useful in the analysis of cultural differences in sense of humour, and the often far-reaching social consequences of those differences.

Social Differences in Sense of Humour

Before elaborating on highbrow and lowbrow humour, I briefly describe the study of humour and its social background on which this paper is based. In so doing, I also explore the various ways in which humour can be related to social background, thus illustrating the use of the concept of humour style.

Between 1996 and 2000 I conducted a study of social differences in the appreciation of humour in the Netherlands.[3] This study was based on a combination of qualitative and quantitative methods: seventy-one people were interviewed, and a survey was done among 340 people from all over the Netherlands. In the interviews and questionnaires people were asked about their appreciation of standardized humour — jokes, comedians, and humorous televisions shows — as well as their appreciation and use of humour in everyday life.

The study showed a clear relationship between humour and social background. What people found funny or amusing was related to gender, age, and, in particular, social class or educational level. Gender differences in sense of humour I found to be differences in the use rather than in the appreciation of humour. Men and women did not differ much in their opinions about comedians and humorous television. However, they were found to have different communication styles,[4] and these give rise to a different use of humour in everyday life. In general, the communication style of men is more exuberant than that of women, and less personal, more competitive, more in compliance with rather impersonal forms of humour such as joke telling. Women tend to favour more personal and interactive, less competitive forms of humour.[5]

Age differences in sense of humour had to do mainly with differences in the tolerance and appreciation of offensive humour. To younger people, calling humour *hard* — which is in fact a Dutch word meaning hard, but also tough, sharp, or shocking — is an extremely positive distinction. The humour liked by younger people was often felt by older people to be offensive and disagreeable. On the other hand, the humour preferred by older people was found by the young to be slow, old-fashioned, and 'corny'.

Although the influence of social class in modern western societies is believed to be diminishing,[6] the relationship between humour and social class was stronger and more inclusive than the relationship with any other variable. Both the interviews and the survey showed a true divide between people of working-class and lower middle-class background on the one hand, and people of upper middle-class background on the other. Analyses of the survey produced two distinct humour 'tastes': a group of comedians and television programmes best described as élite or 'highbrow'; and a cluster of comedians and TV shows that are more lowbrow or popular. The interviews not only corroborated this taste difference between upper and lower middle-class people, they also showed how this resulted in a very different use of humour in daily life.

Underlying these age, gender, and class differences, several mechanisms involved in the appreciation of humour can be discerned. One very important mechanism in humour appreciation is identification: people like humour more if they can identify with it, and if they agree with the purport of the humour. This works on the individual as well as on the group level. For this reason, most sexual jokes are funnier to men than to women, and *Absolutely Fabulous* is funnier to women than to men.

Another mechanism is related to the careful balancing of boundary transgression.

Most humour transgresses a social or moral boundary in some way. This can be very humorous, as long as it 'doesn't go too far'; then it will be offensive. However, jokes that attempt to cross a boundary, but do not go far enough, fail too: they are corny, easy, dull, or stupid. Different individuals, as well as different social groups, have different norms, and this results in a different appreciation of humour. How differences in norms give rise to difference in humour appreciation is best seen in the reaction of older and younger people to each other's favourite comedians. But again, this balancing of boundaries plays some part in all social differences in humour. For instance, in the Netherlands, more highly educated people tend to be more sensitive to, and thus less easily amused by, racist humour, whereas less educated people are less tolerant of religious humour.

Apart from these general mechanisms, the ways in which social background is related to humour were very diverse, and clearly related to the societal roles and norms for men and women. Men tend to use humour in a more competitive way, as a means of gaining status, while women's humour is more focused on personal relationships. I even found that this role difference can lead to some kind of sexual division of labour when it comes to humour: women laughing at men's jokes. More than I expected, my interviews supported an observation made by Rose Coser in 1960:

> A woman with a good sense of humor is a woman who laughs (but not too loudly!) when a man says something witty or tells a good joke. A man with a good sense of humor is a man who makes witty remarks and tells good jokes.[7]

The age difference in sense of humour is mainly a difference in *phase*. People's humour reflects the time in which they grew up. The strong shift in norms and social boundaries in the last fifty years of the twentieth century has resulted in a change in sense of humour: what people found funny fifty or even thirty years ago now seems hackneyed — would-be naughty, contrived attempts to be shocking or rebellious. It is humour based on the transgression of boundaries that people no longer feel strongly about. But apparently, some of the norms learned at a younger age never wear off, and many older people never get a feel for the 'tough' or 'sharp' humour that many young people appreciate today. This can be seen in the mixed reactions to the MTV show *Jackass*, featuring a very provocative and violent humour, which is immensely popular among young people.

Age and phase are related to sense of humour in another way, too. In my view, age differences largely have to do with social changes and the resulting differences in social phase. However, the phases in an individual's life may also have an effect. The older people become, the less they feel the need to explore and transgress boundaries, and this might also negatively affect their taste for transgressive humour.

The class difference could not be reduced to one clear mechanism, such as identification, role difference, or the effects of cultural change. The distinction between highbrow and lowbrow humour was much more comprehensive than the other distinctions, affecting both daily life and television, both creation and appreciation of humour, both form and content. Class differences were found not on the level of individual jokes, but on the level of genres, types of comedian/television show. It is a difference in style: people of different social class have different notions of what good humour is, and should be.

In contrast with age and gender, social class can very well be described in terms of culture.[8] Men and women have different roles, but do not live in different worlds — they share households, workplaces, and, therefore, the same culture, with the same perspective on humour. People of different age groups may have grown up in different times, but they do not lead separate lives. They get to meet each other in daily life, in families, or in the workplace. However, people of different social classes have their own worlds. Research has shown that people usually marry and befriend people of more or less the same educational and professional level, and that people of different classes do not usually meet in the workplace.[9] Thus, it is not surprising that people of different class backgrounds and educational levels should have different lifestyles, norms, tastes — in short, cultures.

Highbrow and Lowbrow Humour Styles

Characterizing humour styles — or any style — is never easy. Characterizing a cultural style for an audience unfamiliar with that culture is even more complicated. Whereas for a Dutch audience, humour styles could be sufficiently described by mentioning the names of comedians and television shows, for a non-Dutch audience, defining a particular style has to start from a more basic and thus more abstract level. Humour styles can be described in several ways. One way is to look at the style itself, at the variety of things that are grouped together as 'good' in one style, at the patterns of choices and evaluations people make. Another way is to look at the norms and expectations underlying the style: What criteria for good and bad humour do people with a specific style have? And finally, one can look at the way a style works: How do humour styles shape humour preferences? How do they guide interpretations of humour?

I have chosen to start with a very general, and thus disputable, impression of highbrow and lowbrow styles. After this impression, I move on to some interview fragments to show the logic underlying these styles, as well as the continuity between humour styles in standardized humour and everyday life. Only after this impression can I move on to specific comedians: the easiest step for 'insiders', the hardest part when writing for outsiders. As will become clear, it is almost impossible to 'explain' a comedian.

These styles as they are described here are based on statistical analyses of the ratings of comedians and television programmes in the survey. This has resulted in two groups of shows and comedians: one appreciated and better known by more highly educated people — the highbrow cluster; the other preferred and better known by less educated people — the lowbrow cluster.

The lowbrow humour style characterizes comedians and television shows in which performance and presentation are very important. Lowbrow comedians rely strongly on impersonations, accents, and the elaborate performance of jokes; lowbrow television comedy is typically sketch comedy or sitcom, genres in which the humour is very strongly based on the humorous effect of specific characters. People who like lowbrow humour usually place high value on performance, and on the personality of the performer.

Highbrow humour is defined more by content than by performance: much, though not all, of this humour could be described as satirical. Highbrow humour has a propensity towards absurdity and ambiguity: the humour is often mixed with other emotions such as shock, sadness, or sympathy. Lowbrow humour is hardly ever ambiguous: it is clearly 'framed' as humour, and very accessible. Highbrow humour, on the other hand, is more 'complicated'. Highbrow comedians and television shows can be very self-consciously confusing, intellectual, and inaccessible. Finally, lowbrow humour is more pleasant or more sociable than the humour in the highbrow cluster, which at times can be quite unsettling.

This description is reminiscent of traditional high–low distinctions in art and culture. Comparable oppositions — between simple versus intellectually challenging; original versus accessible; innovative versus agreeable; unsettling versus pleasing; ironically detached versus exuberant; content-oriented versus performance-oriented — are mentioned in distinctions between élite and popular tastes in fields as diverse as art, literature, clothing, or furniture.[10]

This very general description may not mean much until supplemented by more concrete examples. I provide several of these later, but first I shall look at the 'logic' behind these styles: the criteria to distinguish good from bad humour employed by lovers of highbrow and lowbrow humour. This is best done by citing some of the opinions given by the interviewees on what they consider constitutes good or bad humour.

These quotes also illustrate the thing that makes humour stand out from other cultural domains such as the ones mentioned above: the strong continuity between standardized humour, created by professionals, and the everyday humour of 'normal people'. I asked many of my interviewees to describe someone with 'a good sense of humour'. Not only were the answers they gave much in accordance with their humour style; I also discovered that people judge the humour of comedians more or less according to the same standards by which they judge the humour of people they meet in daily life.

In general, people who liked the highbrow cluster — mainly the more highly educated — described a person with a good sense of humour as follows:

> Somebody who thinks fast [...] Who makes connections real fast. And who is ... well, original in a way. In this sense well, not like what I just said, not like laughing at Laurel and Hardy — not childish, or naïve. (housewife, university educated, 84)

Or, as another woman said:

> There are people who are so witty, but that is not to do with anecdotes; it is more to do with the riposte, or the things they come up with. [...] There is this boy I know who is indeed murderously funny. In a very analytical, straightforward way. [...] A sort of logic carried to the extreme. (freelance writer, 52)

These people see 'someone with a good sense of humour' as someone who is witty: good at wordplay and spontaneous witty remarks, preferably delivered in an ironical tone. Humour, in this perspective, is linked to creativity and intellect.

People with a preference for lowbrow humour describe 'people with a good sense of humour' as essentially sociable people. They do not stress wit or creativity, but rather agreeableness, a good atmosphere, playfulness. As one woman described her son:

> He senses right away that something is funny. And he knows how to present it in a funny way as well. Whenever he enters a room and the mood is down he manages to reverse the mood. Cheer things up. And he senses that and then he throws in a couple of little jokes, real nice ones everybody can laugh at. Which are not offensive in any way. So as to make the mood turn around. He's really good at that. (woman, 62, housewife, retired salesperson)

And another woman says:

> He always has jokes. Always full of them. I don't know where he gets them. Always new ones, too. And well, he is just always up to something ... My sister would tell us that he was pulling everybody's leg and his parents would never figure it out. Always acting silly. And he's never boring. Really someone you could spend a whole day with, someone that is really really nice. Real fun. Because he's always cheerful. (woman, 38, 'planner')

These people are 'the life and soul of the party' — always funny, often good joke-tellers as well. Their humour is described as playful, agreeable, teasing, but never really offensive. Moreover, they are fun to be with. Interestingly, the witty people are not always felt to be that: they are felt to be extremely funny, but not necessarily approachable or friendly.

These descriptions of people with a good sense of humour clearly show the logic behind these humour styles. People with a preference for highbrow humour value originality, absurdity, and ambivalence; they expect humour to provide an intellectual challenge, in the theatre, on television, and in everyday life. 'Humour has to be complicated sometimes', as one informant put it. For people with a lowbrow taste humour doesn't have to be an intellectual challenge: they expect humour to create a good atmosphere, the feel of a pleasant evening with friends. To them, good humour is directly linked to pleasant communication. More highly educated people usually feel that 'good humour' isn't a matter of sociability, but rather of creativity, wit, and intellect.

For this reason, highbrow comedy may be disagreeable, satirical, even confusing — as long as it is interesting. And lowbrow comedy may be overly accessible, repetitive, easy — as long as it is agreeable.

Humour Styles and the Interpretation of Humour

Thus, humour styles are first of all norms, or guidelines: expectations for good humour, and criteria by which to judge humour. These norms structure what humour people like, but also what humour people create. Finally, humour styles also guide the interpretation of humour: people with different humour styles will see the same attempts at humour in a different way.

Very often, this means that some people don't see the humour where other people do: the humour will simply fail to amuse them. This is what happens most of the time when lower-class people see highbrow humour, or when upper middle-class people see lowbrow humour. Such differences in interpretation can be illustrated by the reactions to two of the Netherlands' most popular comedians, André van Duin and Freek de Jonge, who are discussed below. André van Duin is the favourite comedian of people who like lowbrow humour, and is looked upon with some disdain by many more highly educated people. Freek de Jonge ranked highest among people with a highbrow humour style, and is usually described by lower class people as offensive, peculiar, or unpleasant.

In some cases, however, humour manages to appeal to people who do not have the same humour style. For some reason, the humour manages to transcend the criteria of one humour style. In this case, it may well be that people are amused by the same thing for partly, or entirely, different reasons. After describing the comedians that stay within the limits of their own particular style, I shall describe one comedian and one television show that have managed, in various ways, to transcend this high–low division.

The Lowbrow View on Highbrow Humour

I propose to illustrate the lowbrow view on highbrow humour via the example of Freek de Jonge, who is one of the Netherlands' best-known comedians, or *cabaretiers*, as they are usually called. Dutch *cabaret* consists of a humorous performance, by one or maybe two persons, with some political or social comment. *Cabaretiers* are supposed to be funny, as well as 'critical of society' (*maatschappijkritisch*). Freek de Jonge is one of the main proponents of this *cabaret*. The clearest sign of his fame and stature is the fact that he is commissioned to do a show on New Year's Eve, a task that for many years has been the prerogative of the legendary comedian Wim Kan.

De Jonge has a very distinctive style: long and somewhat philosophical tales, interspersed with jokes, short poems, other stories, musings, an incidental song. He moves and talks energetically — too fast to understand, according to some people. His humour is crude and offensive at times, in attempts to 'make people think'. At other times, his jokes and stories are rather ephemeral, full of allusions to politics, literature, art, and especially religion. De Jonge is a self-professed moralist: he wants to be more than 'just funny'.

This is very much in accordance with the highbrow humour style. Most of my upper middle-class informants would admire De Jonge for his sharpness, for the way in which he manages to be critical and poetic as well as funny. Often their praise was worded almost like art criticism: one informant, referring to De Jonge's creative, sometimes literary language, explained how she liked the 'poetry' of his shows. Another said she liked the 'many layers' in his stories.

The interviewees from lower and lower middle-class backgrounds usually showed little appreciation for De Jonge. They felt he was neurotic, over-excited, and that he looked funny and even ugly. They complained he was too complicated, that they 'couldn't follow him', that they 'had to pay attention all the time'. Also, they felt he was being offensive, using coarse language, insulting people. Finally, they complained that his performance was too fast and chaotic. On the whole, they found him disagreeable — unpleasant, both as a person and as a comedian.

And indeed, as any highbrow comedian would, De Jonge is not trying to be nice or agreeable. There is some element of avant-garde provocation in this type of humour: the denying of pleasantness, both in content and presentation. De Jonge likes to create ambivalence, making his audience uneasy while they laugh. Especially when younger, De Jonge used to scold his audience for laughing at 'easy jokes', making them laugh and then exposing them as just as bourgeois, racist, politically correct, and servile as other people. Nowhere does De Jonge try to meet any of the criteria of the lowbrow humour style. He is not sociable or friendly, and at times he is not even ostensibly humorous. He fails the standards of lowbrow humour on all counts.

Educated people might dislike De Jonge as well, but they had very different objections. They usually disliked his moralizing, or they thought he was not provocative enough. This shows how disapproval, as well as approval, is guided by humour style. Humour style provides people not only with reasons to like, but also with reasons to reject humour.

The Highbrow View on Lowbrow Humour

The best-loved comedian among people with a lowbrow humour style is André van Duin. Like De Jonge, Van Duin has been working as a comedian since the 1960s, but his style is very different — in some ways reminiscent of traditional music-hall comedy. He does mainly impersonations and sketch comedy, alone or with others, rather than the critical one-man *cabaret* performances. Van Duin's characters rely largely on stupidity for their comic effect. He often used to perform in a classical duo, with his partner Frans van Dusschoten as the 'clever one'.

Van Duin typically impersonates characters with names such as Herman Wijdbeens ('Herman Legs-Wide'), Dick Voormekaar (a pun that could roughly be translated as 'Al Inorder'), or Flip Fluitketel, a character with a whistling tea-kettle on his head (*fluitketel* — 'whistling tea-kettle'). Even when not doing an impersonation, he alters his voice and distorts his face to look funny; his popular persona has almost become a characterization in itself. His humour is never coarse or overtly sexual, but rather clownish. Van Duin is never offensive to anyone; he stays away from controversial subjects. His jokes range from slapstick and mother-in-law gags to absurd sketches with lots of wordplay. Some of his absurd sketches hardly have a punch line, which sets him apart from traditional music-hall. Aside from these sketches, he also does interviews while impersonating some of his 'stupid' characters, often with a bizarre effect. In an unusual variation on the contrast between stupidity and cleverness, he had a (real) physicist in his show for some time. The physicist would do experiments, with Van Duin interfering, often with a surprising comical effect.

Fans of Van Duin admire him for his pleasant style. They like the fact that he is never offensive or hurtful, that he clearly tries to give people a good time. They enjoy his performance, the 'way he delivers his jokes', and his impersonations. Also, lovers of lowbrow humour appreciate the way Van Duin can make them laugh just by the way he looks. This was a highly valued compliment: 'I only have to see his face and I crack up completely'. In short, people who like Van Duin can be said to describe why they like a *person*, whereas people who liked De Jonge were describing an artist.

People with a highbrow humour style usually find Van Duin *plat*: coarse, vulgar, too simple. People tend to use these words with some degree of hesitation, because they imply a disdain they do not like to show. One informant told me: 'It is too easy [...] Too simple, although with that I imply that humour sometimes has to be complicated. But it is too easy. Too obvious. That's the problem with Van Duin.' This shows the highbrow preference for intellectual challenge, something Van Duin is clearly not trying to do. Also, people who like highbrow humour thought Van Duin too obviously funny. They felt his impersonations were 'too much', that he was trying too hard. They found him lacking in subtlety and ambiguity. Finally, they felt he was hackneyed: his jokes about mothers-in-law and marriage and gender were contrived and would-be naughty.

Again, these objections are very different from those by lower-class people who dislike Van Duin. If they didn't like him, they usually felt that way because they thought his jokes were not sharp enough. These were usually younger people, who have become used to sharper and faster humour. For them, Van Duin was too 'tame'.

Transcending Humour Styles

In the cases I have described above, the humour clearly fails to transcend cultural boundaries. The humour appreciated by one group is misunderstood and disliked by the other. The criteria for distinguishing good from bad humour in these groups are so diverse that the members of the groups fail to see the fun in these comedians. What remains is annoyance and disdain. In some cases, however, humour manages to appeal to both groups. Even though it may have been created with one specific style in mind, there is something in it that makes it work for the other group as well.

Sometimes this enjoyment is very far removed from the original intention of the creator: the appeal may be 'camp' or nostalgic. Or — as has happened to Laurel and Hardy — long after their original popular success, their humour has come to be recognized as 'art'. These are forms of enjoyment that violate the intentions of the creators. They often involve a radical change of interpretation, and even a change in the kind of appeal. The amusement of 'camp' is partly based on the fact that the creator probably meant to be serious. Laurel and Hardy most likely get less laughs in art-house screenings than they used to get when they were mere popular amusement. These strongly revised 'readings'[11] add to (or partly remove) the original humour, but in this way do not do justice to the intention of the creator at all.

Although these are very good examples of the transcendence of humour style, I shall now cite instances that are not as spectacular, but remain more true to the original humorists' intention. The two cases I describe were intended as humour, recognized as humour, and enjoyed as humour. Yet the reasons for the enjoyment were quite diverse, and, in one case, much more diverse than the authors expected.

The first example is Youp van 't Hek, easily the Netherlands' most popular comedian, competing with De Jonge for the New Year's Eve slot. Van 't Hek occupies an interesting position: he fails to meet the standards — though only narrowly — for both highbrow and lowbrow humour, and for precisely this reason he manages to appeal to both. Though sometimes too 'easy', he can be appreciated by people with highbrow tastes because of his wit; and if sometimes rather coarse and unpleasant, he can be enjoyed by lovers of lowbrow humour because he insults only people who 'can take it', and he insults himself as well as others. He is a moralist, but that does not scare people who respond to lowbrow humour, because in contrast with other highbrow comedians, Van 't Hek's moralism is one they recognize and identify with. He is moralistic in a down-to-earth (some would say populist) way. No comedian is praised and loathed for such a broad variety of contradictory reasons: he is described as both complicated and easy, both shallow and profound. He is enjoyed for his straightforwardness, hated for his simplistic judgements, despised for his so-called morality.

What does he do to achieve this position? Mainly he uses the best of both styles. He uses the form of highbrow humour, but takes care not to alienate with highbrow content. He tells stories, and uses a quick wit that educated people appreciate, but he never becomes overly philosophical or ephemeral. And he never causes the ambiguity characteristic of highbrow humour. Unlike De Jonge, he manages to be likeable, without being as completely agreeable as Van Duin.

Of course, even Van 't Hek is disliked. Opinions about him demarcate the social boundary between the intellectuals and the truly progressive élite. The latter still think he is somewhat too vulgar or too easy. And he is disliked by many less educated people because they still think he is being too coarse, insulting, and unpleasant. Nevertheless, it is possible to develop a comic style that combines aspects of several styles without being bland.

Where Van 't Hek probably intends to reach a wide audience, sometimes large audiences are reached by people who are clearly not trying to appeal to more than a very specific group. This can be illustrated by the reaction to a television programme called *Jiskefet*. This sketch comedy show, aired by the alternative/progressive broadcasting corporation VPRO, had already been running for some time when it started a series of sketches called *Debtors/Creditors*. *Debtors/Creditors* showed the dreary daily routine of three men working in an office, and their permanently depressed coffee lady. The main characters were three dull-looking clerks who constantly repeated the same stock phrases — variations on greetings and other ritual phrases which are very hard to translate. For instance, one of the characters would always greet his colleagues rather too enthusiastically, saying 'goedesmorgens deze morgen' ('goods mornings this morning'), which is not only ridiculous in its repetitiveness, but, to Dutch ears, is also reminiscent of the south Netherlands accent. Suddenly, people started repeating and imitating these phrases, and the (vaguely southern) accent the actors used. The creators of the programme, which until then had had a limited and fairly exclusive audience, were amazed to find themselves so popular all of a sudden.

At the peak of their fame, the characters were watched by many people who had never watched VPRO. However, these people appreciated *Jiskefet* for reasons that were rather different from the ones the creators apparently intended. Many of my interviewees explained how they liked this show for reasons that seem to be consonant with the lowbrow humour style. Audiences liked it for the performances — for 'the way the characters delivered the jokes', or for their use of 'imitations'. (As was seen in the description of Van Duin — a typical lowbrow compliment.) A plumber told me how he enjoyed the 'simplicity' of the show: 'The stupider, the funnier.

It's always the same. You would always be waiting for Miss Jannie [the depressed coffee lady] to come in.'

Compare this with the comments of an English teacher, who had already watched the programme before this particular series of sketches, and was probably more typical of *Jiskefet*'s original audience:

> *Jiskefet*, yes, I used to watch that, also *Debtors/Creditors*. After some time, it did get a little limited, I am sorry to say. At first I thought it was a highly original approach, a very original perspective on humour, but well ... After I had seen it several times, the setting seemed too limited. The surprise wore off.

The reason most often given for the appreciation of *Debtors/Creditors*, however, was another, even more unexpected one: recognition. Many of my interviewees told me that they especially liked it because it was exactly like their own office, and their own colleagues. Although this might have been a compliment for many comedians, it must have been something of a surprise in this case. One of the creators of *Debtors/Creditors*, Herman Koch, told me how the sketches originated. They used to do impressions of three men who would laugh very loudly all the time for no particular reason. Indeed, in the sketch, the three men always laugh after greeting each other with the same (nonsensical) stock phrases. The original idea was absurd, even absurdist, as are most of their sketches. Although there were some elements of parody, they never intended to make it lifelike. And yet, this was how most people saw it, and why they felt it was funny.

Conclusion

Although most western countries draw a distinction between highbrow and lowbrow humour, the specific nature of these divisions may differ from one country to another. For instance, in continental Europe highbrow humour often includes a dislike of joke-telling, which is not true of the United Kingdom or the United States. Likewise, the way that Dutch highbrow humour focuses on the creation of shock effects seems stronger in the Netherlands than in most countries — as was illustrated by the shocked and awed responses to De Jonge's performance in Berlin in 2002,[12] which included jokes about Jews and Muslims, as well as rather blunt sexual jokes. This penchant for shock effect may have to do with a fairly well-developed anti-authoritarian streak in Dutch culture and politics, the enduring legacy of the 1960s' cultural revolution in the Netherlands (and which has made Amsterdam so popular). Also, it might well be related to the bluntness and directness for which the Dutch are known, and which, in turn, has been explained in terms of their history of egalitarianism.[13]

Although the precise nature of these distinctions may differ, the general distinction is probably familiar to most people from western countries: humour that is easy and agreeable, in contrast to humour that is more inaccessible and intellectual. And I am quite certain that the mechanisms of high and low culture are visible in the humour of countries other than the Netherlands: humour is one of the strongest means of demarcating cultural and social boundaries.

The social consequences of cultural differences in humour can be considerable. Several of my interviews were with upwardly mobile subjects. They all reported that they had had to get used to a different humour, to different ways of being funny, and all had needed to unlearn some of the humour styles they had learned in their families. As a result, many of them still felt alienated, either among their relatives or in their new social surroundings, or both. A shared sense of humour is one of the strongest signs of 'being on the same wavelength'. Conversely, when someone fails to 'get the jokes', or to joke in ways that appeal to a group, this exposes him/her as an outsider.

This does not apply to class differences alone. The relationship between class culture and humour style merely serves to illustrate the workings of humour in demarcating, and sometimes in transcending, humour styles. The mechanisms of humour style may apply to ethnic and regional differences, as well as differences between national cultures, such as the French and the British. Every culture and subculture has its own standards for good humour, along with its dislike for bad humour. And these styles generate misunderstandings, misinterpretations, annoyance and scorn; but also, sometimes, the pleasant surprise of finding that humour does indeed transcend cultural boundaries.

Notes to Chapter 6

1. See Diana Crane, 'High Culture versus Popular Culture Revisited: A Reconceptualization of Recorded Cultures', in *Cultivating Differences: Symbolic Boundaries and the Making of Inequality*, ed. by Michele Lamont and Marcel Fournier (Chicago: University of Chicago Press, 1992), pp. 58–74; and Herbert Gans, *Popular Culture and High Culture: An Analysis and Evaluation of Taste* (New York: Basic Books, 1999).

2. Pierre Bourdieu, *Distinction: A Social Critique of the Judgment of Taste* (London: Routledge & Kegan Paul, 1984).

3. Giselinde Kuipers, *Goede humor, slechte smaak. Nederlanders over moppen* (Amsterdam: Boom, 2001); Eng. trans. as *Good Humor, Bad Taste: Humor in the Context of Class, Culture, and History* (Hawthorne, NJ: Aldine de Gruyter, forthcoming).

4. Deborah Tannen, *Conversational Style: Analyzing Talk among Friends* (Norwood NJ: Ablex, 1984); and *Gender and Discourse* (Oxford: Oxford University Press, 1994).

5. See also Nancy Walker, *A Very Serious Thing: Women's Humor and American Culture* (Minneapolis: University of Minnesota Press, 1988).

6. Jan Pakulski and Malcolm Waters, *The Death of Class* (London and Thousand Oaks, CA: Sage, 1996).

7. Rose Coser, 'Laughter Among Colleagues: A Study of the Social Functions of Humor among the Staff of a Mental Hospital', *Psychiatry*, 23 (1960), 81–95 (85).

8. Randall Collins, *Theoretical Sociology* (San Diego, CA: Harcourt Brace Jovanovich, 1988).

9. Jan Brands, *Die hoeft nooit meer wat te leren: Levensverhalen van academici met laaggeschoolde ouders* (Nijmegen: Sun, 1992).

10. Gans, *Popular Culture and High Culture*.

11. Stuart Hall, 'Encoding/Decoding', in *Culture, Media, Language: Working Papers in Cultural Studies (1972–1979)*, ed. by Stuart Hall and others (London: Hutchinson/ Centre for Contemporary Cultural Studies, University of Birmingham, 1980), pp. 128–38.

12. Hans Verbeek, 'Freeks harde grappen amuseren Berlijn', *Het Parool*, 17 Jan. 2002. The title can be translated as 'Freek's Hard Jokes Amuse Berlin'.

13. Johan Goudsblom, 'De Nederlandse samenleving in een ontwikkelingsperspectief', in *Taal en sociale werkelijkheid: Sociologische stukken*, ed. by Johan Goudsblom (Amsterdam: Meulenhoff Informatief, 1988), pp. 30–57.

CHAPTER 7

Searching for Jokes:
Language, Translation, and the
Cross-Cultural Comparison of Humour

Christie Davies

The comparative study of humour between modern cultures is best carried out by comparing large numbers of jokes from each culture.[1] Jokes are far easier to work with than other forms of humour since they are short, numerous, uncluttered, and have no authors. They circulate orally, both in face-to-face and telephone conversations, and as they circulate (like all folklore) they vary,[2] usually in ways that are unimportant for our present purposes (though important for other kinds of study);[3] it is pointless, therefore, to search for a pure text. We do *not* remember jokes by rote as entities. We remember only the gist of the story, the punch-line, and possibly a jab-line (a humorous line from the middle of the joke as distinct from the terminal and revelatory punch-line). When we come to tell a joke to someone else, we then reinvent it around the basic skeletal framework that we can remember, often improving on it in the process. Jokes improve as they circulate, through accretion, polishing, and reshaping by a series of good joke tellers. Indeed, this is often their source, for the original proto-joke may be feeble, or else a witticism tied to a specific context.

A particular version of a joke may, of course, become fixed by being written down, published, reproduced as a photocopy, sent by e-mail, or put up on a website. It matters not, for it will again be edited and changed as e-mails get forwarded and publishers plagiarize; it may well go back into oral circulation, change yet again, and then be 'fixed' once more in a new form. At each point, though, it is a text that is being circulated.

I now provide two examples of ways in which jokes can be used in comparative analysis. The first relates to a kind of joke that is almost universal[4] — the ethnic, regional, and local jokes told about the stupidity of a neighbouring group: see Table 1. In this case the task of collection was reasonably straightforward.[5] It was possible to show that such jokes existed in each of the countries in the survey (see left-hand column of Table 1), that they were told about the butts of the jokes (see right-hand column), and that a good proportion of them were local inventions rather than the reapplication of jokes from other countries to a local group. It would not matter particularly if most of the jokes were imports, since the purpose of the research is to examine the nature of the relationship in each case between the joke tellers (first column) and the butts of their jokes (second column). If, for example, most of the French jokes about Belgians were to turn out to be British stupidity jokes about the Irish, minimally altered to fit the Belgians (which is *not* the case), it would still be significant that the French pinned the stupidity jokes on the Belgians rather than, say, on the Japanese, the Parisians, the Algerians, or the Germans.

The second example, which I discuss more fully below, relates to the *absence*[6] of a joke in countries such as Britain, France, and Ireland, but which is present in the USA, Anglophone Canada, Québec, and Switzerland. In the latter group, those about whom stupidity jokes are told are also treated in the jokes as comically dirty, in addition to — perhaps, indeed, as an extension of — being stupid. Some examples:

> Pourquoi c'est marqué C.M.I. sur les trucks de vidange à Montréal?
> Cantine Mobile des Italiens.[7]

> How does a Newfoundlander wipe his mouth after eating?
> He rubs his mouth along his shirt sleeve, then takes his serviette and wipes off the sleeve.[8]

> How do they dispose of the garbage in Polish restaurants?
> They put it on the menu in Italian restaurants.[9]

> Did you hear about the Italian businessman who went broke?
> He imported 200,000 cans of underarm deodorant to Italy — and didn't sell a single one.[10]

Jokes of this kind are not told in French in France, nor in English in Britain and Ireland. Why not? It will be hypothesized that the reason lies in the differing perceptions of the relationship between rationality and hygiene existing in North America and in north-west Europe. However, the possibility of putting forward such a hypothesis depends on our being sure that such jokes did not circulate in any significant number in Britain, France, and Ireland during the period 1960–1990, to which the hypothesis refers. Now, it is more difficult to prove an absence of a set of jokes than to prove their existence, particularly when working in a language other than one's own. It is just possible, for example, that numerous jokes about dirty Belgians circulated underground in France and were not told to visiting English scholars. It is possible that the reason the jokes about other peoples' being dirty do not exist in French jokebooks is that they were censored out for being offensive to liberal sensibilities, or even to Belgians, and exist in France only in diaries, samizdat, and computer files preserved from the decades 1960–1990. If this were the case, then this particular conclusion based on a comparative study would collapse, or at least have to be revised to account for the placing of France in the North American category rather than in the British category as far as jokes about dirt are concerned.

I now look in detail at these two cross-cultural comparative studies, paying particular attention to problems of language and translation, and especially between French and English.

The stupidity joke is very widespread in many different cultures, as may be seen from Table 1. Such jokes are, in essence, of the same kind, but in each case there are also many specific jokes that depend heavily on particular local circumstances or even

TABLE I. Ethnic Stupidity Jokes

Country where joke is told	Identity of 'stupid' group in jokes
USA	Poles (and others locally, e.g. Italians, Portuguese)
Canada (East)	Newfies (Newfoundlanders)
Canada (West)	Ukrainians
Mexico	Yucatecos from Yucatan; Gallegos from Galicia in Spain
Argentina	Gallegos
Colombia	Pastusos from Pasto in Nariño
Peru	Arequipeños from Arequipa
England	Irish
Wales	Irish
Scotland	Irish
Ireland	Kerrymen
France	Belgians, French Swiss
Netherlands	Belgians, Limburghers
Germany	Ostfrieslanders, Saxons
Italy	Southern Italians
Switzerland	Fribourgers/Freiburgers
Spain	Gallegos from Galicia; Leperos, the people of Lepe in Andalucia
Finland	Karelians
Denmark	People of Aarhus
Greece	Pontians (Black Sea Greeks)
Faeroes	People of Klaksvig
Romania	People of Altena
Austria	Carinthians, Burgenlanders
Jordan	Tafilah
Egypt	Sa'idis (Southerners)
India	Sardarjis (Sikhs)
Pakistan	Sardarjis (Sikhs)
Iran	Turks; Rashtis from Rasht
Syria and Lebanon	People of Homs and Hama and of Aleppo
South Africa	Afrikaners (van der Merwe)
Australia	Irish, Tasmanians
New Zealand	Irish, Maoris (North Island), West Coasters (in the South Island)

preferences. Ethnic stupidity jokes can thus be shown to be independently invented *as well as* internationally transmitted, switched, and adapted. There are, for example, many jokes that depend on a play on words in one language that cannot easily be translated into another — as in the following:

> Le 'Newfie' pensait que les crayons à mine (AMIN) venaient d'Ouganda.[11]

> Je suis allé dans un magasin 'Newfie' et j'ai demandé une robe de chambre...
> ... le 'Newfie' m'a demandé: 'Quelle grandeur la chambre?'[12]

> Hé, le Newfie! Où vas-tu avec tes bottes?
> Je vais voir *Histoire d'eau* (O).[13]

> Bogotano (from Bogota, capital of Colombia) on phone to Pastuso:
> 'Como estas?' ('How are you?' But could also mean 'In what position are you?')
> Pastuso: 'I am sitting down.'[14]

> Dialogue Belge:
> ... et quel est votre métier?
> Moi, je travaille dans un bureau.
> Ah bon!... dans quel tiroir?[15]

> Why are Sikhs called Surds?
> Because they are the irrational fraction of India.[16]

It is pointless to try and translate the jokes in French into English, or to seek English equivalents for them.   How would you tell the French jokes in English if you had to precede each of them with a lengthy explanation that would undercut the punch-line, or append an explanation for a non-French speaker who is baffled by it? In the case of the Indian joke that was originally told in English in India, it is easier: the teller merely explains the nicknames for Sikhs casually in conversation and then adds with a straight face, '... of course the *real* reason they are called surds is because they are the irrational fraction of India'. Even then the listener would have to comprehend that stupidity jokes are conventionally told about Sikhs among Indians.

In any case, the jokes do not need to be translated into English in order to establish that they exist. It is enough to note that the same *kind* of stupidity jokes that depend on a foolish misuse or misunderstanding of words exist in English, French, and Spanish, and indeed in other languages. These language-based jokes are a subset of stupidity jokes in general. There is, though, one speculation I wish to put forward which someone else may care to test. I would suggest that the proportion of all stupidity jokes that are dependent on errors of language has declined over time, whereas the number of jokes that depend on a stupid ignorance of the material world, and particularly modern artifacts, has greatly increased. The latter phenomenon is easily explicable. It is partly that the number and importance of these artifacts has increased and that our understanding of the material world has become more complicated, and partly that these jokes can be more easily transferred through translation and adaptation between countries with different languages. Thus, when many German *Ostfriesenwitze*[17] were turned into Danish jokes about the people of Aarhus,[18] it seems likely that it was the 'material' jokes, rather than those depending on wordplay in German, that were adopted and adapted by the Danes, because they can be rendered more quickly into Danish. Educated and cultured Danes will, of course, have an excellent knowledge of

German, the language of their immediate, respected, and overwhelming neighbour, but they may well take a pride in exchanging the language-based jokes in the original German and transmitting only the material jokes in Danish to the humbler classes. However, I am making a stronger and more general claim. I suggest that there has been over time, in English at least and probably in other languages also, a stagnation or even a decline in the numbers of ethnic stupidity jokes rooted in language.

With regard to the stupidity jokes about the material world, for the reasons indicated earlier, it does not really matter in what language they are told or published. I cannot understand Arabic, Turkish, or Farsi, but for present purposes it is sufficient to be told many such jokes in English by a more or less bilingual local informant (itself confirmation that such jokes exist in substantial numbers), and then later to demonstrate that many of them are unique to the local people. The weak test of the existence of jokes unique to a particular country is that an outsider with a knowledge of several thousand ethnic stupidity jokes from other countries can say that he or she is unfamiliar with some of the jokes; it is a test that is vulnerable for obvious reasons. The strong test is that the jokes require local social or cultural knowledge if they are to be properly understood. An example of the application of the weak test would be to take the following Syrian jokes about Homs, Hama, and Aleppo (collected by the author in Damascus in 1996), whose general thrust is similar to jokes existing in English or French but which are unfamiliar, and ask whether they have a different and perhaps local twist to them:

> A man from Homs found £500 Syrian in very new notes lying on the ground. He looked around carefully to make sure nobody was watching, took them and put £500 down in old notes instead.

> A Homsiot took part in a race in which he was the only competitor. He came in second.

> Why does a Homsiot put a cucumber under his pillow but not a tomato?
> A tomato would get squashed.

> The people in Homs decided to save time by giving all their jokes numbers and shouting out the numbers. Someone shouted 'Number 6', and everyone laughed. Another person shouted 'Number 9', and everyone laughed. Somebody then shouted 'Number 27', and everyone laughed for a short time, but one man went on and on laughing. The other Homsiots asked him why he laughed so much. He replied, 'Because I had never heard it before'.

> Why does a Homsiot sleep with one eye open and the other closed?
> He took half a sleeping pill.

> A man from Homs and a man from Hama quarrelled. The man from Homs unscrewed the other man's door and ran away with it. The man from Hama chased after him. The man from Homs got tired and stopped, putting the door down in the road between them. The man from Hama caught up with him and knocked on it saying, 'Open the door'. The man from Homs refused to open it.
> Just then a man from Aleppo came along who was carrying a large jar of olive oil. He asked the man from Hama, 'Why do you want him to open the door?' 'Because he stole it', came the reply. He then asked the man from Homs if this was true. 'Yes,' said the man from Homs, 'It is — so I'm not going to open the

door.' The man from Aleppo poured all the olive oil out of his jar onto the ground, banged the empty jar, and said: 'Your heads are as empty as my jar.'

Yet in *assuming* that these are local jokes, one is giving a hostage to fortune. It may well turn out that identical jokes exist in other countries with connections of one kind or another with Syria, such as, say, Iraq, Turkey, or France, and that the jokes are in international circulation and possibly not even of Syrian origin.

The strong test is more secure, as may be seen in the following Indian jokes about Sikhs, collected in India between 1974 and 1981.

> A Gujarati merchant sold a watch to a Sikh. At 12.00 noon the Sikh came back very angry and said: 'You have swindled me. You have sold me a watch with only one hand.'
>
> The Gujarati took the watch, told the Sikh to wait for two minutes and went to the back of the shop pretending to look at it through a lens. On his return he gave the Sikh his watch back and said: 'No, it's fine. As you can see it has two hands.'

> A Sikh was sitting in a crowded train in India. Suddenly he stood up, waved his sword over his head and cheered loudly.
>
> 'Why are you so excited?' said the other passengers.
>
> The Sikh replied: 'Because it is twelve o'clock and I haven't done anything stupid.'

Both these jokes depend on the conventional Indian script for jokes, that at twelve o'clock, in the heat of the day, the Sikhs go crazy because their heads get overheated. The supposed reason for this is that orthodox Sikhs never cut their hair, but bundle their long hair on top of their heads and hold it in place with a turban. In the second joke, reference is made to the Sikh carrying a sword. It is unusual for anyone to carry a sword on a train, but an orthodox Sikh is obliged by his religion to wear some kind of sword (*kirpan*) at all times. Like having uncut hair and beard (*kesh*), it is one of the five Ks, the key symbols of Sikhism.[19] Indians and probably Pakistanis are likely to know this, but people from outside the subcontinent of South Asia are not, and so the joke is unique to the region.

Despite the problem of working out the meanings of jokes in languages that are unfamiliar and, indeed, incomprehensible, and where one is reliant on a native speaker in translating the joke into a world language such as French or English, we can be sure that the stupidity joke is a phenomenon specific to each of the countries in the first column of Table 1. We can now ask the further crucial question: What is the nature of the relationship between the peoples of the first and the second columns?

It has often been hypothesized that the joke tellers are in conflict with the butts of their jokes, and that they use the jokes to put the latter down.[20] This thesis collapses for two reasons. First, only in some cases is there such a conflict between those in the first column and those in the second. In most cases the relationship is one of reasonable amity or of indifference. Secondly, the members of the groups in the first column often feel and express more serious hostility towards, or alienation from, some other group about whom stupidity jokes are not told. As Mina and André Guillois put it:

> [...] il existait une forte communauté de travailleurs immigrés, supposés sales, paresseux, stupides et n'inspirant aux femmes que répulsion et mépris: les Porto-Ricains aux Etats-Unis, les Nord-Africains en France, les Jamaïcains en Angleterre.
>
> Pourquoi n'en a-t-on pas fait les tristes héros de ces histoires que nous appellerons 'belges' pour la commodité?
>
> [...] Ces individus au teint bistré ne nous sont pas assez proches pour que nous nous considérions en eux comme devant un miroir déformant.
>
> En revanche, les Belges sont quasiment des frères, sur lesquels il est bon de s'aiguiser l'esprit.
>
> Le plus drôle, c'est qu'ils ne récoltent peut-être que ce qu'ils ont semé.[21]

These resolute French sentiments are perhaps a little too strongly expressed for everyone's taste, and it is not necessary to concur with them entirely in order to understand the central point being made. The two Guillois have thoroughly invalidated the conflict–hostility theory of ethnic stupidity jokes, and have *independently* come to the same conclusion as the present author, namely that the joke tellers see the butts of their own stupidity jokes as similar to themselves and as a distorted version of themselves, and that they amuse one in the same way as a distorting mirror on a pier or in a fairground.

There is an asymmetry of status between those in the first column of Table 1 (the more elevated) and those in the second. The asymmetry may be based on a difference in economic dominance or in socio-economic class, as in the case of the Laz in Turkey, the Newfoundlanders in Canada, the Irish in Britain, or the Poles in America. The butts of the jokes are rustics or blue-collar workers. However, this does not apply in many other cases, such as the French jokes about Belgians or the French-speaking Swiss (Ouin Ouin), for these countries' income per capita exceeds that of France. Indeed, in these terms Switzerland is the richest country in the world and Brussels is at the economic heart of Europe, whereas much of France is at the economic periphery.

The asymmetry lies, rather, in the fact that the French, and particularly the Parisians, are the arbiters of the French language. It is an asymmetry of cultural power that extends to neighbouring French speakers, but not in the same way to other neighbours such as England, Germany, Spain, or Italy, who have their own language, culture, and literature. This is why the Belgians and the Swiss are singled out as the butts of French jokes. The Walloons acquiesce in their subordinate position, for they are fighting a losing battle within their own country against the more numerous and economically dominant Flemish speakers. They, therefore, seek to rely on the prestige of the pure French of French high culture, and there are on sale in Belgium books such as *Chasse aux belgicismes*,[22] which instruct Belgians how to speak a French free of bits of Flemish or Bruxellois or Picardisms. Yet, on the other side of Belgium the Flemings have to defer to the Dutch version of the two countries' common language; it is the form used in the Netherlands that today decides meaning and usage. The Dutch laugh at the way Belgians speak, which they describe as old fashioned, much as the Greeks joke about the way Pontians speak or used to speak Greek.[23] In many of the other cases listed in the second column of Table 1, the butts of the jokes speak the joke teller's language in a way that is seen as inferior, either because they speak it as their second language (as with Afrikaners speaking English), or because they speak a frontier version contaminated by another language or an unsophisticated dialect from a peripheral province.

There may well be a great deal of variation in the degree to which the distinctive ways of speaking of the butts of the jokes are incorporated into the jokes themselves. In British jokes about the Irish, the use of Irish ways of speaking English is common. British joke tellers, and particularly comedians, will put on an Irish accent (or even two different Irish accents, such as those of Dublin and County Antrim, respectively) to tell jokes about the Irish; and Irish uses of English may be central to the very structure of the joke. In the past, verbal blunders known as 'Irish bulls' were the basis of very many jokes about the Irish,[24] and they have been traced either to the problems that arise for those switching from speaking Gaelic to speaking English,[25] or to a love of figurative language[26] that made Irish conversation singularly attractive but which was also apt to go wrong. Despite the shift to stupidity jokes relating directly to the material world, many language-based jokes remain. For instance:

> Cunnilingus is not an Irish airline. No, it's a tongue twister.[27]

> Car sticker in O'Connell Street, Dublin: Brush up your Erse.[28]

> I'm a tinker.
>   Oh! An what are you tinking about?[29]

> How to speak Irish in one easy lesson:
>   Say very quickly:
>   WHALE OIL BEEF HOOKED.[30]

By contrast there seem to be very few French jokes about the Belgians that rely on the idiosyncrasies of speech of Belgians speaking French. As far as I can tell, French joke tellers do not usually put on a Belgian accent to tell a joke about the Belgians. If this *is* the case, it is curious that the Belgians, who are identified as peripheral from a French point of view mainly for reasons of language, should be the butt of jokes that do not depend on their mode of speech, whereas the Irish, who are peripheral to the British in many spheres, notably the economic, are the subject of jokes that stress their distinctive speech patterns. There are probably three reasons for this. First, the British tradition of telling jokes about the Irish is much older that that of the French joking about the Belgians, and has preserved not just the older stupidity jokes about language but also the tradition of inventing such jokes. Secondly, the Irish, and notably Irish comedians, are much more prominent in the British entertainment business, and particularly in comedy, than is the case with the Belgians in France. Thirdly, Walloons in France, especially if appearing on radio or television, would tend to adhere to or imitate the French of the metropolis, whereas the Irish take a pride in the distinctiveness of their English, which, though mocked, is also appreciated and enjoyed. Irish ways of speaking can be an asset to an entertainer, even though strongly Irish forms of speaking carry low status because of their association with the poor peasantry of the West of Ireland, who go to Dublin or to Britain to work as labourers. The urban middle classes in Ireland, whose speech is closer to standard English, tell jokes about the Kerrymen[31] from the remote south-west of Ireland, who have a strong brogue. In doing so, these Irish joke tellers concede that the dominant form of English is that of their English neighbour.

> What do you call a Kerryman with a Cork accent?
> A social climber. (Ireland, 1980s)

Yet the prestige in Ireland of speech patterns leaning towards middle-class England jostles with a local pride in distinctively Irish forms of English and a strong sense of national identity. By contrast, Belgium has no secure identity and remains a mere aggregate created for political reasons by outsiders: it had been Spanish, Austrian, French, and Dutch in turn. In 1830 Belgium was created as a neutral buffer state in a strategically important area, an uneasy bundle of secular French speakers and Roman Catholic Flemings united only by a wish to escape from Dutch rule. Like a nineteenth-century African colony, Belgium was created without regard to tribal boundaries, and is now paying the price for this. Belgium is not a nation but a 'scrap of paper', and an inflammable one at that. *Les Wallons* define themselves not against non-Belgians but against the 'other' Belgians, *les Flamands*. Thus, it is not strictly necessary for an English translator of French jokes about Belgians to know much about the ways in which Belgians speak, or are supposed to speak, French, or to ponder the difficulties of rendering it in English; whereas jokes based on Irish English, such as those listed above, would be difficult to render into French.

The most distinctive characteristic of French stupidity jokes about the French-speaking Swiss is the slowness of speech ascribed to the Swiss. In other countries very few stupidity jokes depend directly on slowness in this way. In the jokes the French-speaking Swiss are being reproached for speaking French slowly, and those who are slow of speech are, by implication, slow-witted. By extension, everything about the Swiss and Switzerland is stupidly slow.

> Un Français pénètre chez un cordonnier suisse, une paire de chaussures à la main. Il lui demande de changer le talon droit, ressemeler le gauche, poser des fers à l'une mais pas à l'autre. Le Suisse se retourne alors et dit:
> — Entrez![32]

> Un express arrive en gare de Lausanne: le chef de station sort lentement de sa guérite, se dirige vers la motrice et annonce:
> — Ici Lausanne. Puis il va a l'arrière du train et dit:
> — Ici aussi![33]

> Un 'Suisse' rencontre un ami. Soudain il se retourne et écrase du pied un escargot:
> — Pourquoi fais-tu ça? lui demande son interlocuteur.
> — J'en avais assez, répond-il, cela fait trois heures qu'il me suit![34]

> Par décret cantonal, la chasse aux escargots est réservée aux ressortissants suisses à l'exclusion de toute autre personne.[35]

> On croit généralement que l'inscription S.B.B.–C.F.F. qui figure sur les wagons des trains suisses signifie Chemins de Fer Fédéraux. En réalité cela veut dire: Ça fa fite, c'est bas bossible.[36]
> [This could be translated as 'Shlowly bush bast, coing fast's forbidden.']

> Un capitaine suisse passe ses hommes en revue:
> — Garde à vous! ordonne le sergent.
> Personne ne bouge et la troupe continue à fumer et à bavarder.

— Eh bien, demande l'officier au sergent, vos hommes n'ont pas entendu l'ordre?
— Si, mon capitaine, mais attendez un peu que le bruit se répande.[37]

It would not be difficult to translate any of these jokes into English, yet they might well not be fully understood by a British audience, who would not have available to them a 'script' or comic image[38] of the Swiss, the Irish, or any other group as speaking or responding too slowly. The jokes might have to be explained in order to make them funny. Presumably there is a cultural difference here, with the French but not the British seeing intelligence as linked to rapidity of speech and verbal response. Perhaps this is the reason why at a bilingual conference the British will deliberately speak more slowly, so as to be more intelligible, and thus, hopefully, to appear more intelligent, whereas the French speak very quickly, as they would anyway in France, because to do otherwise would be to lose caste. The English, by contrast, tell jokes about the dangers of speaking too quickly.

> A train had a ten-minute stop at a junction, and an Irishman went into the station bar for a drink. As he was finishing his third Guinness he realised that the train was leaving. He ran down the platform after it, shouting: 'Stop, stop, there's a man on board who has been left behind.' (Britain, 1920s)

> During the dispute over the disestablishment of the Anglican church in Wales, David Lloyd George spoke in the hall of a chapel in a small Welsh village. A Nonconformist worthy introduced him, saying:
> 'Well, we all heard the disgraceful remarks made last week by the Bishop of St Asaph's, who I have to say is the biggest liar in creation. Fortunately we have here tonight Mr David Lloyd George who will be more than a match for him.'[39]

What we can see from the contrast between these French and English jokes is that the humorous link between stupidity and speed of speech depends on arbitrary cultural assumptions and preferences. Where the material world and its artifacts are concerned, jokes about stupidity are uniform; but the same is not true of this subset of the stupidity jokes. Rather, it reflects a particular set of the French preferences, a forced dichotomy between *élan* and *esprit* on the one hand, and the heavy, stolid, and phlegmatic on the other, the latter qualities being arbitrarily linked to stupidity. It is perhaps significant that the former terms cannot be easily and exactly translated into English. Somehow, 'jabbering verbosity' or 'doubleplusgoodduckspeaker' does not carry quite the same evaluation of these qualities.

> Un Suisse feint de l'hypertension.[40]

> Quel est le principal défaut des Suisses?
> L'enthousiasme.[41]

It is perfectly possible to perceive solidity and stolidity not as the qualities of an inert, stupid, unimaginative people, but those of of a calm, reflective, sensible, intelligent people, one not carried away by verbosity and excitement. The truths of culture, unlike those of the everyday material world, are problematic, and so, therefore, are the supposed stupidities that mark a departure from them. Only the French are likely fully to appreciate French jokes about the Swiss.

The same point may be made concerning those American jokes about ethnic stupidity that deal with dirt. The relationship between dirtiness and stupidity is not straightforward. There are certain respects in which rationality, modernity, and cleanliness are obviously connected. In the wealthy, developed countries, people live far longer than their ancestors mainly because they have a clean water supply and better sanitation, as well as aseptic surgery, and doctors who wash their hands between patients. Yet beyond some ill-defined optimal point, the rationality of yet greater cleanliness can and should be questioned. It is merely a matter of visual, olfactory, and ideological preference.

Herein lies the reason why stupidity and dirtiness are linked in North American jokes, but not in French, British, or Irish ones. The Americans have an *ideology* of rational hygiene not shared by the latter peoples, which they believe can enable them to defy the decay of ageing and even the victory of the grave.[42] Within such an ideological framework the striving for cleanliness can become a form of 'value rationality' and not just a means to an end. Americans must eliminate even the suggestion of the existence of the smell of sweat, and in consequence a far greater proportion of American men purchase deodorants than is the case in Europe.[43] Even the dead must be clean and free from decay and dissolution; and so Americans are carefully embalmed and buried in treasure caskets (not coffins) placed in concrete-lined bunkers.[44] However strange this behaviour may appear to Europeans, it is part of a coherent system, not a universally accepted one but one peculiar to America, one that is an outgrowth of specifically American cultural assumptions about the nature of a world that Americans believe is infinitely malleable, reformable, and ready for cleaning up in a war against dirt.

The theory has interesting implications for French speakers in North America and Switzerland. Does the fact that the Québécois tell jokes about Newfoundlanders being dirty as well as stupid indicate that they have been thoroughly Americanized and are part of a single North American culture of rational hygiene along with Anglophone Canadians? Do the Swiss, who tell jokes about the 'stupid–dirty' people of Fribourg/Freiburg, also have an ideology of rational hygiene, though one with different origins and implications from the American one?

Jokes about the stupid–dirty did not thrive in Britain in the period 1960–90. The American researcher Sandra McCosh,[45] when comparing jokes in oral circulation among British and American school children, noted that the latter told jokes about the dirty as well as stupid Poles, but that British children told only stupidity jokes about the Irish. This was not a product of censorship, for the politically correct American teachers tried to suppress such joking, whereas the British teachers were indifferent to it. If the dirtiness jokes were absent from the repertoire of her sample in the mid-1970s, at the height of the Irish joke craze, then it is likely that they were absent altogether. What is notable is that the American jokes about dirtiness did *not* transfer to Britain, despite the common language of the two countries and the ease and frequency of communication between them.

It can easily be shown that an attempt was made to introduce American-style jokes about dirtiness into Britain and to pin them on the Irish, but the attempt failed and the jokes did not go into general circulation; quite simply the jokes did not fit British cultural assumptions. In 1978 Peter Hornby produced his second collection of

British jokes about Irish stupidity, *The Official Irish Jokebook No. 3 (Book 2 to Follow).*[46] In this best-selling book Hornby tried to introduce the British to jokes about Irish dirtiness by taking a large set of American jokes about filthy Polacks from the obscure American jokebook *Polish Jokes* by Pat Macklin and Manny Erdman,[47] substituting the word 'Paddies' for 'Polacks' in these jokes, and unleashing them at the high point of the Irish joke cycle. Given the justified popularity of Hornby's excellent books, this ought to have launched a new wave of jokes about the dirty Irish in Britain. It did not. The jokes never got into oral circulation, which is proof that they did not fit into the British framework of thinking. A German-speaking Swiss student of the author's from Berne, who did not believe that the English could ignore such jokes, tried telling the British students, in English, a series of jokes of German-Swiss origin about the dirty–stupid people of Fribourg/Freiburg. She reported back that the British students did not respond to them with high amusement in the way that Swiss students would have done. A deep cultural difference had been demonstrated.

In the case of the French in France, it is difficult to be so sure that the dirtiness jokes were completely absent. They are absent from the published joke books, but this could be due to the pressure of indirect censorship. In English-speaking Canada, where jokes about dirty Newfoundlanders abound, relatively few of these jokes get published in printed joke books, owing to the social power of the politically correct. Those jokes about 'dirty Newfies' that do get published are often bowdlerized.[48] Freedom of expression in Canada is far more limited than outsiders know. At the site of the Canadian version of Speakers' Corner in Toronto, consciously named after the one in Hyde Park in London, there is a notice dedicating the area to freedom of speech, followed by a long list of what may not be said there. Canadian joke books, both English and French, unlike those of other countries, all carry a disclaimer at the beginning, saying that they are not intended to offend anyone. It is presumably a ploy to avoid being harrassed by the state for breaking one of Canada's numerous rules laying down what may not be said in print. It was only after extensive study in the folklore archives of Canada that I was able to uncover the full rich range of ethnic dirtiness jokes about Newfoundlanders and about Italians. If I had relied only on printed sources, I would have been unsure of how important these jokes were. This is in complete contrast with the British case, where ex-American jokes about dirt appeared in print (they were not censored) but did not enter the oral repertoire of the British public. Things are not quite what they seem. In France, one is probably on safe ground in assuming that during the period 1960–1990 jokes about dirty Belgians were not removed from, or toned down in, joke books, either by official censorship or by self-censorship under external pressure, as had happened in craven Canada. Given that French jokes about exotic foreigners and immigrants, such as those from *l'Afrique noire*, were easily available in French printed jokebooks of that period, why should jokes about dirty Belgium have been omitted?

Unfortunately, so far as I know, France has no major archive of jokes collected by folklorists to compare with those in North America, from which one can retrieve the jokes that do not get into print. Also, there have been no significant empirical studies of how French people, and in particular young people, told jokes in the 1970s and 1980s; so how sure can we be that jokes about the 'stupid–dirty' did not exist in France? It is always difficult to search for something that is absent, particularly when one is searching in someone else's language and culture and does not know where things may be hidden. Nonetheless, I am willing to predict that no French jokes about dirty Belgians will be discovered for the period 1960–1990.[49] It is just possible that the explanation for this is that the French had little exposure to jokes in English or French from North America, and were simply unaware of the possibility of telling dirtiness jokes about the Belgians; but such an explanation is very unlikely, particularly given that some of the main editors of French jokebooks, such as André and Mina Guillois,[50] knew English very well indeed and were well acquainted with the American jokebooks about 'dirty–stupid' Poles.

Finally, it should be stressed that the relationship being postulated here between the strength of a culture obsessed with 'rational hygiene', and the prominence of the stupid–dirty ethnic joke between 1960 and 1990 is based on two *independent* pieces of data: (*a*) the existence or non-existence of the jokes, and (*b*) the presence or absence of a cult of hygiene and bodily perfection expressed through differences in funeral practices and in the use of soap and deodorants etc.

The explanatory models advanced here are of interest in themselves, but they also impinge on the work of translators. In the case of most ethnic stupidity jokes, there probably already exists a similar joke in one's own language that gives a good indication of how it might be translated. In the case of those stupidity jokes that depend upon a play on words within the language in which it is told, the jokes may be difficult to translate. It may also be the case that the humour of any stupidity joke is enhanced by the use of dialect throughout, or specifically in, the punch-line. How is this to be rendered?[51] There is a different problem with jokes whose meaning is quite straightforward but which depend on cultural assumptions and a knowledge of scripts that are not going to be shared by the readers of the translated jokes. How are you going to get through to the British that the Swiss are seen as slow for the purpose of the jokes, and that this is a hilarious departure from the French ideal of celerity of cerebration? How are you going to convey to the French that American jokes depend on the equation of dirtiness with stupidity?

Notes to Chapter 7

1. Christie Davies, *The Mirth of Nations* (New Brunswick, NJ: Transaction, 2002).
2. Alan Dundes, *Holy Writ as Oral Lit: The Bible as Folklore* (Lanham, MD: Rowman and Littlefield, 1999).
3. Richard Raskin, *Life is Like a Glass of Tea: Studies of Classic Jewish Jokes* (Aarhus: Aarhus University Press, 1993).
4. Christie Davies, *Jokes and their Relation to Society* (Berlin: Mouton de Gruyter, 1998).
5. Among the published sources used in compiling Table 1 are:
    ALLARD, LOUIS-PAUL, *Le Coin du Newfie* (Montréal: Héritage, 1976)
    —— *Le Coin du Newfie No. 2* (Montréal: Héritage, 1978)
    BIRON, FRANÇOIS, and GEORGE FOLGOAS, *Eh bien raconte* (Paris: Mengès, 1977)
    BRAMIERI, GINO, *Io Bramieri ve racconto 400 barzellette* (Milano: De Vecchi, 1980)
    —— *Il Grande Libro delle barzellette* (Milano: De Vecchi, 1980)
    BUTLER, TONY, *Best Irish Jokes* (London: Wolfe, 1968)
    CAGNEY, PETER, *The Official Irish Joke Book No. 4* (London: Futura, 1979)
    —— *Positively the Last Official Irish Joke Book* (London: Futura, 1979)

CARVER, JOHN, *Ag Shame, Van der Merwe* (Johannesburg: Lorton, 1980)

CHITROUFLET, JEAN, and MAURICE VAN DER FRIED, *Encyclopédie pratique des jeux belges* (Paris: Garnier, 1981)

CLIMENT-GALANT, JACKIE, *Les Meilleures de Lui* (Paris: Filipacchi, 1979)

COLLEVILLE, VICOMTE DE, and FRITZ DE ZEPELIN, *Contes grotesques du Danemark* (Paris: Chamuel, 1896)

DOWNEY, JAMES, *The Great Canadian Joke: Towards a Sociology of Ethnic Joke-Telling in Canada* (Ottawa: Carleton University Press, 1986)

DRAITSER, EMIL, *Taking Penguins to the Movies: Ethnic Humor in Russia* (Detroit: Wayne State University Press, 1998)

DUPONT, JEAN-CLAUDE, and JACQUES MATHIEU, *Héritage de la francophonie canadienne: traditions orales* (Sainte-Foy: Presses de l'Université Laval, 1986)

EARLE, GEORGE, *Old Foolishness ... or Folklore* (St John's, Newfoundland: Harry Cuff, 1987)

EL-SHAMY, HASAN M., *Folktales of Egypt* (Chicago: University of Chicago Press, 1980)

GAIDOZ, HENRI, and PAUL SÉBILLOT, *Blason populaire de la France* (Paris: Léopold Cerf, 1884)

HARVEY, WILLIAM, *Irish Life and Humour* (Stirling: Eneas Mackay, 1904)

ISNARD, ARMAND, *Les Bonnes Blagues des petits Suisses* (Paris: Mengès, 1977)

―――― *2000 histoires belges* (Boulogne: Détente, 1979)

JERROLD, WALTER, *Bulls, Blunders and Howlers* (London: Brentano's, 1928)

KOENDERMAN, TONY, JAN LANGEN, and ANDRÉ VILJOEN, *Van der Merwe* (Hillbrow: Lorton, 1975)

KOWALSKI, MIKE, *The Polish Joke-Book* (New York: Belmont Tower, 1974)

KRÖGERSEN, EIBE, *Ostfriesenwitze* (Frankfurt am Main: Fischer, 1977)

KUIPERS, GISELINDE MANIOUSCHKA MARIJE, *Goede humor, slechte smaak* (Amsterdam: University of Amsterdam Press, 2001)

LABELLE, RONALD, *Inventaire des sources en folklore acadien* (Moncton, New Brunswick: Université de Moncton, Centre d'études acadiennes, 1984)

MACHALE, DES, *The Worst Kerryman Jokes* (Dublin: Mercier, 1977)

―――― *More of the World's Best Irish Jokes* (London: Angus Robertson, 1984)

MACKLIN, PAT, and MANNY ERDMAN, *Polish Jokes* (New York: Patman, 1976)

MULIERO, PEPE, *Chistes de Gallegos* (Buenos Aires: Planeto, 1994)

―――― *Chistes de Gallegos 2* (Buenos Aires: Planeto, 1997)

MURTIE, KEVIN, *At Last! The Official Irish Joke Book No. 2* (London: Futura, 1985)

NÈGRE, HERVÉ, *Dictionnaire d'histoires drôles*, 2 vols (Paris: Fayard, 1973)

O'LEARY, SEAMUS, and O'LARRY, *Irish Graffiti* (London: Futura, 1983)

OSHIMA, KIMIE, 'Ethnic Jokes and Social Function in Hawaii', *Humor: The International Journal of Humor Research*, 13 (2000), 41–57

PETROPOULOS, E., 'Oi Pontioi', *Scholiastis* (July 1987), 46–47

RASKIN, VICTOR, *Semantic Mechanisms of Humor* (Dordrecht: Reidel, 1985)

ROCKWELL, JOAN, *Evald Tang Kristensen: A Lifelong Adventure in Folklore* (Aalborg: Aalborg University Press, 1981)

STEEMAN, STÉPHANE *Raconte... une fois, les vraies histoires belges* (Paris: Mengès, 1978)

THOMAS, GERALD, 'Newfie Jokes', in *Folklore of Canada*, ed. by Edith Fowke (Toronto: McClelland and Stewart, 1976), pp. 142–53

VAN DEN BROECK, WALTER, *Minder Cola met nog meer rietjes* (The Hague: Manteau, 1976)

VAN DER BOUTE-HEN TRAIN (pseud.), *Anthologie de l'humeur belge* (Paris: Garnier Frères, 1980)

WELSCH, ROGER L., 'American Numskull Tales: The Polack Joke', *Western Folklore*, 26 (1967), 183–86

WILDE, LARRY, *The Official Polish/Italian Joke Book* (Los Angeles: Pinnacle, 1973)

―――― *More: The Official Polish/Italian Joke Book* (Los Angeles: Pinnacle, 1975)

―――― *The Last Official Polish Joke Book* (Los Angeles: Pinnacle, 1977)

―――― *The Last Official Italian Joke Book* (Los Angeles: Pinnacle, 1978)

―――― *The Absolutely Last Official Polish Joke Book* (New York: Bantam, 1983)

WISE WILLY, *Wise Willy's Newf Dictionary* (St John, New Brunswick: East Coast, 1991)

YEARHOUSE, H. A. (pseud.), *De bedste Aarhus Historier* (Copenhagen: Chr. Erichsen, 1979)

ZENNER, WALTER P., 'Joking and Ethnic Stereotyping', *Anthropological Quarterly*, 43 (1970), 93–113

ZEWBSKEWIECZ, ED., JEROME KULIGOWSKI, and HARVEY KRULKA, *It's Fun to be a Polack* (Glendale, CA: Collectors, 1965)

6. Christie Davies, 'The Dog that Didn't Bark in the Night: A New Sociological Approach to the Cross-Cultural Study of Humor', in *The Sense of Humor*, ed. by Willibald Ruch (Berlin: Mouton de Gruyter, 1998), pp. 293–306.

7. Folklore Archive, Université Laval, Québec, file F. 513. Collected by Hélène Joncas in 1961.

8. Memorial University of Newfoundland Folklore Archive, file 70–22. Collected by Bernice Bartlett.

9. Wilde (1975), p. 12.

10. Wilde (1975), p. 55.

11. Allard (1976), p. 69.

12. Allard (1976), p. 91.

13. Allard (1976), p. 97. The Newfoundlanders are fishermen and wear long rubber boots for working in water and at sea. They are somewhat different from the kinky rubber boots worn by the fetishists.

14. Colombia, 1980s.

15. Van der Boute-Hen Train, p. 7.

16. Surd, Sardar, Sardarji are terms used in India for the Sikhs. A surd is a particular kind of irrational number, namely one that cannot be expressed as an exact ratio of two finite natural numbers. The Welsh by contrast are the vulgar but rational fraction of England. The joke was told to the author in 1963 by Mani Shankar Aiyer, from Tamil Nadu, then living in Delhi and studying in Cambridge.

17. Krögerson, *Ostfriesenwitze*.

18. Bengt Holbek, 'The Ethnic Joke in Denmark', in *Miscellanea Prof Em. Dr. K. C. Peeters: Door Vrienden en Collega hem aangeboden ter gelegenheid van zyn emeritaat*, ed. by W. van Nespen (Antwerp: Govaerts, 1975). See also Yearhouse, *De bedste Aarhus Historier*.

19. J. Singh Uberoi, 'On Being Unshorn', in *Sikhism and Indian Society*, Transactions of the Indian Society for Advanced Study, 4 (Simla: Rashtrapati Nivas, 1967), pp. 89–100.

20. Robert B. Klymasz, 'The Ethnic Joke in Canada Today', *Kentucky Folklore Quarterly*, 25 (1970), 167–73; Seth Kravitz, 'London Jokes and Ethnic Stereotypes', *Western Folklore*, 36 (1977), 275–301.

21. Mina Guillois and André Guillois, *Histoires belges et méchantes* (Paris: Mengès, 1979), p. 15.

22. Joseph Hanse, *Chasse aux belgicismes*, (Brussels: Fondation Charles Plisnier, 1971).

23. Petropoulos, 'Oi Pontioi' .

24. Jerrold, *Bulls, Blunders and Howlers*.

25. James Orr Bartley, *Teague, Shenkin and Sawney* (Cork: Cork University Press, 1954).

26. Richard Lovell Edgeworth and Maria Edgeworth, *Essay on Irish Bulls* (London: J. Johnson, 1802).

27. O'Leary and O'Larry, *Irish Graffiti*.

28. Murtie, p. 47.

29. O'Leary and O'Larry, *Irish Graffiti*.

30. *Whitelands Rag* (London: Whitelands College Students Union, 1985).

31. MacHale (1977).

32. Van der Boute-Hen Train, p. 230. See also Isnard (1979).

33. Van der Boute-Hen Train.

34. Van der Boute-Hen Train, p. 231.

35. Van der Boute-Hen Train, p. 231.

36. Isnard (1979), p. 19.

37. Van der Boute-Hen Train, p. 229.

38. Raskin, *Semantic Mechanisms of Humor*.

39. Christie Davies, *Welsh Jokes* (Cardiff: John Jones, 1978). See also George Gordon Coulton, *Four-Score Years* (London: Cambridge University Press., 1945).

40. Van der Boute-Hen Train, p. 233.

41. Van der Boute-Hen Train, p. 230.

42. James P. Spradley and Michael A. Rynkiewicz, *The Nacirema: Readings in American Culture* (Boston: Little Brown, 1975); Christie Davies, 'Denying Dirt, Decay and Death in Britain and America', in *Contemporary Issues in the Sociology of Death, Dying and Disposal*, ed. by Glennys Howarth and Peter Jupp (Basingstoke: MacMillan, 1995), pp. 65–71.

43. Heron House Associates, *The Book of Numbers* (London: Pelham, 1979).

44. Davies, 'Denying Dirt, Decay and Death'.

45. Sandra McCosh, *Children's Humour* (London: Granada, 1976).

46. Peter Hornby, *The Official Irish Joke Book No 3 (Book 2 to Follow)* (London: Futura, 1978), pp. 61–62.

47. Macklin and Erdman, pp. 23–24.

48. Christie Davies, 'The Newfoundland Joke: A Canadian Phenomenon Viewed in a Comparative International Perspective', *Humor: the International Journal of Humor Research*, 10 (1997), 137–64.

49. The limits of the time period are deliberately specified. Before 1960 there were no ethnic jokes about dirtiness in North America anyway, nor had the cult of rational hygiene become fully established. Since 1990 the joke cycles about stupidity have been in decline and there has been a commercial attempt to sell American-style rational hygiene in Britain, France, and Ireland. American firms have bought up family undertaking businesses, particularly in East London, and are trying to create a market for embalming. Deodorants for men have been advertised in Britain using the former boxing champion Henry Cooper to give them an image congruent with British ideas of masculinity. In this way the entire culture is being changed, and so the discovery of brand new jokes about the dirty Irish today would be irrelevant for the thesis being advanced here.

50. Guillois and Guillois, *Histoires belges et méchantes*; Mina Guillois and André Guillois, *Les Meilleures Histoires écossaises, anglaises, irlandaises, galloises* (Paris: Mengès, 1979).

51. Christie Davies, 'The Humorous Use of the Contrast between Standard Educated English and Local Dialect in Scottish Jokes', *Stylistyka*, 10 (2001), 111–23.

CHAPTER 8

And What If They Don't Laugh?

Ted Cohen

I know more about jokes than about any other vehicle of humour — at least I have thought more about them, and so they are mainly what this essay is concerned with. And I shall, mainly, be concerned with only one aspect of joking, namely, what to make of it when a joke doesn't work.

There are, no doubt, many reasons why one might tell a joke, but a basic, central reason must be in order to induce laughter in the joke's audience. In my small book *Jokes*,[1] I attempted, in one brief section, to establish that all jokes are conditional in the sense that they can succeed only if the audience meets certain requirements, that is, satisfies certain conditions. I won't rehearse any of that here, but will repeat only that the conditions can range from being very slight to being extremely rich and complex. In all kinds of joke failure, I think, it is reasonable to suppose that in some way or another the target audience has failed to meet the requisite conditions. This may sound as if it is always the audience that is to be blamed, but in fact it is characteristically the fault of the teller, who has somehow mistaken his or her audience and presumed in them something that is not there. Or, in what may be the most interesting case, the teller has not been aware of something that *is* there. Let me give an example:

> Late one night Abe and Sarah are asleep, when Sarah wakes up needing to use the bathroom. When she has not returned to bed for quite a while, Abe hears her calling softly, and he goes to the bathroom to discover that Sarah, who has been growing increasingly plump, has in fact gotten herself stuck in the toilet. She is wedged in and simply can't get herself out. Abe does his best, tugging and prying, but he can't extricate his wife. At his wits end, finally, it occurs to Abe that this is, after all, a problem in the bathroom, and so he calls Ole, the Norwegian plumber. Because it is an emergency, Ole agrees to come over, even though it is nearly 3 a.m. When he arrives, and Abe has let him into the house, Abe suddenly realizes that Sarah is sitting naked in the bathroom and Ole is about to see her. Thinking as quickly as he can, Abe runs ahead, removes the yarmulke from his head, and places it over Sarah's most private parts just before Ole gets to the bathroom. Ole surveys the situation carefully, walking round and round the toilet, saying nothing, until Abe asks, 'Well, can you do something?'
>
> 'Yes', says Ole, 'with the equipment I've brought, I can get her out all right. But the rabbi: he's a goner.[2]

I will not rehearse the list of conditions required of those who get this joke, beyond mentioning that, of course, they must recognize 'Abe' and 'Sarah' as Jewish names. The joke never says that they are Jewish, and unless they are, Abe's wearing a skullcap makes little sense. And unless Ole takes Abe and Sarah to be Jewish, and has some idea that a rabbi might wear such a cap, his final remark is unintelligible.

So, an audience that doesn't recognize the Jewish practice of covering one's head, and therefore has no sense that someone with a rather flimsy sense of this practice might associate it with Jewish rabbis, will not, as we say, 'get' this joke, will not understand it. If they do understand it, but still don't find it funny, I'm not sure what to say (assuming, of course, that this is an audience that finds at least some jokes funny, and that it isn't a joke-audience equivalent of the tone-deaf listening to music). But what if it is another kind of failure? The audience does get it, does find the wit in it, does appreciate how totally unexpected the wonderful punch-line is, but doesn't laugh. Perhaps this is an audience that, though not unduly solemn or reverential, still finds it in some way offensive to be offered, even if only by implication, an image of a rabbi somehow lodged beneath a woman's bare bottom, presumably being crushed and/or drowned as he succumbs to a flush. Or it might be an audience that never likes Norwegian jokes, and that is particularly distressed at having a Norwegian portrayed as someone making an utterly fantastic inference in order to explain what he sees — a woman on a toilet seat with a yarmulke between her legs.

Now in all these cases in which a joke has not worked, something has gone wrong, and as a devoted student of J. L. Austin, I incline towards thinking that it may be more profitable to ask what has gone wrong when something has, than to try to say what has gone right when something works.[3] So, what has happened with this joke-telling? Has there been a misfire, a hitch, a flaw? Has there been a failure to 'secure uptake'? Wittgenstein says that a joke gone wrong is like a ball thrown to someone who puts it in his pocket and does not throw it back.[4] This is far too crude. Perhaps the fellow caught it and won't throw it back; but why? Does he think you don't want it back, or, perhaps, that you can't catch it? And did he catch it to begin with? It may be that the ball was not caught, and it may not have been caught for various, quite different reasons, and it is worth inquiring into as many of these as we can. If the ball was not caught, did he not see it coming? Was he not looking? Did he see it well enough but have insufficient hand–eye coordination to catch it? Was it thrown so badly that it was virtually impossible to catch? We might look into as many of these possibilities as we can think of. It is possible, you know. Austin once wrote this, speaking not about ball catching or joke telling, but the uses of language:

> I think we should not despair too easily and talk, as people are apt to do, about the *infinite* uses of language. Philosophers will do this when they have listed as many, let us say, as seventeen; but even if there were something like ten thousand uses of language, surely we could list them all in time. This, after all, is no larger than the number of species of beetle that entomologists have taken the pains to list.[5]

Now I am not going to get anywhere near seventeen items, but I am going to try to list some ways in which jokes can fail.

A joke gone wrong (or perhaps we should say, a joke gone nowhere) has fallen stillborn for at least one of these three general reasons:

1. The audience didn't understand the joke.
2. The audience did understand the joke, but found no fun in it.
3. The audience did understand the joke, and found the fun in it, but was somehow constrained not to laugh; that is, something overwhelmed what might otherwise have been a laughing response.

The first kind of failure, a failure by the audience even to understand the joke, is not particularly complex, although if we had time we might go into just what features of a joke might go not understood; that is, just what the audience has failed to do (not understanding words in another language, or not securing geographical and historical references, or not recognizing the invocation of stereotypes, or failing to recognize a particular accent — thus not realizing, for instance, that one of the characters in the joke must be Irish, or a number of other possible breakdowns). I shall not go into these, however, for, as interesting as they are, they are not as hard to describe and understand as other kinds of failure.

The second kind of disaster is one in which the audience does indeed understand the joke but doesn't find any fun in it. This is not so hard to describe, but it is difficult to find much to say about it that is not obvious. An example is needed. Here is one taken from my book. It is one of those rare jokes that tend to succeed with both children and adults.

> What do Alexander the Great and Winnie the Pooh have in common?
> They have the same middle name.

This joke usually does succeed, and it is a surprise to me how many of those who have written about my book have cited this as a favourite joke. But it does not always work. It is virtually always understood. The joke is not without its craft. For instance, it is better to pair Alexander the Great with Winnie the Pooh, than to pair Alexander with, say, Peter the Great, or Attila the Hun, and it is not so difficult to say why it is better. It is a pleasant exercise to try explaining why it is better, and it is a more difficult exercise to find what to say when the joke is in its best form; and yet people who understand it do not find it funny. They do understand everything that seems relevant: they know who Winnie and Alexander are, they are familiar with historical nomenclature, they realize that Winnie and Alexander have nothing whatever in common, and so on. But they don't find the joke funny. All I have thought to say is that this is just a rock-bottom fact about the world and us humans: that two of us might understand something perfectly and yet only one of us be moved to laugh. What else is there to say?

Even more pressing is the question of what to say about a failure of the third kind, when the audience gets the joke, sees exactly what is funny in it, but does not, as it were, *feel* the fun, does not laugh, does not even give a grudging smile. What has happened here? Perhaps it is something like this. I am reminded of a kind of experience that was part of my childhood. I don't mean to burden you with my autobiography: I hope to be reminding you of an experience you've had. On some occasions I would be moved to inappropriate laughter. Either it seemed to me inappropriate to be laughing at the thing at all, or, although the thing was a fit object of laughter, it seemed inappropriate to be laughing in the circumstances. So I didn't want to be laughing then and there. I found it almost impossible to stifle the laughter directly, and so I would try to overcome it, as it were, by turning my thoughts to something as sober as I could imagine. I would recall the death of a grandparent, or I would imagine something infinitely sad. Often this would not work, and I would laugh on, but sometimes it did work, at least after a fashion, and my laughter was subdued.

I had no 'theory' of why this laughter-killing might work, and I don't have one now. But something happened, and it may be reasonable to think of it like this: it is as if something X might produce laughter in me, and something else Y might produce great sobriety or even tears. Given that X was already at work, if I could introduce Y into my mental life, I might create a vector, as it were, the resultant of X and Y, and so my ultimate reaction might not be utter sobriety or weeping, but it would be something less than laughter. This seems reasonable to me, if not as a 'Newtonian' theory of inertia, momentum and motion, at least as a useful description of moments in the mind of a laughing animal. It is one thing to be struck by the vulgarity, obscenity, unspeakability of some joke, and thus think that one should not laugh, even though without these strictures one would laugh freely, because, after all, the damned thing is funny; and it is yet another thing, and a different kind of thing, to have a negative reaction to the joke so strong and pointed that this reaction undercuts any response of amusement.

I'm not sure of the plausibility of this description, but it does seem to me a description that matches, for instance, the experience that my appreciation of the music of Wagner and of some of the poetry of T. S. Eliot is often strangled by the anti-Semitism I find in those works. *Should* one's appreciation of this music and this poetry be subdued by their offensive politics? In *Jokes* I argued that there is no final answer to this question, that those whose appreciation is not affected are entirely legitimate in their responses; but so are those, like me, who find their appreciation undercut. I wonder if that is how it is with humour. I have no doubt that that is exactly how it is in some cases, cases in which one should admit the existence of the fun but also insist that one wants nothing to do with it.

As I recall my childhood efforts to stifle my own laughter, it seems to me that these efforts, whether or not they worked, occurred in two markedly different kinds of situations. One was a case in which I found something genuinely funny but thought it utterly inappropriate that I should be exhibiting mirth under the circumstances. I might be at a funeral, for instance, when something funny either occurred to me or presented itself, and I felt a strong inhibition against laughing or even smiling during that sad occasion. This is not so complicated, I suppose, because the question of whether something is genuinely funny, or even only funny to me, didn't arise. It was indeed funny, but it was inappropriate to respond to the fun. In other cases, however, it seemed to me that perhaps there was something wrong in me to find something funny — even though I did — and I was, as it were, trying to kill that response in myself once and for all. It wasn't that I thought it inappropriate to laugh then and there, but that I thought it inappropriate to laugh at this thing ever.

And then there is a kind of mixed case, which still leaves me unsure what to say. My mother once took a friend and me to a ballet performance when we were ten to twelve years old. I had never before attended one, neither had my friend, and I was largely unable to make any sense of it whatever. When some of the female dancers did a routine during which they stood erect on one leg, toe curved and pointed downwards, with the other leg bent so that its toe touched the extended leg, I was suddenly struck by the image and whispered to my friend that the dancers looked as if they had fleas. Of course this convulsed the two of us, and I bent every effort to suppress my giggling. As little as I understood ballet, I understood absolutely that I was not supposed to be laughing at this display while seated amidst an attentive and appreciative audience. No question about that. But there is a question of whether it would be right or apt or decent to find this exhibition funny under any circumstances whatever. It is, one might say, a *wrong* response to the dance. What do you think?

I distinguish that case, and cases like it, from a case such as the following. In a movie I last saw dozens of years ago, an inconsequential movie called *Cat Ballou*, Lee Marvin plays a hired gunfighter who has been engaged to protect a man named Frankie Ballou. He does not succeed, and although Lee Marvin is unaware of it, Frankie Ballou is shot to death. His daughter, Cat Ballou, played by Jane Fonda, has her father laid out in a casket with memorial candles burning nearby. Lee Marvin stumbles drunkenly into this scene, assesses it, and then blows out the candles while singing 'Happy Birthday' to Frankie. Here there is simply a mistake. Lee Marvin has mistaken a bier for the trappings of a birthday party, and has failed to realize that the birthday boy is dead. I *did* understand, if very dimly, what ballet is, and, unlike Lee Marvin, I understood perfectly well that laughter was an inappropriate response to the occasion. So if I made a mistake, it was not Lee Marvin's kind of mistake, and it was a deeper and more significant error.

Exactly what kind of error is this? We are now concerned with humour, and this error is one of laughing at the wrong thing, or at the wrong time, but the question of when it is right to laugh is an instance of the larger question of the appropriateness of feelings and reactions. When is it right, or wrong, to feel sadness, to feel fright, to feel disgust, or, to feel amused? Hume says there is a sense in which a feeling is never right or wrong, it just *is*; but Hume goes on to say that feelings can be appropriate or not, or, as he says, they can be the 'natural' responses to things.[6] Some things are, in Hume's words, 'fitted by nature' to produce certain human responses. Should we agree with Hume in this? There is a temptation to do so. Ask yourself what you would like to say of someone who has strong erotic feelings in the presence of young children, or who is amused by the pain experienced when animals are tortured. Such people seem pathological, somehow not right, and it is tempting to say that their responses are 'unnatural'.

But the history of denominating things natural and unnatural is not, in general, a history of very sound philosophy, and it is not always an entirely savoury history. Homosexual attraction has been called unnatural. Slavery has been called natural. It has been called natural to believe in the Christian God. Hume thought it somehow natural to prefer the poetry of Milton to that of Ogilby, natural to feel more pleasure from Milton's verse than from Ogilby's. He also thought the same about Bunyan and Addison. Those who have read Ogilby probably share Hume's comparative responses to him and to Milton, but most of us can only guess about Hume's opinion of the relative merits of Bunyan and Addison. (In fact, Hume thought Bunyan something of a bumbler, while he thought Addison a master stylist.)

It seems clear to me that this natural/unnatural business is very slippery, and maybe not a little dangerous. I think it won't do to take as natural what is typically or usually thought or felt. In the first place, it has not been uncommon in history for a majority to have a sensibility later thought misguided; and in the second place, Hume would like to say that the proper response to a work of art is somehow the natural one, but Hume also notes that often only a few people are capable of this proper response. But then what are we to say of those who laugh at the wrong things, or — my official topic — those who don't laugh at genuine fun? There is one thing we can say, and although it may be disappointing, it is very interesting if this is all we can say. We can say that these eccentrics are *not like us*. I laughed at this joke. You don't. You are not like me. Are you, in addition, somehow unnatural, defective, inadequate? On what possible grounds could I say that? I could take myself as a measure, an index, and judge everyone else in terms of my personal responses, but, of course, you might do that just as well. So what is left to say?

For the past few years, when thinking and writing about figurative language, art in general, and jokes in particular, I have been forced to the conclusion that in the end there just is nothing to say but that we sometimes are the same in our responses, sometimes different, and when these differences arise, sometimes we can explain the differences and sometimes we can't, but that we are often unable to make sense of the idea that someone is right and someone wrong. If that conclusion disappoints you, and you would like something more definitive, more classically 'philosophical', then I invite you to find it, and share it with me.

In closing, I should like to point out that a great deal of humour, especially of joking humour, in fact portrays people responding eccentrically, having inappropriate or somehow skewed responses. Here is an example. First, however, I shall give one item of background that you may need. Among some Jews there is a particular practice employed when a death occurs: it is called 'sitting Shiva'. For seven days after the burial, the bereaved family opens its house to sympathizers, with the house itself prepared for the occasion in various ways dictated by various versions of this practice, but always, and typically, with food and other refreshments for those who visit. The family is said to be sitting Shiva.

> Greenberg, an elderly New Yorker, with few financial resources, hits on an ingenious way to supplement his food supply. He reads newspapers regularly, attending to the obituaries, and when he finds a Jewish name, he checks the address of the deceased and then goes to that place, where he is always welcomed as a fellow-mourner and invited to eat and drink.
>
> One day he finds the address of someone recently passed, and he sets out in the early evening for East 57th Street. He has mistaken the address, however, and he should have gone to West 57th Street. When he arrives, unknown to him, he has come to a house of ill repute. When the Madam answers the door, Greenberg says, 'I've come for the Shiva.'
>
> 'Shiva?' asks the woman. 'I don't know about Shiva, but Brandy knows a lot of tricks. Go up to the second floor and ask for Brandy at the first door to the left.'
>
> Greenberg goes to the door, and when Brandy opens it, he says, 'I was told to come up here for the Shiva.'

'Shiva?' asks Brandy. 'I don't think I know that one, but I know a lot and I'm sure you won't be disappointed. Come in.'

Greenberg enters the room, and half an hour later he emerges, Brandy behind him, and he hears her say, 'That was swell, mister, you just come back any time you like.'

'Yes,' says Greenberg solemnly, 'I will. But on a happier occasion.'

I find this story funny, and I hope you do, but there is more than a little at work in that story that is not so funny — or not *just* funny. Accepting death, acknowledging it, taking time out to feel one's loss, but not an indefinite time, asking others to help but also helping them, perhaps by feeding them, perhaps in other ways. All those things are in the background, along with the presumption — at least something I presume — that Greenberg is not a bum. He is not just freeloading when he attends these Shivas: he is participating in deep, complicated, incomprehensible strategies invoked in order to live through impossible losses, and, having gone to many Shivas, he is accustomed to encountering new and novel ways of doing this. All this was noted by Stanley Cavell when I gave him this story.

So what do you make of Greenberg? No doubt he has been lucky. He has made some kind of mistake, I suppose, and certainly he and Brandy have not had exactly the same response. Maybe we should say that sometimes things just don't work out. But sometimes they do. And then again, as Stanley Cavell remarked, soon enough Greenberg is going to remember he's hungry.

Notes to Chapter 8

1. *Jokes: Philosophical Thoughts on Joking Matters* (Chicago: University of Chicago Press, 1999).
2. I owe this story to my friend Professor Henry West of Macalester College, St Paul, Minnesota. I have been told that Professor West told the story to open an academic conference a few years ago. I do not know the topic of the conference. I wish I had been there.
3. In his 'Performative Utterances' (and again in *How to Do Things with Words*), Austin catalogues ways in which a speaker can fail to effect the act purportedly being performed when he speaks. In 'A Plea for Excuses' he argues that to say of an act that it is 'voluntary' is, in general, to deny that it is involuntary in one of a number of ways in which an act may be qualified. The two essays are to be found in J. L. Austin, *Philosophical Papers*, 3rd edn (Oxford: Oxford University Press, 1979), pp. 175–204, 233–52. The book is a reconstruction of Austin's William James Lectures, published by Harvard University Press (Cambridge, MA, 1962).
4. Ludwig Wittgenstein, *Culture and Value*, ed. by C. H. Von Wright, trans. by Peter Winch (Oxford: Blackwell; Chicago: University of Chicago Press, 1980), 83e. The book was first published as *Vermischte Bemerkungen* (Frankfurt: Suhrkamp, 1977).
5. Austin, 'Performative Utterances', p. 221.
6. 'Of the Standard of Taste', in David Hume, *Essays Moral, Political and Literary* (Indianapolis: Liberty Classics, 1985, 1987), pp. 226–49. Hume argues that judgements as to beauty are based, not on properties directly found in objects, but on feelings of pleasure induced in judges. But different judges experience these pleasures differently, of course, and so Hume locates what he calls a 'standard of taste' in the feelings of specially qualified judges, which judges, he claims, can be identified by empirical testing. I have attempted to explain some of the subtleties in Hume's marvellous essay in 'Partial Enchantments of the *Quixote* Story in Hume's Essay on Taste', in *Institutions of Art: Reconsiderations of George Dickie's Philosophy*, ed. by Robert J. Yanal (University Park, PA: Pennsylvania State University Press, 1994), pp. 145–56.

CHAPTER 9

Without the Rape the Talk-Show Would Not Be Laughable

Iain Galbraith

Several years ago I was asked to speak about my German version of a stage adaptation of Irvine Welsh's *Trainspotting* to a translation research forum at the University of Oxford. Here is a passage from that talk that provoked some debate:

> As far as I can make out, the complex issue of humour has frequently been neglected in productions [of the German version] ... with a pronounced tendency among directors and actors, themselves engaged in a type of translation — and possibly flattered by the social and political topicality of the drugs issue, to play down what might be referred to as the 'Rabelaisian' aspects of the work in a well-meaning attempt to expose the subject's harrowing core. In this context, it is perhaps worth remembering just how far away from the original text a stage adaptation can 'stray', and for reasons that may be quite beyond the translator's control. The complexity of a stage performance owes much to the composite structuring of the material in a series of interlinked, collaborative and exploitative processes, reflecting the specific, and always dynamic, juncture of aesthetic, social and commercial interests. Ideally, then, if we are to speak of the translation of the text from its Scottish setting to the German stage milieu, it would be necessary to analyse the full spectrum of formative influences on the text at different stages of the process. One source of factors that generally remains outwith the translator's grasp is the way in which the theatre itself, both in a specific sense (directors, actors, stage designers, rehearsals etc.) and in its traditions (aesthetic, literary, social, local, historical), is brought to bear on the text with each new performance, so that the process even of textual translation is never fully concluded. For it is rare that a production can afford to have a translator on hand, contributing advice to actors and director on the consequences of the textual changes frequently made during rehearsals, or in the course of a season's exposure to the rigours of performance.

One might expect the ensuing discussion to have centred on the manner in which humour — the grotesqueries of *Trainspotting*, for example — can be attenuated or lost altogether in that complex and prolonged process of 'translation' to which dramatic texts are generally subjected. However, if the passage I have just cited proved contentious (and it was not intended to be so), this had less to do with problems of translation *per se*, than with the vexed question of textual authority, and, by implication, with the authority 'accruing' to the translation, or to the translator as author's advocate. How, I was asked, could I allow anyone to tamper with my translation once I had considered it finished? Is it not the very task of the translator to ensure that the closest possible rendering of an author's text be heard in the target language? Further, and by logical extension, is it not the translator's job to resist all intermeddling on the part of dramaturges and directors?

These questions, and their implications, are well worth examining. Unable to offer an adequate solution at the time, I have been forced to question my own practice as a translator — and 'invisible' component of the theatrical ensemble — ever since, only to find that the same questions arise in almost every theatrical production, and that each production can offer a different set of answers. Perhaps it is unsurprising that the difficulties we encounter in discussing the instability of humour in translated dramatic texts should be interlaced with questions about textual authority posed by the theatre as an institution, or as a whole, for the interests and occupations of the theatre — unlike those of a translator — extend far beyond those of establishing a written text. In what follows I propose to investigate and, briefly perhaps, to unravel the loops of that knot by reference to another play I have translated into German, a play whose milieu, it might be argued, has at least a passing resemblance to that of *Trainspotting*. Performed for the first time at the Abbey Theatre in Dublin in September 1997, *Sucking Dublin* was written by the young Irish dramatist Enda Walsh, whose *Disco Pigs* — the ill-fated struggle of a teenage 'Bonnie-and-Clyde' to transcend what they perceive as the unremarkable expectations of a life in (Walsh's native) Cork — has been one of the most widely produced plays in German of recent decades. Before addressing Lukas Langhoff's popular *mise-en-scène* of *Sucking Dublin*[1] at the Bremer Theater, however, I wish to explain why I think that the volatility of humour in translation for the stage is linked to two factors which — although we also have reason to think of them separately — are, in this case, inextricably intertwined.

First, the transportation of humour into a new cultural environment entails its insertion into an unforeseen field of tension whose social, political, aesthetic, and linguistic coordinates may differ quite considerably from those whose relations generated laughter in the source milieu. Consequently, although we may wish to identify various types of humour as specific to different texts or situations — types suggested, for example, by what might be referred to as the Superiority (Aristotle, Hobbes, Bergson), Incongruity (Hutcheson, Schopenhauer), and Release (Hutcheson, Kant, Freud) theories of laughter — common sense is likely to predicate these and other explanations of the phenomenon on a dialectic that includes the contingent perceiver as well as the perceived object of laughter: 'Nothing is laughable in itself', writes the psychologist John Y. T. Greig, for 'the laughable borrows its special quality from some persons or group of persons who happen to laugh at it'.[2] The transliminal instability of whatever humour we might attribute to a source text is thus the *repository and perpetual part* of a dynamic negotiated by all texts in their iridescent relation to an ever-changing, linguistically, and socially pluralistic milieu. It is the utopian task of the translator to anticipate and body forth that dynamic as it unfolds in a new linguistic and cultural environment — utopian because the translator's attempt to *predict* the outcome of such a process, like the physicist's attempt to probe the quantum world, must inevitably, by exclusion, or via determination of the parameters, limit the percipient, assimilatory potential of the translated text.

Secondly, the instability of the humour implicitly held in a dramatic text, whether translated into a different language or not, must be seen as a consequence of the role attributed to texts in the context of theatre as a process. In other words, it must be seen in terms of the difficulty of resolving the textual and non-textual aspects of theatre. In the case of a *translated* dramatic text, the link between 'heteroglot' (in the Bakhtinian sense) and theatrical destabilization is self-evident, since the theatrical process itself, in so far as it belongs to a local or national culture, is part of the target milieu to which the source text has been exposed and in dialogue with which its potential humour now must develop — if indeed it can develop at all.

Summarizing the relations between page and stage we should always start by reminding anyone with a literary, rather than specifically dramatic, interest in texts that allegiances to the authority of the written word have rarely been clear-cut in the history of theatre. Theatre is a process in which the text and everything that is essential to theatre but is non-textual — dress, stage design, actors, directors, locality, etc. — influence one another as the production gets under way and the shape of a performance emerges. Of the tensions, especially those between page and stage, that have characterized theatre since the advent of literacy, the American theatre historian Jennifer Wise has written that it is 'theatre's knowledge of but stubborn non-absorption by writing which has guaranteed for it a special, even privileged position within the family of literary genres. Precisely because it is not textual itself, theatrical performance can 'display' or represent writing in a way that a written medium itself cannot; in the theatre there is an 'outside' of writing'.[3] As an example of the way non-textual elements in the theatre have influenced the theatrical text as performed and, indeed, the text as transmitted to later eras, Wise also cites Denys Page's work *Actors' Interpolations in Greek Tragedy*, which surveys hundreds of examples in Greek tragedy in which actors 'appear to have added lines, cut speeches, altered stage directions, written their own prologues, changed sad endings to happy ones, transposed speeches from one character to another and even from one play or other written work to a separate piece'.[4] As far as modern theatre is concerned, too, I would agree that 'the identity of drama as a literary genre depends on its maintenance of a certain freedom from itself qua literary text'.[5] The extent to which that freedom is actually exploited, however, depends on factors that go beyond the scope of this discussion; suffice it to say that the ebb and flow of what in Germany are often referred to as *Autorentheater* (author's theatre) and *Regietheater* (director's theatre) have much to do with an irresolvable dialectic that can probably be traced to a dilemma already in place at a time when the Athenians, as Plutarch tells us,[6] felt impelled to pass a law against textual deviance.

Returning to the twenty-first century, it was immediately obvious to me when I saw the German première of my translation of *Sucking Dublin* in Bremen on 11 November 2000 that the director, Lukas Langhoff, had invoked all the freedoms of his trade. *Sucking Dublin* had taken longer to sell to a German theatre than other plays by Enda Walsh.[7] Speculating as to why that might have been so, I shall suggest it was the kind of play Hélène Cixous had in mind when, in a text entitled *Aller à la mer* (1971), she gave her reasons for having stopped visiting the theatre altogether:

> With even more violence than fiction, theatre, which is built according to the dictates of male fantasy, repeats and intensifies the horror of the murder scene

which is at the origin of all cultural productions. It is always necessary for a woman to die in order for the play to begin. Only when she has disappeared can the curtain go up; she is relegated to repression, to the grave, the asylum, oblivion and silence. When she does make an appearance, she is doomed, ostracised or in a waiting-room. She is loved only when absent or abused, a phantom or a fascinating abyss. Outside and also beside herself. That is why I stopped going to the theatre; it was like going to my own funeral, and it does not produce a living woman or (and this is no accident) her body or even her unconscious.[8]

What Cixous has to say of theatre in general more or less summarizes the plot of *Sucking Dublin*: a flat full of penniless characters evidently bound to hurt each other in their struggle for survival in a Dublin milieu that is entirely gridlocked by drugs and various other forms of material compensation for lack of love and meaning. Very close to the beginning of the play Little Lamb, celebrating her eighteenth birthday party, is raped in full sight of the other characters, who do not intervene, by drug-dealer Steve, married to Lamb's sister. Things get worse from there: a 'fascinating abyss', and Little Lamb is the only character who seeks, and possibly finds, a way out: in flight, literally, *à la mer*. The play ends with Little Lamb at the airport, driven by the forlorn hopes and volatile energies of the truly desperate, deserting her baby in its pram on an empty stage, in transit to a commercial pipedream of sea and sand on a ticket paid for with money stolen from her parents' savings: 'Leave her for someone ta be a good mammy and daddy!! Might seem fuckin nasty but I gotta be hard!!'

We do not have to be Hélène Cixous to fear that a visit to the theatre on an evening for which this play was billed would be unlikely to produce a challenge to the naturalistic gloom of a perspective that refuses redeeming commentary or resolution of any kind. In a German cultural context, in which theatre has long been seen, and often vigorously contested, as an institution whose aesthetic and moral consensus reflects the values and fickle tolerance of the 'educated' middle classes, this kind of material has to be handled with kid gloves. Lukas Langhoff may well have considered that any 'serious' German production would be forced to hazard a course between maudlin sentimentality, as the likely response to social realism, and the moral condescension of a didactic drama. Contrary to expectation, then, the Bremen performance turned out to be comic; it also allowed the characters' despair, and the actors' visceral rendering of human frailty, to seep — disturbingly and incongruously — through the multiple layers of media trash and recycled 'MacFun' which the production, aping a repressive function of the entertainment industry, 'dumped' on top of them.

Examining the relationship between page and stage, the French semiologist Patrice Pavis has expressed their interdependence in terms of a negotiable dialectic: on the one hand, the *mise-en-scène* need not be faithful to a dramatic text; on the other, the *mise-en-scène* does not dissolve or annihilate the dramatic text.[9] Certainly, the Bremen production did not annihilate the text of *Sucking Dublin*, but it seemed very close, on a number of occasions, to dissolving it in a welter of apparently arbitrary additives: the actors *chez eux* talking about the experiences of one of them as a TV-part in the *Teletubbies*; an improvised talk-show in which participants discussed the shapes and sizes of kidney stones in different German *Länder*; a civic disquisition of prolix probity by Steve, the dealer and rapist, alleging that Communist, or at any rate Eastern, intelligence agencies had flooded the West with drugs, killing our children in a bid to finance their other operations; a fragment of Euripides' *Medea*; a passage from the *Revelation of St John*; music and dance; masks; a pseudo-critical 'discussion' with the audience; a live rock band, and 'lots, lots more'. The baby was not left in a pram, as required by a textual stage direction, but was visible at the end of the play through the distortions of a giant ice-cube.

Why, then, did the Bremen *mise-en-scène* incorporate such apparently extraneous matter? What questions was it trying to address, or indeed to answer? Surely every dramatic text has space, or must make space, for the questions the actors and director address to it? The French theatre theorist Anne Ubersfeld sees the dramatic text as *troué*,[10] composed — like a piece of Swiss Emmental cheese, perhaps — partly of 'holes', which, in a performance, are filled by the 'text' of the *mise-en-scène*, both texts contributing to a larger ensemble of signs that ultimately includes the activity of the audience. In this ensemble, character is understood as the locus of mediation between director and author, text and performance. I would argue that the Bremen production supported an ensemble of this kind — in which the audience, too, finds it has assumed a certain role. Before taking their seats, the spectators — whether deliberately or by prior unconscious agreement, so to speak — seem to have answered a question: How much cynicism do we need in order to live in the world as it is? We may not exactly knit while enemies of the state mount the guillotine, yet we have become accustomed, possibly for want of a better alternative, to munching our takeaways while watching 'our bombers' reduce distant cities to rubble in the news-breaks between soaps. Why then should we come to the theatre at all? Do we not have the world-theatre we need? Or to put it plainly: how shall we — as an audience in our time — be moved by a hyper-realistic illusion of another cage of junkies wasting away?

The junk, of course — and at one point in the performance an enormous can of trash really was emptied over the stage — is also in our heads. The burgers in our mouths and the bombs falling on the screen may be part of that junk. But where are we now — how do our feelings sit alongside the trash? Maybe we feel some confusion; or pleasure, at the taste of the relish on the burger, for instance. Or perhaps we sense a sort of satisfaction, or justification, in the image of destruction of people we take to be our enemies. At the same time, we may feel grief, or fear, or helplessness, even anger, at the thought that our lives should have led to this. But we don't know what to do with the feelings; it is not clear what kind of engagement could break a vicious circle that includes our inability to respond directly to the suffering our societies produce. So while mediation sets the parameters for our cynical integration of such phenomena, need ironic distancing itself imply a cynical response? An answer to the question of how much cynicism we need is implicit in the 'text' of the *mise-en-scène*. One synonym for cynicism is heartlessness, but the Bremen production of *Sucking Dublin* responds that (in theatre, at least) our heart is not primarily engaged by the object of the text (characters and their predicament), but rather struggles to find its place, or range, in a fully mediated encounter between the audience and that object. In other words, it is not the way the object of the text itself is managed that concerns us in the theatre, but the way we manage our relations with that object. With the freedom it maintains 'from itself *qua* literary text',[11] theatre as an interdependent process is capable of reflecting, and of countering by reflection, systematic objectification.

The humour, too, derives from the uneasy correlation we perceive between our quotidian experience of the *absence* of theatre, and the recognition of our own predicament *in* the theatre: in our baulking at, and simultaneous desire for, a life in which there would be a palpable and manageable link between the ubiquitous trash, the unbearable states of being we intuit or know may lie behind that trash, and our own feelings. Without the trash, however, without this reflection of our own indifferent lifestyles, or indeed of our own indifference, the portrayal of the predicament behind, or buried in, the trash would be unlikely to affect us so intensely; and, conversely, it is the ludicrous incongruity of a trash we recognize as 'ours' — the way it sites, and sits alongside, the harm and hurt — that induces our laughter. Without the rape the talk show would not be funny, or even laughable; and without both, we would have no sense of ourselves in relation to either.

In retrospect I would add that a certain humour perceived in the text itself (a humour with its roots in the process that culminated in the original Abbey Theatre production) — much of which consists of sarcastic repartee — helped to generate the 'holes' through which the 'text' of the *mise-en-scène* (Ubersfeld) was able to work. The humorous aspects of the authorial text are compounded, significantly I think, by the way in which several of its stage directions organize the contiguity of trash with surreal expressions of horror:

> *Noise of the city bellowing up and down in volume as lights fade up on an extremely frightened* LITTLE LAMB *as she 'walks'. The noises take on a strong rhythmic beat. Sounds of footsteps, talking, cars, sirens, various radio stations (one of which plays 'The Flower Song' from Lakmé at one point). We hear Larry Gogan's 'Just a Minute' quiz which indicates the time as noonish.* [...] *Loud noise/music as the* BOY *and* GIRL *drag* LITTLE LAMB *to the ground and kick the fuck out of her.*[12]

Because of what I take to be the history of theatre as a genre and as a process, I have attempted to justify what could equally be seen as a director's cavalier disrespect for the letter of the text. At the same time, however, I cannot deny that if I had been the author of the play (and to some extent the translator invisibly shares authorship of the text in the target language), I would probably have felt as disturbed by this unauthorized and promiscuous use of my text as Enda Walsh was when I mailed him with details of the production, reminding him of a reaction to this sort of thing attributed to his compatriot, Samuel Beckett. Beckett is reported to have said that he wished to shoot interpretative theatre directors in the testicles, one shot every five minutes, until they got the message. Enda Walsh wrote back — I asked him if he minded this going on record, and he did not:

> I'm just a little pissed off. I would have expected that the Bremen crowd would have asked for permission. How my name could have been associated with such a hotch-botch of ideas is terrifying. I understand small changes and certain scenes cut. I have no problem with this. But when my play becomes a part of a larger plan you really wonder why the director just didn't write his own play and scrap my words completely. Or perhaps he needed my name to hang some of these ideas to. Similarly to Beckett I would like to meet this fucker and fry him.

In any case, the play sold out for the season.

Notes to Chapter 9

1. Enda Walsh, *Sucking Dublin*, trans. by Iain Galbraith (Berlin: Felix Bloch Erben, 1999).

2. John Y. T. Greig, *The Psychology of Laughter and Comedy* (New York: Dodd, Mead and Co., 1923), p. 71.

3. Jennifer Wise, *Dionysus Writes: The Invention of Theatre in Ancient Greece* (Ithaca and London: Cornell University Press, 1998), p. 231.

4. Wise, p. 99. Wise is quoting from Denys Page, *Actors' Interpolations in Greek Tragedy* (New York: Garland, 1934), pp. 10, 16.

5. Wise, p. 115.

6. See Rosalind Thomas, *Oral Tradition and Written Record in Classical Athens* (Cambridge: Cambridge University Press, 1989), p. 48.

7. In their order of performance: *Disco Pigs* (Co-production by Deutsches Schauspielhaus, Hamburg, and Baracke des Deutschen Theaters, Berlin, 1998); *Misterman* (Schaubühne, Berlin, 2000); *Ginger Ale Boy* (Staatstheater, Mainz, 2000); *Bedbound* (Münchner Kammerspiele, 2001), all trans. by Iain Galbraith.

8. 'Aller à la mer', trans. by Barbara Kerslake, in *Twentieth-Century Theatre: A Sourcebook* ed. by Richard Drain (London: Routledge, 1995), p. 133.

9. *Theatre at the Crossroads of Culture*, trans. by Loren Krüger (London: Routledge, 1992), pp. 26–28.

10. *Lire le théâtre* (Paris: Editions Sociales, 1978), p. 24.

11. Wise: see note 4.

12. Walsh, *Disco Pigs/Sucking Dublin* (London: Nick Hern Books, 1997), pp. 45–47.

CHAPTER 10

Translating a Great Feast of Languages

Jean-Michel Déprats

It is common knowledge that Shakespeare delighted in punning and word games — what Johnson called his fatal Cleopatra. With ingenuity, some of these puns can be transposed into French, but many remain untranslatable (those on *sun* and *son*, for example). However, there is a particularly tricky category of puns: those that imply two or more languages. Incidentally, the difficulty of translating bilingualism or multilingualism (as found in Joyce, for instance) goes beyond the question of puns. There are many instances of inserted foreign words or phrases in Shakespeare, such as the utterances in Italian and French in *Twelfth Night*; and those in Latin, French, and Italian in *Love's Labours Lost*, with multilingual polysemy in names and words (for example, the name Longueville playing on the French *ville* ('town'), the English *veal* ('calf flesh'), and the German *Viel* ('plenty') etc.). We also have the case of *Merry Wives*, with its Latin lesson[1] and its string of barely translatable Latin–English/ English–Latin bilingual puns (Pulcher/Polecats; hing, hang, hog/bacon; caret/carrot; horum/whore; quies, quaes, quods; keys, case, cods), not to mention the insertion of an imaginary Greek-sounding, Russian/Moldavian gibberish in *All's Well That Ends Well*,[2] although that is easily translatable, since it can be left as it is.

But when you have to translate a play into French that already contains scenes written in French, even if it is Shakespeare's curious French — a mixture of fifteenth-century authentic French and pidgin, dog French — the difficulty of translating laughter and comedy is uppermost. *Henry V* is the play in question here, and it is probably Shakespeare's most polyglot work. Any translation into French will erase or attenuate its bilingualism. The difficulty one faces when translating *Henry V* has been well described by Jacques Derrida; although his argument relates to James Joyce's novel *Finnegan's Wake*, it summarizes the problem in *Henry V* quite adequately:

> Even if by some miracle one could translate all of the virtual impulses at work [...], one thing remains that could never be translated: the fact that there are two tongues here, or at least more than one. By transplanting everything into French, at best one would translate all of the virtual or actual content, but one could not translate the event which consists in grafting several tongues on to a single body.[3]

But, over and above the more common difficulties of Shakespearean translation, *Henry V* confronts us with a number of specific linguistic problems and oddities that can baffle the (French) translator, at many points leaving him or her with little choice but to adapt, transpose, or recreate, 'undertranslating'[4] in some instances (dealing with dialectical accents), or leaving the actors to translate the untranslatable.

Some passages of *Henry V* defy not only translation but even comprehension, seemingly suffering the curse of Babel. One such instance is Pistol's macaronic line 'qualtitie calmie custure me' (Folio text), in response to the French prisoner Monsieur Le Fer's 'Je pense que vous estes le Gentilhomme de bon qualitee' (Folio text spelling).[5] Editors, commentators, and translators still wonder what this 'word pudding' is supposed to mean. According to Warburton (1747), Pistol actually says 'Qualtitie call you me, construe me!', or even perhaps 'Qualtitie, cullion, construe me!'. Some later commentators have suggested that the odd statement may be in Irish Gaelic. As Sylvère Monod states, 'Pistol begins by repeating a twisted version of the last word he's heard, then, so as not to be wanting in jargon, he cites the first words of an Irish song, as it appears in printed form around 1565 (in Clement Robinson's *Handeful of Pleasant Delites*)'. The exact text, confirmed in 1939 by Gerard Murphy, was 'Caitlin o tSiure mé' ('I am a maid from the river Suir').[6] J. H. Walter (in the 1954 Arden Edition) and T. W. Craik (in the 1995 Arden Edition) both point to an Irish origin, too, but they trace Pistol's 'calmie custure me' to a deformation of 'Cailin ôg a' stor' ('Young maid, my treasure').[7] The following play on the words 'moi' and 'moy' (French soldier: 'O prenez miséricorde! Ayez pitié de moi!'; Pistol: 'Moy shall not serve, I will have forty moys') poses the same type of question. According to Andrew Gurr, 'Pistol hears the French "moi" (pronounced as "moy" in Middle French) as a half, a moiety'.[8] But for Walter and Taylor 'moy' refers to a unit of measure roughly equivalent to a bushel.[9] Other commentators argue that Pistol, having talked about a ransom, believes it is a currency[10] (although probably not the Portuguese *moidore*, which was not introduced into England until the eighteenth century).[11]

In fact, the whole scene is interspersed with bilingual wordplays, more or less subtle but all based on Pistol's miscomprehension. One instance plays on the French word 'bras' and the English word 'brass'[12] (I rendered this as the monolingual pun: 'Que je t'embrasse, roquet? Sacré bouc lubrique des montagnes, tu veux que je t'embrasse?') Another case turns on the prisoner's name Monsieur Le Fer, to which Pistol responds with a series of homophonic terms: 'Master Fer? I'll fer him, and firk him, and ferret him'.[13] In this scene, all the comic effects stem from communication problems caused by the linguistic barrier. The French soldier speaks French, the Boy speaks to Pistol in English and to the prisoner in French, and, of course, Pistol speaks English, even if he begins one of his lines with 'Owy, cuppele gorge permafoy', which he does seem to understand. Even then, to say that the French soldier and the Boy speak French is to simplify matters a lot. They speak an old Lingua Franca, half sixteenth-century French, half gobbledygook, made up by Shakespeare with the main aim of entertaining a British audience.

Four scenes or sequences pose particular translation problems. They are, in chronological order:

1. The dialect scene (III. 3) between three Officers: one is Welsh (Fluellen), one Irish (Macmorris), and the third Scottish (Jamy); and all speak in regional-specific ways.

2. The scene of the English lesson between Catherine and Alice (III. 5), in which the drive to find obscenities in the foreign language runs throughout (as we all know, language learning begins with the 'dirty words').

3. The scene we have already discussed (IV. 4), between Pistol, Monsieur Le Fer, and the Boy, which is often not performed, the actors regarding it as the result of Shakespeare's all-too-complacent punning.

4. The seduction scene (V. 2), in which Shakespeare intertwines Catherine's and Alice's broken English and odd French, together with Henry's poorly mastered French, into a more standard, 'Shakespearean' English.

In the scenes of tragedy, the French language appears only briefly, and, one could say, decoratively. Besides a citation from the Bible (III. 8 — the Dauphin: 'Le chien est retourné à son propre vomissement et la truie[14] lavée au bourbier'), it mostly takes the form of exclamations (III. 6. 5, 11, 15 — the Dauphin: 'O Dieu vivant!', Bretagne: 'Mort de ma vie', Constable: 'Dieu des batailles'; IV. 5. 1, 2, 3, 6 — Constable: 'O diable!', Orléans: 'O seigneur! Le jour est perdu, tout est perdu!', the Dauphin: 'Mort de ma vie! [...] O méchante fortune'; III. 8 — the Dauphin: 'Ch'ha! [...] Le cheval Volant, the Pegasus, qui a des narines de feu'). The comic scenes use plays on words that only an audience with a knowledge of both languages can fully understand. As Jean-Claude Sallé writes:

> The use of the French language in several scenes reveals the same critical intention, the same questioning of theatrical conventions [as does the presence of a Chorus]. Indeed, the bilingualism may seem required by the subject: eighteen of the twenty-three scenes in the play take place in France. But in the first part of *Henry IV*, the characters who speak in Welsh do so on the side (III, i) during an interlude which remains outside of the English dialogue, as the Welsh text is not given. *Henry V* is thus exceptional in taking a double stand: the decision to follow the tacit convention according to which the audience will not be surprised if one party speaks the enemy's language, and at the same time, the position of realism, which allows for comic effects due to the problems of communication across the language barrier.[15]

While Shakespeare's French king speaks in English, he has the three other French characters, Alice, Catherine, and Monsieur Le Fer, speak a half-authentic, half-fanciful French. But it is not irrelevant that these three characters are two women and a prisoner: the defeated speak French, whereas the language of the conquerors — indeed, of the conquest itself — is English. And thus the telling scene in which Henry tries to conquer the heart of the French princess Catherine turns into a linguistic battle meant to reaffirm the supremacy of the English language.

Faced with this, the French translator has to decide between two perhaps equally unsuccessful alternatives. On the one hand, the decision to retain the original French — which is, after all, full of fancy and charm, even if at the expense of a certain degree of chaos — will result in only three characters speaking a bizarre French: the princess of France, her attendant lady, and a captured officer, while all of the British characters speak a fully understandable modern French! On the other hand, to 'translate' Shakespeare's French into everyday French loses most of the exotic and exquisite sweetness and old-fashioned coloration of the former. For the dubbing of Branagh's film, I had opted for the first alternative, because it was a British film with British actors. For Jean-Louis Benoit's French staging in Avignon,[16] I decided to adopt the second alternative: to translate Shakespeare's French into modern French.

Another option would be to translate the whole play into sixteenth-century French, but this exercise would be of more theoretical than practical value, as the result would be a literary curiosity that would not lend itself to a viable performance for the present day. What is more, the result would succeed only in disguising the fundamental untranslatability of the effect of a foreign language inserted within a given text. Whichever option is resorted to, any translation of *Henry V* into French erases the bilingualism of the play. As Ton Hoenselaars forcefully states: 'With a macaronic, Babylonian text, it is impossible to provide a fully convincing and satisfying translation'.[17]

Most translators acknowledge this impossibility, and simply transcribe, if sometimes in italics (a graphic solution that loses all meaning in performance), the parts in 'Shakespearean French', correcting the more glaring errors without actually rewriting the text. Geneviève and Daniel Bournet, two translators from Marseilles, chose to translate Shakespeare's peculiar French into medieval French. In a note, they explain their choice:

> In a French translation, the distance between Catherine's language and the words she is learning obviously runs the risk of vanishing. The idea of a theatre performance in French demands that this distance be kept. Given that theatrical convention allows Shakespeare's English to be turned into French for the French stage, and given that the princess and her attendant are medieval French characters, we shall transcribe the few English words into modern French, and Catherine and Alice's lines into old French, which, one can surmise, will have, for a French audience, the exotic character of French words for an English audience.[18]

Accordingly, Catherine's English lesson becomes a lesson in modern French. This is how it begins:

CATHERINE	Alice, tu fus chieux les Anglois, et ben paroles li langaige.
ALICE	Alques, madame.
CATHERINE	Jo toi prie m'enseigniez, me faust apenre à paroler... Coument est appeled le paulme, en anglois?
ALICE	Le paulme? Il est appeled 'main'.
CATHERINE	'Main'? Et li deies?
ALICE	Li deies? Meie feid, jo m'oblie li deies, mes me sovenira. Li deies? Jo crei que sont appeled 'doives'. Oil, 'doives'.
CATHERINE	Le paulme, 'main'. Li deies, 'doives'. Jo crei que je suis li buen escoulier. J'ai gaigned dous moz anglois vistement. Coument est appeled les grifz?
ALICE	Les grifz? Nos les appelons 'oncles'.
CATHERINE	'Oncles'. Oyez, diste-mei si jo parole ben: 'main', 'doives', 'oncles'.
ALICE	Cel est ben dist, madame: forz buen anglois!

At the very least, it is a 'forz buen françois' that was to be expected here. But given how far into crazy inventiveness the translators have got, good sense is hardly *de rigueur* any more. No doubt this medieval version of *Henry V* is rather delightful, but its paradoxical result is that Catherine's and Alice's French is a lot less understandable than even the original was. What is more, this translation option greatly accentuates the contrast between, on the one hand, the French princess and her attendant, and, on the other, the rest of the characters who speak in a twentieth-century French. One cannot uphold both linguistic truthfulness and theatrical convention.

At any rate, the question of the relative authenticity of Shakespeare's French and the problems it poses for the translator become less acute at the moment of the actual staging, when gesture can take over from where linguistic translation leaves off. In Jean-Louis Benoit's stage adaptation, the English lesson scene turns into a little marvel of theatrical and linguistic humour. The actress playing Catherine, Marie Vialle, invented a series of comic gestures to sum up the English words she is learning, gestures that veer towards the explicit to better make her point. A closed fist with raised middle finger, illustrating the word 'fingers', summons up an obscene imagery that runs the course of the scene, culminating in the titillating discovery that the English words 'foot' and 'gown' sound dangerously like the French 'foutre' and 'con' ('cum' and 'cunt').

The scene during which Henry courts Catherine (v. 2) poses more complex linguistic questions, as it is a matter not simply of alternating between English and French, but also of introducing a string of intermediary steps, involving more or less monstrous intermixings between the two languages. Sylvère Monod[19] opted to warn the reader of the original form, with notes in italics. There are six different modes of enunciation:

1. Statements in English: most of Henry's lines.

2. Statements in bad English: for instance, Catherine's 'Your majesty shall mock me, I cannot speak your England' (which I left in the original, whereas Sylvère Monod translated it as 'Votre Majesté va se rire de moi, je ne peux pas parler votre langue Angleterre').

3. Statements mixing French and bad English: for instance, Catherine's 'Pardonnez-moi. I cannot tell vat is "like me"'.

4. Statements in French: for instance, Catherine's 'O bon Dieu, les langues des hommes sont pleines de trumperies'.

5. Statements alternating between English and bad French: for instance, Henry's 'No, Kate, I will tell thee in French. [...] Je quand sur le possession de Fraunce, & quand vous aves le possession de moy' (Folio spelling).

6. Statements mixing English and French: for instance, Catherine's 'Your majesty ave fausse french enough to deceive de most sage demoiselle dat is en France'.

In this scene it does not seem to me appropriate — any more than in the one discussed earlier — to have Catherine and Alice speak in dog French when, following theatrical convention, Henry speaks in perfect French (except when, in the more 'realistic' moments, he tries a few 'beginner's French' words).[20] In order to maintain this bilingualism, I kept some English lines in Henry's part, a few simple phrases that any French audience can follow, and I left in English — in bad English as it is transcribed — the lines in which Catherine and Alice try to speak the language of the conqueror. This solution was taken up by the actors and worked all the better, since the staging emphasized the comic effect of the interlocutors' imperfect comprehension. As is often done in front of foreigners, the character made up for the miscomprehension by miming the simplest phrases: to die, to speak, to kiss, and so on.

The most acute translation problems stem from the scenes in dialect. The short sequence that brings together the Welshman Fluellen (or, as Andrew Gurr calls him, Llewellyn),[21] the Irishman Macmorris, and the Scotsman Jamy, is of great political import, as it portrays both the diversity — linguistically represented — and the unity of the Kingdom, gathered in the patriotism of the war effort. The most developed of the three Officers, Fluellen, displays comic traits to emphasize the king's role, as Falstaff did with respect to Prince Hal in *Henry IV*. Fluellen's lines contain stylistic and morpho-syntactic idiosyncrasies that are perfectly translatable (strings of synonyms, circumvoluted run-on sentences, erroneous agreements — for instance, 'The mines is not according to the disciplines of war'). But they also contain phonetic distortions (for example, 'digt' for 'digged', 'aunchient' for 'ancient') that prove much more difficult to translate or transpose. Fluellen uses unvoiced plosives for voiced ones (*b* is pronounced *p*, *v*, is pronounced *f*, *j* is pronounced *ch*), and as a result says 'Cheshu' for 'Jesus', 'athversary' for 'adversary', and so on. But these distortions are neither constant nor systematic, and, as a matter of fact, they do not sound particularly Welsh to a modern English-speaking audience.

Neither Macmorris's use of fricatives for sibilants (for example, 'Be Chrish' for 'By Christ'), nor Jamy's specific vocalizations ('gud' for 'good', 'baith' for 'both', 'wad' for 'would'), seem to be attested in the historical documents available for the period represented in *Henry V* (among them, for instance, a letter of the king of Scotland to Henry IV concerning his son James's captivity).[22] One can thus surmise that Shakespeare's dialects are stylized — theatrical Welsh, Irish, or Scottish, meant to *present* a linguistic difference rather than *characterize* it in any precise fashion.

Most of the time, French translators try to transpose these British local ways of speaking into French or French-speaking equivalents. Accordingly, François-Victor Hugo gives Jamy a Creole accent, supposed to account for the Scottish rolled *r*.[23]

> JAMY   Ce seha pafait, su ma paole, mes baves capitaines. [...] Par la messe, avant que ces yeux-là se livrent au sommeil, ze fehai de la besogne ou je sehai poté en terre: oui-dah! Je sehai mort; je paiehai de ma personne aussi vaillamment que ze pouhai, ze m'y engaze, en un mot comme en mille. Mobleu! Ze sehais bien aise d'ouïr une discussion entre vous deux.[24]

This rather strange option seems to us neither 'politically correct', nor, more decisively, linguistically or intellectually convincing. Nevertheless, the drive to find French-speaking equivalents to these dialects is found in later translations too. If M. J. Lavelle[25] transcribes the Officers' lines into standard French, Marcel Sallé[26] gives Jamy a lisp and Fluellen something of an Alsatian accent: 'Che vous en brie [...] Foyez-fous [...] la discibline'.[27] Jean-Claude Sallé[28] has Macmorris speak with an Auvergne accent: 'Che n'est pas le moment de discourir [...] Que le Chricht me garde'. When translated by Sylvère Monod,[29] the same Macmorris now speaks a North-African French straight out of the Casbah: 'Té, par le Chrisse, c'est un beau gâchis'. Monod explains his choice in a note:

> Our translation attenuates, without being overly systematic, the irregularities in the written pronunciations (sometimes turning grammatical oddities into particularities in the spoken form). Moreover, in order to give French readers a sense more or less equivalent to what happens in the original text, we have taken Fluellen's phonetic and psychological particularities to be like those of an Eastern Frenchman, those of Macmorris like those of a Southern Frenchman, and those of Jamy like those of a Normandy Frenchman.[30]

I, for one, am totally opposed to these transpositions into French local ways of speaking. All vernacular languages are specific and cannot be transported or transposed.[31] To have Fluellen, Macmorris, or Jamy speak like a Frenchman from Alsace, Brittany, or Picardy, or like a Belgian or Swiss, makes no sense in any case. This will never evoke a Welshman, an Irishman, or a Scotsman for a French reader or theatre-goer. Even supposing that Welsh, Irish, or Scottish people have a particular accent when they speak French, nothing indicates that this accent is the same when they speak English; so to transcribe faithfully such distortions in consonants can only lead to utterly contrived and ridiculous-sounding ways of speaking. It is part of the actor's role to find the specifics of pronunciation that will particularize his character. I wholly agree with Monod's suggestion that the many erroneous, heavy, or fanciful forms 'are interspersed in an irregular fashion through Fluellen's lines because Shakespeare probably deemed it enough to indicate only now and then the type of pronunciation which the actors should adopt'.[32] Accordingly, in my translation, I reproduced Shakespeare's transcribed distortions only where they arose, and if they occurred on the same consonants in French, thus avoiding artificial manners of speaking. For the solution is not a written, but an oral one.

In Jean-Louis Benoit's *mise-en-scène*,[33] the problem of the Welsh, Irish, and Scottish accents disappeared, as the whole scene was cut (so as to lighten and shorten the play as a whole). But the problem remained, transposed into the French-speaking sphere, since the director had asked several actors playing French characters to put on regional accents. Indeed, fifteenth-century France was a mosaic of languages and dialects. As a result, for the première in Avignon, the Governor of Harfleur spoke with a vaguely northern-French accent, and one of the French nobles had a southern accent.[34]

Although, as we have seen, some translators desperately try to invent homogenized parlances and distinct mannerisms in French, it is my absolute conviction that there can be no valid, purely *linguistic* translation of regional accents — genuine or artificial — into another language; only a temporary, individualized, and always to be reinvented, *scenic* translation.

To put it in Jakobson's terms,[35] intersemiotic translation (from word to gesture, from speech to acting) takes up where interlinguistic translation leaves off. This could be the conclusion to a discussion of the failings and limits in translating a bilingual text. When the text at stake is meant for the theatre, a purely verbal translation can never be complete in and of itself. It has to be completed by a scenic translation that fills in the gaps, and, above all, actualizes the potential effects — on condition that the translator thinks in terms of transposition and adaptation, rather than simply interlinguistic translation.

Notes to Chapter 10

Editors' note: Jean-Michel Déprats refers throughout to his own translation: Shakespeare, *Henry V*, traduction nouvelle de Jean-Michel Déprats, édition bilingue présentée par Gisèle Venet, folio/théâtre No 59 (Paris: Gallimard, 1999). His present paper was given as a contribution to a round-table discussion of laughter in the theatre.

1. *The Merry Wives of Windsor* (Arden edn), IV. I. 103 f.
2. *All's Well That Ends Well* (Arden edn), IV, 3. 116, 121, 122: Portotartarossa/Bosko chimurcho/Boblibindo chimurmurco, etc.
3. Jacques Derrida, *The Ear of the Other: Otobiography, Transference, Translation*, ed. by Christie V. McDonald, trans. by Peggy Kamuf (New York: Schocken, 1985), p. 99.
4. On the notions of 'undertranslation' and 'overtranslation' see Jean–Michel Déprats, *Antoine Vitez: le devoir de traduire* (Montpellier: Editions Climats et Maison Antoine Vitez, 1996), pp. 45–47.
5. William Shakespeare, *Henry V*, trans. by Déprats, pp. 271–79 (IV. 4).
6. *Henry V*, trans. by Sylvère Monod, in William Shakespeare, *Œuvres Complètes*, VI, Collection Formes et Reflets (Paris: Le Club français du livre, 1957), pp. 238–39. On this question, see *Hebridean Folksongs*, ed. by J. L. Campbell and Francis Collinson, II (Oxford: Clarendon Press, 1977), pp. 200–09.
7. *King Henry V*, ed. by T. C. Craik, The Arden Shakespeare (London and New York: Routledge, 1995); this edn replaces that by J. H. Walter for The Arden Shakespeare (London: Methuen, 1954).
8. *King Henry V*, ed. by Andrew Gurr, The New Cambridge Shakespeare (Cambridge: Cambridge University Press, 1984), p. 171 (note to line 11).
9. *Henry V*, ed. by Gary Taylor, The Oxford Shakespeare (Oxford: Oxford University Press, 1984), 235 (note).
10. *King Henry V*, ed. by Craik, p. 298.
11. This was Johnson's hypothesis in *Shakespeare's Plays*, 8 vols, ed. by Samuel Johnson (1765; repr. Menston: Scolar Press, 1969).
12. *King Henry V*, ed. Craik, p. 299.
13. I translated this freely in my translation as: 'Je vais me le faire, le ferrer et le faire taire', cf. *Henry V*, p. 275 (note, p. 441).
14. The Folio text gives 'La leuye' (la laie).
15. William Shakespeare, *Œuvres complètes. Histoires*. Edition bilingue (Paris: Laffont, 1997), I, 760.
16. Premièred on 9 July 1999, at the Cour d'honneur du Palais des papes. It was the first French production of the play — indeed, *Henry V* is the only History play that had never before been performed in French.
17. Cf. Ton Hoenselaar's very interesting article on François-Victor Hugo, translator of *Henry V*: 'Shakespeare for "the People": François-Victor Hugo Translates *Henry V*', *Documenta*, 13 (1995), 243–52.
18. William Shakespeare, *Théâtre complet* (Lausanne: L'Age d'homme, 1992), IV, 371.
19. In his translation (see note 6 above).
20. The audience has no problem in accepting the rules of this game, and the passage from a conventional language to an 'actually spoken' language. If they speak some phrases with an English accent and cite some 'English' Latin, the actors can help this movement from one register to the other.
21. *King Henry V*, ed. by Gurr, p. 63.
22. *King Henry V*, ed. by Gurr, p. 62.
23. He is perhaps hinting at a similarity in their colonial situations.
24. Shakespeare, *Œuvres complètes*, I (Paris: Gallimard, La Pléiade, 1959), pp. 782–83.
25. *Henry V*, trans. by M. J. Lavelle (Paris: Aubier-Montaigne, 1947).
26. *La Vie de Henri V*, trans. by Marcel Sallé (Paris: Les Belles Lettres, 1961).
27. To French ears, the result sounds more like the caricatures of German soldiers in comedies about the Second World War.
28. In William Shakespeare, *Histoires*, I, trans. by Jean-Claude Sallé (Paris: Laffont/Bouquins, 1997).
29. *Henry V*, trans. by Monod.
30. In his translation of *Henry V*, for Shakespeare, *Œuvres complètes*, VI, p. 237.

31. Cf. *Actes des quatorzièmes assisses de la traduction littéraire (Arles 1997)* (Arles: Actes Sud, 1998), pp. 95–128 (round-table discussion on the translation of dialects and regionalisms for the theatre, chaired by Jean-Michel Déprats).

32. Speaking of his translation of *Henry V* for Shakespeare, *Œuvres complètes*, VI.

33. Revived at the Théâtre de l'Aquarium in Paris, 12 Dec. 1999 to 5 Mar. 2000.

34. Paradoxically, this Southerner plays the role of Brittany in the original — which only proves again that everything is a matter of stylization in the theatre. Accuracy has little to do with artistic success.

35. See Roman Jakobson, 'On Linguistic Aspects of Translation', in *Selected Writings*, II: *Word and Language* (The Hague: Mouton, 1971), pp. 260–66.

CHAPTER 11

Traduire le rire

Paul J. Memmi

Dans une pièce de théâtre, dans un compte rendu, le rire est indiqué sous forme de didascalies:"Ici, le personnage rit", "Rires divers dans l'assemblée", etc.

Dans le corps d'un texte, le rire est indiqué sous forme de "Ha ha ha", ces mêmes "Ha ha ha" qui, c'est à craindre autant qu'à espérer, figureront dans les Actes de ce colloque, et qui indiqueront que nous aurons ri.

Le rire ainsi annoté pose peu de problèmes de traduction. Traduisons "Ha ha ha" par "Ha ha ha"! Ma communication est-elle terminée? Ce serait très amusant de vous remercier dès maintenant et de quitter l'estrade. Mais un plaisir plus grand me retient, celui de réfléchir avec vous dans une université aussi prestigieuse que celle d'Oxford.

Est-il possible, au-delà de la traduction des procédés comiques, de traduire le rire, en le prenant au pied de la lettre, là où se trouve encore la chose, ses viscères, ses muscles, son souffle, sa bouche?

La question ainsi posée peut sembler vaine au traducteur littéraire, et même au traducteur de théâtre. Ni l'un ni l'autre n'ont le corps, le visage et la voix. Ils ne travaillent pas avec les outils du comédien. N'ayant pas les outils, le rire ne fait pas objet pour eux.

Pourtant, il existe des traducteurs qui travaillent avec les moyens mêmes de production du rire: les traducteurs pour le cinéma dont je suis, traducteurs des versions doublées et sous-titrées.

Le traducteur d'une version doublée doit offrir une traduction fidèle au texte source mais qui, une fois jouée, semble sortir de la bouche du comédien à l'écran. Pour réussir cette illusion, il doit fournir au comédien du doublage une partition textuelle mimologique qui permette à celui-ci de reproduire à l'identique ce qu'a physiquement dû faire le comédien à l'écran.

Ainsi outillé et s'il interprète bien sa partition, le comédien du doublage devient tel un ventriloque qui projette sa voix dans le corps et la bouche de lumière muette apparaissant à l'écran.

Pour composer sa partition textuelle mimologique, le traducteur doit analyser en détail le mode de production corporel et buccal du texte source et de tous les gestes et sons buccaux qui l'enchâssent.

Il tient compte des positions et des mouvements du corps: position couchée, marche, course, qui rendent une voix calme, oppressée, haletante, etc.

Il respecte synchroniquement tous les appuis et les élans du souffle, toutes les positions, qui ont produit la parole source: fermetures des occlusives, semi-fermetures des fricatives, tensions latérales des sifflantes des "é", des "i", ronds des "o", des "on", etc.

C'est ainsi que se fabrique la prosodie. La partition offerte est prosodique.

Mais pas seulement: elle reprend tout ce que la bouche a pu produire et qui a été enregistré: déglutitions, bégaiements, baisers, bâillements, murmures, rires, etc.

Dans ce métier singulier, quel est l'objet de la traduction?

Certes, un texte. Mais un texte incarné, joué, et à incarner, à jouer. Peut-on dire alors que le traducteur doit aussi traduire un bégaiement ou un rire? Ne se contente-t-il pas de répliquer analogiquement ces formes physiques en les inscrivant dans un même temps synchronisé?

Si c'était le cas, même au cinéma, on ne traduirait pas, on se contenterait de reproduire le rire en tant que forme corporelle brute.

Mais observons des lèvres qui laissent échapper un rire bref entre deux phonèmes. Si on coupe le son, il arrive fréquemment qu'on voie sur les lèvres autre chose qu'un rire: on croit y lire une articulation de parole. Un rire peut parfois être lu erratiquement en phonème, et réciproquement un phonème peut parfois être vu en rire.

Pour trouver ses solutions, le traducteur maquille constamment des phénomènes physiques en phonèmes articulés. Et réciproquement, la production d'un phonème devenu inutile à la traduction du contenu textuel peut être proposée comme geste buccal non textuel: une grimace muette ou un bruit.

Tirons-en une règle: enchâssé dans une activité verbale, mais je dirai plus généralement "textuelle", tout geste buccal, comme le rire, s'offre à la textualisation. Et sa réciproque: enchâssé dans une production buccale, tout texte s'offre à la détextualisation.

La traduction au sous-titrage nous offre un autre angle de visée et va nous permettre d'enrichir cette notion de textualisation, encore purement formelle.

Le sous-titrage repose sur une contrainte particulière: il est impossible de lire la totalité d'un texte parlé dans la durée qu'il faut à celui-ci pour être prononcé, a fortiori quand les yeux sont aussi requis pour découvrir une image mouvante. En moyenne, il faut économiser un tiers des signes typographiques pour offrir au spectateur un temps de lecture suffisant. Ici, l'art du traducteur se distingue en un mot: Concision. Comment traduire concis?

La démarche est différente: elle renvoie moins au jeu sur les signifiants ou les pseudo-signifiants buccaux explicites, qu'au jeu d'implicitation des contenus linguistiques qui seraient aussi manifestés par le corps.

Qu'est-ce qui, dans la gestuelle de l'acteur à l'écran, est porteur de sens? Et qu'est-ce qui, parmi ce sens, peut permettre d'être concis dans la traduction linguistique qu'on proposera dans le sous-titre?

Le traitement linguistique des expressions non- ou pseudo-linguistiques n'est pas la préoccupation majeure du spectateur normal, il est pourtant primordial dans nos métiers.

Artistiquement et techniquement, qu'est-ce que le cinéma? L'intrication organique de trois champs de sens: verbal, visuel et sonore.

Sans l'image et le son, un texte d'audiovisuel se révèle toujours lacunaire. Son sens profond est en grande partie incompréhensible, privé ici d'un thème, là d'un prédicat. Ses formes, qui renvoient à des référents absents, où manquent des actualisateurs, sont intraduisibles.

Le traducteur doit donc se représenter synthétiquement le sens pertinent pour la narration comme une configuration d'origine triple, et mettre en cohérence les différents champs de sens. Comment ne pas qualifier cette opération singulière de première traduction? Celle de l'univers filmique en "contexte", au sens textuel du terme, pour s'épargner de parler de "co-texte".

L'opération de textualisation apparaît comme un pont entre sémiologie et linguistique. Elle est indispensable à la traduction à l'audiovisuel, autant qu'elle permet de distinguer en quoi celle-ci diffère de la traduction littéraire. Reste à savoir dans quel ordre ce pont est praticable.

Si ce qu'exprime le corps de l'acteur et le discours qu'il prononce se rapportent au même univers, il y a cohérence entre le texte corporel et le texte verbal, il y a éventuelle suppléance entre les deux, et possible économie dans le verbal partout où il y a redondance.

Dans le cas différent où il n'y a pas isotopie, le texte corporel et le texte verbal ont des cheminements parallèles et aucune économie par prise de relais de l'un par l'autre n'est possible.

"Texte corporel", avons-nous risqué? Ceci mériterait en soi l'organisation d'un colloque. L'art oratoire montrerait que la beauté et l'efficacité d'une tirade, d'une prière, mieux encore d'une chanson, se mesurent à leur habitabilité corporelle. Le langage des signes à l'usage des sourds montrerait qu'on sait traduire par des gestes un discours politique. Le mimodrame, les masques du théâtre Nô, la commedia dell'arte montreraient la richesse des expressions corporelles.

Laissons l'exemple complexe et limite du langage des signes. Ce dont il est question au cinéma, comme dans la vie de tous les jours, relève de l'expression naturelle. Répondons à notre précédente question: qu'est-ce que le corps de l'acteur exprime, que nous puissions traiter dans nos traductions?

N'étant pas plus bêtes que nos chiens, admettons que nous comprenons de nos gestes au moins tout ce qu'ils en comprennent: le corps désigne les corps présents, les objets à portée de regards et de membres, les directions, les actes et les états concrets, les expressions comme précurseurs d'actions.[1]

Mais nous faisons mieux que nos chiens. Pour nous, les points dans l'espace expriment par métaphore les points dans le temps. Nous racontons des histoires par rébus gestuels. Nous affirmons, nions, conditionnons par de simples mouvements de tête.

A nous, linguistes, de lire sur le corps le renvoi aux noms, communs et propres, les fonctions sujets, compléments, l'envoi des verbes, leurs temps et modes fondamentaux, des modalisations adverbiales, des pré- et des postpositions, des ponctuations, des incises, en bref, le vocabulaire et la grammaire corporels formant des assertions dans l'ordre du Discours, et même une stylistique.

A nous, linguistes, de traduire en nos catégories ces signifiés corporels et de réfléchir à la façon dont ils s'intègrent intimement à l'expression verbale, pour lui donner son sens complet.

Paraphrasons Jakobson:[2] le décodage va du geste au sens. Mais entendu que le geste fait déjà sens, et que ce sens vaut déjà mot.

Nous apercevons en quoi la textualisation des expressions corporelles n'est pas une opération forcée.

Mais étonnons-nous peut-être de la position singulière de ce texte corporel restreint vis-à-vis du langage verbal: on peut l'y intégrer, mais il en reste extérieur par la substance charnelle de ses vecteurs de signification. Il relève de la linguistique, à cette différence substantielle près, grâce à laquelle il est doté d'une précieuse expression de l'extériorité au langage.

A ce titre, l'étude du rire occasionne quelque surprise.

Tentons donc, pour finir, de textualiser le Rire, pour pouvoir à l'avenir mieux traduire les rires.

Est-on en droit de poser le Rire comme Signe linguistique?

Notons qu'il suffit qu'on ne puisse pas tout écrire sur un rire. Réciproquement, il suffit que tout rire exprime un texte identique, suffisant de lui-même et nécessaire au langage.

Un bébé rit quand il voit sa maman s'approcher de trop près. Voilà qui révèle le rire comme réponse satisfaisante à une menace. Mais un bébé autiste ne rit pas. Voilà qui indique que le rire présuppose une capacité de représentation et de communication achevée ou dans un devenir normal. Tel est le socle.

Maintenant, prenons les exemples d'un gag puis d'une blague qui font rire:

> Un gag: "Un gros mange, mange, mange et explose" (dans le film "Monty Python's The Meaning of Life", de Terry Jones).

Ce gag met en scène une loi aisément textualisable: "Il faut manger pour vivre". Mais ici, cette loi a été renversée et semble être devenue "Il faut vivre pour manger". Le corps soumis à cette loi déraisonnable finit par en mourir. Mais ce n'est pas cela qui fait rire, c'est l'explosion du corps qui fait rire, car celle-ci est imaginaire, elle ne peut être que fictionnelle.

> Une blague: "Elle voulait que son bébé réussisse dans la vie, elle l'a promené sur la voie rapide de l'autoroute" (dans la série "KYTV", de John Kilby et John Stroud, sur la BBC).

Cette blague relève du comique de mots: une mère applique à la lettre un précepte social, le résultat est fatal pour un corps. Mais c'est l'invraisemblance fictionnelle de la catastrophe qui fait rire.

Tout effet comique présuppose une loi physique ou psychique, objet de la Raison, ou une loi laïque ou religieuse, objet du Droit ou de la Morale, et ces lois sont par nous textualisables.

Ces lois viennent menacer un sujet parce qu'elles sont ou risquent d'être exécutées de façon déraisonnable, sans limitation, sans relativité, bref sans conscience.

Qu'est-ce que l'humour, ou le comique dont Bergson a écrit "qu'il s'adresse à l'intelligence pure"?[3] C'est l'ensemble des procédés qui permettent de stigmatiser les faussetés internes d'une loi, les déraisons internes de la Raison, en les tournant sur elles-mêmes, pour s'en distancer.

Qu'apporte le rire? La marque de son extériorité corporelle! Là où l'humour dit de l'intérieur du langage: "Il y a erreur ou abus", le rire nous sert à dire depuis une position à la limite extérieure du langage: "Ce n'est que de l'esprit!", et par là, nous nous évadons avec un plaisir physique des prisons de l'esprit.

Les animaux ne parlent pas, ils expriment. Ils crient, ils pleurent comme nous, mais cela ne fait pas la parole. Et s'ils sont incapables de rire, c'est qu'ils sont incapables d'émettre cette parole d'animal pensant. Car tel est le paradoxe: le rire est une parole, et elle est sauvage. Par extension, le rire est le modèle de toute parole sauvage, et s'offre à toutes les rébellions. Job ne l'ignorait pas.[4] Et Kafka fait rire les Tchèques.[5]

Par cette parole qui dit le corps jouant le divorce d'avec l'esprit, le rire dit l'animal en nous jouant le divorce d'avec l'homme, et l'homme jouant le divorce d'avec le sujet de la Loi. Le rire est plus qu'un signal, même plus qu'une preuve d'intelligence. Du corps d'où il sort, à une distance reprise, le Rire marque la désinscription. Ce faisant, il marque la nature inscrite, construite, de toute loi, y compris de langage, de toute Raison, en signant leur limite substantielle.

Accueillons le Rire dans notre linguistique. Il mérite d'être reconnu comme signe. Rappelons l'intérêt d'avoir admis la négation comme assertion, et le zéro comme nombre.

Par le signe Rire, l'homme se démarque du Verbe en se proclamant Chair. Par l'éclat de rire, la chair se défait Verbe, dans un jeu réciproque.

Le "Rire" est le Signe du plaisir à ce que toute loi présentée comme naturelle, totalisante, prétexte à des mises en actes outrancières, ne soit qu'une "fiction anthropologique", au sens que lui donne Pierre Legendre.[6]

C'est un cri de victoire, une vengeance du corps qui se consacre en Tiers-garant, mais c'est le Texte qu'au final le rire consacre aussi. En cela, il est essentiellement humain, car noué à la structure morale de l'être parlant.

Un condamné à mort voit les fusils se braquer sur lui et il rit... Son rire ne dit-il pas que la loi au nom de laquelle on veut le faire mourir n'a rien d'absolu, qu'elle n'est qu'un tissu textuel que l'homme, seul parmi les animaux, sait déchirer de ses dents? Et n'est-ce pas l'extériorité relative de son rire qui lui permet de dire l'indépendance de sa raison et la déraison coercitive autant que dérisoire de ses bourreaux?

Le rire a cette force conceptuelle de créer le comique même là où il n'est est pas.

Déchirure de la bouche, irremplaçable hoquet sonore qui déchire cordes vocales et tympans, le rire est une déchirure du texte, en cela il échappe au traducteur. Mais il signe le triomphe de la Fiction. En cela, il nous revient — et au sein de la textualité même.

Rire franc ou simulé, rire jaune, rire ironique, rire gras ou sardonique, voilà autant d'expressions avec lesquelles ou sur lesquelles on peut écrire, qu'on peut textualiser en contexte, et au final qu'on peut traduire dès lors qu'on examine le déroulement du procès avec toutes ses parties, où une loi est jouissivement dénoncée comme abusive par une parole à la sauvagerie reconquise.

Je vous remercie de ne pas avoir ri.

Notes

1. Charles Darwin, *L'Expression des émotions chez l'homme et les animaux*, trad. de Dominique Férault (Paris: Payot & Rivages, 2001).
2. Roman Jakobson, *Essais de linguistique générale*, trad. de Nicolas Ruwert (Paris: Editions de Minuit, 1963).
3. Henri Bergson, *Le Rire. Essai sur la signification du comique* (Paris: Presses universitaires de France, 1940).
4. Job, in *La Bible*, trad. d'André Chouraqui (Paris: Desclée de Brouwer, 1989).
5. Franz Kafka, *La Colonie pénitentiaire*, trad. d'Alexandre Vialatte (Paris: Gallimard, 1948).
6. Pierre Legendre, *La 901e Conclusion. Etude sur le théâtre de la Raison* (Paris: Fayard, 1998).

CHAPTER 12

Rire et désir dans les comédies américaines de Lubitsch: l'exemple de *Ninotchka* (1939)

Natacha Thiéry

Ernst Lubitsch (1892–1947) fut le maître de la comédie hollywoodienne des années trente et quarante.[1] Ses films américains parlants, de *Haute Pègre* (*Trouble in Paradise*) à *La Folle ingénue* (*Cluny Brown*), en passant par *Sérénade à trois* (*Design for Living*), *La Veuve joyeuse* (*The Merry Widow*), *Ange* (*Angel*), *La Huitième Femme de Barbe-Bleue* (*Bluebeard's Eighth Wife*), *Ninotchka, The Shop around the Corner, Illusions perdues* (*That Uncertain Feeling*), *To Be or Not To Be*, ou *Le Ciel peut attendre* (*Heaven Can Wait*), réalisés entre 1932 et 1946, sont des comédies. En passant du cinéma muet au cinéma parlant, Lubitsch, qui avait auparavant exploré des genres divers, s'est en effet conformé à l'univers des *sex comedies* — que l'on peut traduire en français par "comédies de mœurs" ou "comédies conjugales". Pour faire surgir le rire du spectateur, le genre comique recourt à divers procédés: chez Lubitsch, c'est essentiellement l'usage de la parole, et plus largement l'ensemble de la bande sonore, qui produisent un effet comique. Si la période concernée coïncide certes avec la naissance du parlant, Lubitsch ne se contente pourtant pas de faire parler ses personnages dans des situations comiques, c'est la parole même, ainsi que la façon dont elle est proférée et mise en scène, qui donnent à ses films leur caractère humoristique.

Une analyse du lien entre l'humour et l'usage de la parole dans les films suppose une définition de la spécificité de la place du spectateur face à ces derniers. Parler de rire au cinéma, c'est en effet se placer au point de vue du destinataire de l'humour, en l'occurrence le spectateur. Un rappel préalable de l'exigence comique de Lubitsch, de son humour et de sa mise en scène du verbe, permet d'une part de considérer plus spécifiquement la fonction du rire et le rapport ambivalent entre le cinéaste et le spectateur, et, d'autre part, d'évaluer précisément dans quelle mesure le rire est lié à la question du désir, elle-même au cœur des films. Quelques exemples précis seront convoqués, en particulier celui de *Ninotchka,* réalisé en 1939.

Exigence comique et mise en scène du verbe

Parce que nul n'est plus rigoureux dans l'écriture qu'un auteur de comédies, Lubitsch s'entourait des scénaristes les plus talentueux.[2] Mais il participait aussi très activement à l'écriture de ses films. Extrêmement attentif à la qualité des dialogues, il s'enfermait des heures durant avec ses collaborateurs. Cette exigence comique a été décrite par Charles Brackett et Billy Wilder, deux des scénaristes qui travaillèrent avec lui:

> Il était capable d'aborder chaque fragment avec cette déclaration effrayante: "Il faut que cette scène soit hilarante... ". Là-dessus, tous les esprits concernés se concentraient et se mettaient au travail pour rendre la scène "hilarante", se maintenaient à la tâche avec la régularité d'un marteau pneumatique jusqu'à ce que, bon sang, la scène soit hilarante.[3]

C'est dire si Lubitsch avait le souci de la qualité comique des films, et s'ils étaient *écrits*, jusque dans leurs plus infimes détails. Or il est justement frappant de constater à quel point, dans ses films, la parole est soignée dans sa forme. Les personnages se congratulent d'ailleurs régulièrement lorsque la parole est non seulement juste mais bien tournée. Aussi, même une insulte peut-elle être appréciée si elle est élégamment formulée: dans *The Shop around the Corner* (1940), Kralik (James Stewart) reçoit les propos humiliants de sa collègue Klara (Margaret Sullavan) avec ce commentaire: "Voilà qui est très joliment tourné!". Et ce n'est pas un hasard si c'est la qualité de leur correspondance qui séduit ces deux épistoliers qui s'ignorent.

Plus largement, la maîtrise de la parole est un trait caractéristique des protagonistes des films. Non seulement volubiles, ils sont aussi polyglottes et capables de manipuler par les mots les interlocuteurs encombrants. Chez Lubitsch, la capacité des personnages à arriver à leurs fins est tributaire de leur virtuosité langagière. Parfois même, leur salut en dépend. Au point que lorsque dans *To Be or not To Be* (1942), Joseph Tura (Jack Benny) laisse échapper un lapsus en disant "je" à la place de "il" et perd le contrôle de la situation périlleuse dans laquelle il se trouve, il commet un réel faux pas et trahit, auprès d'un espion nazi, son identité véritable.

Plus que la seule parole, c'est l'ensemble de la bande sonore qui sert un but comique. Les bruits, les onomatopées et la musique, comme la parole, souvent répétée dans des situations différentes, deviennent des objets ludiques et circulent d'un personnage à un autre, voire d'un espace à un autre. Leur expressivité surprend et fait rire. En ce qui concerne les bruits, on pense par exemple au hoquet persistant de Jill (Merle Oberon) dans *Illusions perdues* (1941), qu'un psychanalyste ne tarde pas à identifier comme l'expression somatique d'un malaise conjugal, le symptôme de la frustration d'une épouse délaissée; ou encore à la mère du pharmacien Wilson qui, dans *La Folle ingénue* (1946), n'articule à aucun moment le moindre mot, mais émet des bruits étranges qui ressemblent à des borborygmes. Quant à la musique, même si elle accompagne les images, elle n'est pas, la plupart du temps, redondante ou tautologique par rapport à ce qui est vu. Au contraire, elle dit souvent autre chose que les images et possède une fonction contrapuntique. Ainsi, elle se moque des personnages et provoque un effet de distanciation. L'ironie musicale indique au spectateur le jeu de ces derniers, le met en garde contre des feintes, des dissimulations ou des mensonges qu'elle contribue même à souligner, et participe pour une large part au plaisir des films.

Complicité du cinéaste et du spectateur

Si les dialogues des films sont irrésistibles, c'est aussi et surtout parce qu'ils sont servis par la grâce et la malice de la mise en scène de Lubitsch. Comme un objet, la parole circule, se déplace et donne au récit son rythme soutenu. Suivre un personnage, c'est suivre les tours et les détours de la parole. Le spectateur, partenaire du déroulement de la narration, est intégré à la mise en scène par la connivence ludique que Lubitsch entretient avec lui, jouant sur ce qu'il laisse voir et sur ce qu'il préfère dissimuler. La mise en scène des portes est particulièrement représentative de ce rapport entre Lubitsch et le spectateur. Littéralement "mis à la porte", celui-ci est souvent forcé d'imaginer ce qui se passe derrière, dans un hors-champ auquel il n'a pas accès et où l'essentiel a pourtant lieu. Dans une séquence de *Ninotchka* (1939), les trois Russes poussent des exclamations de contentement à l'arrivée d'une première femme de chambre vendeuse de cigarettes, puis de deux autres (une pour chacun), ce qui redouble leurs cris. L'aspect comique de la scène vient moins de ces rires d'enthousiasme que du fait que l'on ne voit pas les six personnages, hors champ. La caméra, et le spectateur avec elle, restent dans le couloir, voyant la porte s'ouvrir et se fermer. La frustration du regard va donc de pair avec une curiosité accrue pour ce qui advient derrière cette porte close, et l'on rit autant de l'effet indirect de l'humour de Lubitsch (les cris des Russes) que de la malice du cinéaste. Si ce procédé permet évidemment à Lubitsch de contourner la censure — notamment celle du "code Hays", établi dès 1932 —, il suggère aussi, en les soulignant, les comportements les plus impertinents et les plus hardis de ses personnages. La relation étroite entre parole et mise en scène induit ainsi des effets de continuité ou d'ellipse, auxquels le spectateur participe. Et lorsque des écarts se font sentir entre la parole et l'image, lorsque l'une et l'autre ne signifient pas la même chose mais au contraire se contredisent, c'est encore le spectateur qui, par sa complicité avec le cinéaste, comprend l'implicite. Ce dispositif de mise en scène des portes place donc le spectateur dans une position d'exclusion, de frustration et d'attente. Mais cette frustration se trouve compensée et finalement dépassée par la stimulation de son imagination dont l'activité (opposée à la passivité du voyeur) procure un plaisir infiniment supérieur à celui de l'assouvissement du désir de voir tout, tout de suite. A la fois privé de certains éléments du film et intégré à eux par ces manques, le spectateur participe activement à la mise en scène lubitschienne.[4] De cet inconfort premier naît le plaisir de la contribution, en aval, à la création du film.

Par définition, la comédie sollicite la complicité du public, sans laquelle elle ne peut fonctionner. Mais chez Lubitsch, il ne s'agit pas de flatter le sens du grotesque chez le spectateur, mais plutôt de postuler son intelligence, c'est-à-dire de faire le pari qu'il comprendra ce qu'il cherche à lui signifier, le plus souvent de manière indirecte ou détournée. Et si Lubitsch ne cesse de déconcerter le spectateur en optant fréquemment pour la solution qu'il n'envisageait pas, cet esprit de contradiction ne conduit pas le film à se dérouler à son insu. Au contraire, le spectateur est à ce point inclus dans le film que l'on a parfois l'impression que les personnages, conscients de sa présence, s'adressent autant à lui — à mots couverts — qu'à leur interlocuteur, dans l'espace du plan filmé.

Avec Lubitsch, le spectateur est donc à la fois dérouté et sujet d'une certaine liberté. S'il se laisse surprendre, il n'en demeure pas moins maître de ses émotions et Lubitsch l'encourage à une prise de distance vis-à-vis de ce qu'il voit et entend. Une véritable connivence le lie au cinéaste pendant le déroulement du film. Mais plus encore, Lubitsch incite le spectateur à porter son attention sur autre chose que ce qui l'attirerait par habitude ou par penchant naturel, et d'une certaine manière à se méfier de ce qui s'offre à son regard et à ses oreilles. Ce procédé de double énonciation qui place le spectateur dans une position ambivalente, est au cœur des films. En définitive, le spectateur prend conscience de la nature du film en tant que jeu, et Lubitsch met celui-ci en évidence en soulignant les artifices, les coulisses, les codes sur lesquels repose sa narration.

L'humour, notion complexe, prend des formes et relève de registres différents pratiquement à chacune de ses manifestations. La réflexion de Freud, dans son bref essai consacré à cette notion — issu du recueil intitulé *L'Inquiétante Etrangeté et autres essais*[5] —, peut aider à appréhender l'enjeu de l'humour pour un réalisateur de comédie (et en l'espèce, pour Lubitsch), ainsi que pour le spectateur de ses films. Selon Freud, l'humour constitue une *économie* de dépense de plaisir et par là un gain de plaisir. "L'essence de l'humour", note-t-il, "consiste à économiser les affects que la situation devrait occasionner, et à se dégager par une plaisanterie de la possibilité de telles extériorisations affectives",[6] postulant que l'humour se manifeste comme une attitude de défense. Mais l'humour a aussi à voir avec le narcissisme, qu'il nourrit:

> L'humour n'a pas seulement quelque chose de libérateur comme le mot d'esprit et le comique, mais également quelque chose de grandiose et d'exaltant. [...] Le caractère grandiose est manifestement lié au triomphe du narcissisme, à l'invulnérabilité victorieusement affirmée du moi. Le moi se refuse à se laisser offenser, contraindre à la souffrance par les occasions qui se rencontrent dans la réalité [...]; il montre qu'ils ne sont pour lui que matière à gain de plaisir.[7]

Cette dérivation de la souffrance en plaisir peut être un angle d'analyse possible pour un film comme *To Be or Not To Be*, dont la toile de fond est pourtant grave et douloureuse, comme si Lubitsch, en leur donnant une tonalité comique, lançait un défi aux circonstances: "L'humour n'est pas résigné, il défie", précise encore Freud.[8] Chez Lubitsch, les personnages se protègent d'une situation périlleuse, des affres douloureux d'une sentimentalité débridée ou des abîmes d'amertume d'une blessure amoureuse, pour la simple raison qu'ils donnent la primauté à leur plaisir. Ce trait caractéristique suscite une impression de légèreté et d'aisance, même dans les moments difficiles auxquels ils n'aliènent jamais la liberté du plaisir.

Dans la conclusion de son essai, Freud rappelle le caractère plus "intériorisé" et plus subtil de l'humour par rapport à d'autres moyens de rendre la réalité plaisante: "Il est exact que le plaisir humoristique n'atteint jamais l'intensité du plaisir pris au comique ou au mot d'esprit, qu'il ne se prodigue jamais en francs éclats de rire".[9] De fait, avec Lubitsch, la plupart du temps on sourit plus qu'on ne rit véritablement. Et le spectateur sourit du plaisir de se sentir flatté par la connivence qu'il décèle entre lui et le cinéaste. Le narcissisme atteint celui qui reçoit l'humour au même titre que celui qui le prodigue: il y a là une sorte d'accord tacite, d'intelligence entendue entre personnes qui croient parler le même langage.

L'analyse de la parole chez Lubitsch met en évidence son goût du verbe. Cette satisfaction verbale perceptible à tout moment dans les films, le spectateur la fait sienne. Les personnages paraissent se faire plaisir en parlant et ne cèdent jamais à un autre leur "temps de parole". Ainsi, les trois protagonistes de *Haute Pègre* (1932)[10] revendiquent ce plaisir, non seulement parce qu'ils parlent beaucoup et avec aisance mais aussi parce que le seul fait de faire venir les mots à leur bouche est une source de satisfaction physique, sensuelle, presque érotique. La façon dont Lily (Miriam Hopkins) se fait passer pour une comtesse au début du film, en usurpant son identité véritable, illustre bien cette volupté des mots. C'est le fait de dire qui rend le plaisir possible. La réciproque se vérifie également: on ne peut éprouver de plaisir si l'on ne peut *dire* les choses. Finalement, seuls les personnages qui ressentent le plaisir de la parole et expriment par elle leur désir, trouvent grâce aux yeux de Lubitsch et finissent par avoir... le dernier mot.

Le désir: *Ninotchka* et le rire du spectateur

Il n'est question, dans les films américains de Lubitsch, que de séduction et de désir. Les personnages jouent à se séduire en permanence, et le cinéaste, pour signifier leur attirance, recourt à des figures telles que le double sens, la litote et l'antiphrase, ou à de nombreux sous-entendus scabreux. Un bel exemple de ces derniers intervient dans *To Be or Not To Be*. Quand Stanislav (Robert Stack), le jeune aviateur amoureux de Maria Tura (Carole Lombard), vante les performances de son bombardier, il dit: "Je pilote un gros bombardier. Je peux lancer trois tonnes d'explosifs en deux minutes!... Sans être prétentieux, me permettriez-vous de vous le montrer?". La métaphore sexuelle est évidente, mais le jeune homme n'en paraît pas conscient, tandis que Maria, très impressionnée, semble y voir la promesse d'une sexualité hors du commun. Le but de ces figures touche encore à la complicité qui s'établit entre le cinéaste et le spectateur. On s'aperçoit d'ailleurs que les mots dans ces films possèdent une faculté tactile. L'effleurement des mots précède et prolonge celui des corps. Le "grain de la voix" — pour reprendre l'expression de Roland Barthes[11] — stimule l'excitation et le plaisir, tout comme le grain de la peau dont il est une sorte de double immatériel, fantasmé. Accepter la parole séductrice d'un interlocuteur c'est déjà accepter un contact physique, simplement différé.

Pour approfondir l'analyse du rire et du désir dans les films de Lubitsch, l'exemple de *Ninotchka* est particulièrement significatif. En effet, ce film est, littéralement, l'histoire d'une métamorphose, déclenchée par le rire. Or chez Lubitsch, rares sont les personnages qui rient. La plupart du temps, on rit des personnages, des situations, des dialogues, de la malice du cinéaste, mais dans ce film, le rire est sur l'écran avant d'être dans la salle, et produit des effets décisifs sur le personnage principal, Ninotchka, interprétée par Greta Garbo. Le film s'ouvre sur l'arrivée à Paris de trois émissaires russes dont la délicate mission consiste à vendre les bijoux de la grande-duchesse Swana (Ina Claire), grâce auxquels le gouvernement communiste espère se réapprovisionner. Les Russes rencontrent Léon (Melvyn Douglas), un bourgeois parisien volage, amant de la duchesse qui veut bien sûr les récupérer. Il les manipule et les empêche de vendre les bijoux. C'est alors qu'une autre envoyée soviétique, Ninotchka, est dépêchée sur place, très décidée à honorer sa mission. Léon cherche d'abord à la séduire puis tombe amoureux d'elle, mais elle lui résiste. Or c'est à partir du moment où il réussit à la faire rire que Léon déclenche une véritable métamorphose chez la jeune femme.

Dans ce film les mots sont explicitement désignés comme une source de plaisir. Cela est évident dans la manière dont Léon séduit la jeune femme russe, par un flux de parole ininterrompu, compulsif. Chez lui, l'usage euphorique des mots semble indissociable du fait qu'il se voue entièrement au plaisir. En effet, il ne travaille pas et se définit lui-même comme un séducteur hédoniste.[12] A l'inverse, Ninotchka se maintient dans la rétention des mots et le refus du plaisir, ce qui lui fera dire à Léon, dont la parole séductrice "ne prend pas": "Vous êtes très bavard". Pour la jeune femme, toute parole doit avoir une destination, une utilité, et il est impensable de parler pour rien — ou pour le plaisir, ce qui revient ici au même... Ninotchka a une conception économique de la parole. Un mot n'est bon à dire que s'il sert à quelque chose. Aussi son vocabulaire est-il amoindri et son verbe rare, car Ninotchka oppose sa résistance à toute une partie du langage, celle du plaisir et du désir. Rien d'étonnant donc à ce qu'elle refuse de sourire et *a fortiori* de rire, comme le constate avec regret Léon qui, déçu et à court d'histoires drôles, affirme: "Vous n'avez aucun sens de l'humour!".[13] L'incapacité à rire chez Ninotchka vient de ce que le rire n'a pas de fonction, sinon celle de se faire plaisir autant que d'exprimer son contentement. Elle oppose au principe de plaisir de Léon un principe de réalité par définition dysphorique. Et lorsqu'elle accepte de rire, elle découvre enfin le plaisir et la volupté de la parole.

D'autre part, l'opposition établie dans le film entre communisme et capitalisme se manifeste moins dans un discours théorique, d'ailleurs caricatural, ou dans des préoccupations sociales divergentes, que dans un rapport antagoniste au rire: le communisme interdit le rire tandis que le capitalisme l'exige et en jouit — et l'érige presque au rang de bien, échangeable au même titre qu'un objet. Le rire est explicitement coextensif du plaisir, et le système communiste est ici désigné (schématiquement) comme ce qui nie toute forme de plaisir. Or, c'est au cours de la séquence où l'on voit les trois Russes céder à l'euphorie du rire, que l'on comprend la faille ouverte dans leur idéologie: déjà minée, elle est dès lors atteinte, inopérante. Chez Ninotchka, la résistance au rire est le symptôme le plus significatif d'une rigidité générale, aussi bien idéologique que physique. Le film joue d'ailleurs sur la froideur inaccessible du visage de Garbo et sur son appartenance presque ontologique à la sphère des stars, analysée par Roland Barthes.[14] Ce visage, jusqu'alors déshumanisé et à la sexualité incertaine, Lubitsch le fait passer du masque à l'expressivité. Avant de considérer cette mutation, il faut rappeler qu'à l'époque où le film fut tourné, à la fin des années trente, Garbo représentait en effet l'essence de la star.[15] Et Lubitsch, en choisissant d'identifier Ninotchka à Garbo, joue de cette image en la soumettant à un véritable renversement.[16]

Dans le film, Ninotchka affiche un refus de céder au rire, non seulement parce qu'il n'est rien de plus inutile et de plus gratuit, mais aussi parce qu'elle pressent sa force subversive. Ce refus va de pair avec sa résistance au discours amoureux de Léon auquel elle se montre longtemps imperméable. Or le rire possède une dimension érotique indéniable, que Ninotchka tient à distance, de la même façon qu'elle arbore les symptômes de la frigidité. Le rire est issu du désir et le fait croître en retour. Le psychanalyste Daniel Sibony a analysé la contiguïté entre l'érotisme et le rire dans son livre *Jouissances du dire*:

> Même la contagion du rire reflète la contagion érotique ou inconsciente. Plus généralement, être en proie à l'objet de désir qui file et qui circule avec sa mécanique implacable non seulement prête à rire, mais incite à penser *le rire comme objet de désir*, désir de ce que le rire pointe au croisement, entre faire *l'amour* et advenir à la langue du désir [...]. Le jet du rire lui-même, sillon entre amour et parole, s'élabore comme support érotique et signifiant.[17]

Ainsi, lorsque Ninotchka, dans la séquence du restaurant, accepte enfin de rire, elle s'assume elle-même, simultanément, comme objet de désir, et passe de la désincarnation apparente à l'incarnation. Par ce rire qui lui échappe, elle devient une femme, consent à sa féminité et fait disparaître le masque de la star, fissuré par ces éclats spontanés de plaisir.[18] Et le rire de Garbo est d'autant plus jubilatoire que l'on ne s'y attend plus et qu'il fuse à contre-temps, par l'échec du rituel de la séduction. D'abord, Ninotchka rit *de* Léon, ridiculisé par sa chute au restaurant, puis elle rit *avec* lui, lorsqu'il comprend qu'en riant ensemble, sans motif, et en participant à l'euphorie collective, ils jouissent d'une proximité physique définitive.

La métamorphose de Ninotchka se traduit par des changements subtils: dès la séquence suivante, Garbo imprime à son visage et à son corps des nuances charnelles. Elle semble rêveuse, sourit et se met à rire en pleine réunion avec ses compatriotes. Sa voix n'est plus la même, modifiée par des inflexions plus douces, plus expressives, relâchée par la détente dont tout son corps semble ressentir la volupté. Son espace s'ouvre à de nouveaux repères: il s'élargit et se réduit en même temps. Il s'élargit car pour la première fois elle éprouve le besoin d'ouvrir la fenêtre et de respirer l'air du printemps, et prend le temps de regarder ce qui l'entoure autrement que d'un point de vue scientifique. Il se réduit au moment où, ses amis venant de quitter la pièce, Ninotchka s'enferme et, après s'être assurée que nul ne peut la voir, sort d'un tiroir l'un des chapeaux parisiens dont elle avait dit le plus grand mal au début du film, et se regarde, sereine, dans le miroir. Tout se passe comme si Ninotchka s'appropriait enfin un espace et, par ces gestes simples, acquérait une intimité propre. La transformation est aussi d'ordre vestimentaire: une robe du soir blanche et légère, aux épaules découvertes, remplace ses tenues antérieures, sévères et presque asexuées. Plus tard, arrivée chez son amant, Ninotchka prétend ne jamais être venue, ce qui confirme bien sa "métamorphose". Elle explique que les histoires drôles de Léon la font encore rire, même si elle les trouve stupides: c'est que pour rire, la connivence est nécessaire de part et d'autre. Plus tard, elle danse, radieuse, avec son amant, ce que l'on n'aurait jamais pu imaginer du "camarade Yakouchova". Ainsi, le rire ouvre une large brèche dans la forteresse où se maintenait Ninotchka — mais aussi Garbo dont Lubitsch démythifie entièrement l'image figée, transformant "la Divine" en une femme vivante. Il marque aussi pour elle l'apprentissage d'un plaisir situé à la frontière de la parole et du corps, entre le déferlement d'un bruit sans signifié et une euphorie physique sans objet.

Avant de revenir, à l'appui de ce film, sur la place du spectateur, il faut rappeler que Lubitsch s'amuse constamment à mesurer l'écart ou la proximité entre les êtres. Dans ses films, les corps se touchent ou se frôlent, se caressent et s'enlacent. Les personnages s'embrassent volontiers, sans s'attarder trop durablement sur les préliminaires — qui, finalement, viennent après, lorsque les jeux sont faits, pour le plaisir. Si une distance se maintient entre les corps, les mots, dont la faculté tactile et érotique a été soulignée, se chargent de la combler symboliquement. L'usage à la fois ludique et érotique de la parole dans les films maintient les personnages dans un état de désir toujours reconduit sitôt satisfait. Nous l'avons vu, entendre et accepter ces mots c'est déjà établir un contact physique avec l'autre.

Il se joue pour le spectateur une expérience assez similaire pendant la durée de la projection. A la fois présent comme l'un des destinataires de la parole et absent car privé de parole propre, il devient le sujet d'un désir comparable à celui des personnages. Il désire le film, par son intérêt, ses anticipations, ses émotions. L'acuité particulière du regard et de l'écoute sollicite l'excitation de ses sens. En définitive, le spectateur se trouve dans une situation similaire à celle de Ninotchka, dans la mesure où Lubitsch le conquiert et le séduit par des voies auxquelles il ne s'attendait pas, en le surprenant et en lui donnant à éprouver la malice du sourire et le plaisir du rire, un rire qui le met dans une position peut-être inconfortable, mais le "renarcissise" en même temps, grâce à la connivence qu'il postule avec le cinéaste.

> Le rire, écrit encore Daniel Sibony, ébranle le narcissisme tout en lui donnant satisfaction; *rire, c'est se secouer le narcissisme* (comme on dit se secouer les puces) tout en lui accordant de petits orgasmes, à la surface (non seulement du corps: chatouillements, mais plus généralement à la surface des langues, des corps collectifs, à la frontière qui les coupe des autres et prétend les distinguer, les affirmer).[19]

Les films de Lubitsch revendiquent donc le plaisir du texte proféré. Ce qui importe, c'est la parole, toujours considérée dans son acception à la fois ludique et érotique, dont la mise en scène intermittente, entre masquage et dévoilement, fait de ce cinéma un objet de désir exemplaire. Aussi, comme Ninotchka, par le rire, le spectateur se place dans une situation de disponibilité érotique et s'offre au film en tant que corps désirant; aux corps projetés de l'écran répond la projection du corps du spectateur vers les personnages, vers les films. Cette disponibilité est à la fois la cause et l'effet du rire et augmente le plaisir du spectateur.

Notes

1. D'origine allemande, le cinéaste quitta l'Allemagne pour Hollywood en 1923, sur l'invitation de la comédienne américaine Mary Pickford.
2. Outre Samson Raphaelson, son collaborateur le plus régulier, Ben Hecht, Charles Brackett, Billy Wilder, Walter Reisch, Edwin Justus Mayer, pour ne citer qu'eux, écrivirent ses scénarios.
3. Billy Wilder et Charles Brackett, *Et tout le reste est folie. Mémoires* (Paris: Robert Laffont, 1993).
4. François Truffaut a remarqué à juste titre ce dispositif — "Pas de Lubitsch sans public, mais attention, le public n'est pas *en plus*, il est *avec*, il fait partie du film [...]. Les ellipses de scénario, prodigieuses, ne fonctionnent que parce que nos rires établissent le pont d'une scène à l'autre. Dans le gruyère lubitschien, chaque trou est génial": "Lubitsch était un prince", *Cahiers du cinéma*, numéro spécial Lubitsch (1985), 95–96.
5. Sigmund Freud, "L'humour", *L'Inquiétante Etrangeté et autres essais* (Paris: Gallimard, 1985).
6. Freud, pp. 322–23.

7. Freud, p. 323.

8. Freud, p. 324.

9. Freud, p. 328.

10. Gaston (Herbert Marshall), Lily (Miriam Hopkins) et Mariette Colet (Kay Francis).

11. Roland Barthes, *Le Plaisir du texte* (Paris: Seuil, 1973).

12. "Ninotchka: Que faites-vous pour l'humanité? — Léon: Pas grand-chose. Mais je fais beaucoup pour les femmes...".

13. Ce reproche pourrait signifier, si l'on se rapporte à la définition de l'humour par Freud, que Léon trouve qu'elle n'a aucun sens du défi et, finalement, de la transgression.

14. Roland Barthes, "Le visage de Garbo", "L'acteur d'Harcourt", *Mythologies* (Paris: Seuil, 1957).

15. Notamment par l'image que les films de son Pygmalion, Joseph von Sternberg, avaient construite: *Blonde Vénus* (1932), *L'Impératrice rouge* (1934), *La Femme et le pantin* (1935).

16. Peu après, George Cukor fit d'ailleurs de cette représentation désormais dédoublée de Garbo, le sujet même de son film *La Femme aux deux visages* (1941).

17. Daniel Sibony, *Jouissances du dire* (Paris: Grasset, 1985), pp. 307–08.

18. Le rire de Garbo fut d'ailleurs un argument "promotionnel" lors de l'annonce du film.

19. Sibony, p. 309.

CHAPTER 13

What's So Funny? On Being Laughed At...

Adam Phillips

I

Laughing at the same jokes is evidence of far-reaching psychical conformity
SIGMUND FREUD, *Jokes and their Relation to the Unconscious*

One of the oddly striking things about Primo Levi's initial impression of Auschwitz, which he describes in the first fifty or so pages of *If This is a Man*, is his sense that this must be some kind of joke. On entering the camp, he writes:

> They make us enter an enormous empty room that is poorly heated. We have a terrible thirst. The weak gurgle of the water in the radiators makes us ferocious: we have had nothing to drink for four days. But there is also a tap — and above it a card which says that it is forbidden to drink as the water is dirty. Nonsense. It seems obvious that the card is a joke, 'they' know that we are dying of thirst and they put us in a room, and there is a tap, and *Wassertrinken verboten*. I drink and I incite my companions to do likewise, but I have to spit it out, the water is tepid and sweetish, with the smell of a swamp.[1]

The scene has a kind of archetypal resonance; they are thirsty but they cannot drink. And it is Levi's instinct, so to speak, to work out why people would do such a thing. He is in search of an explanation for something unbearable, and the idea he comes up with is that the card itself must be a joke. The water is surely fine, but the sign is actually the sign of someone's sense of humour. It must be a joke for Levi because the world can't be this incoherent and cruel; if people are thirsty no one shows them a tap and says, but you mustn't drink the water. In short it is a joke for Levi because it is so cruel; and because it must be a joke, it can't be true. So he drinks the water and it is so disgusting he has to spit it out. The sign is telling the truth; and it is there, in a certain sense, to protect them. Why did it occur to Levi to think of this as some sort of joke? And the answer is that he believes that there are people who might play such jokes on others, but there can't be people in the world who would refuse people water for four days and then put them in a room with a tap they can't drink from. In other words, there is something about human cruelty that Levi cannot imagine. And, of course, something else about human cruelty — the joke — that he can. People can joke about such things, but they could never do them. As he intimates, the joke was on him. But it is the joke that is Levi's preferred form of explanation; that there are jokes and jokers in the world makes this experience, at least initially, intelligible to him.

If jokes and mockery are one motif in his grave and horrifying book, the other motif is to do with teaching and learning, as though there are two ways Levi organizes his experience: on the one hand there is mockery, and on the other there is something we might call, for want of a better phrase, moral education. When Levi is not describing the ridicule of camp experience, he is using the language of pedagogy ('One learns quickly enough to wipe out the past and the future when one is forced to', p. 42). In Auschwitz, Levi is at once a student of human experience in extremity, and the object — both in reality, and in his own interpretation — of an unbearable, an inconceivable, taunting and teasing.

The camp, in Levi's account, is, among other things, a kind of anti-university, a brutal parody of humanistic learning. 'We have learnt other things, more or less quickly, according to our intelligence,' he writes, 'to reply *jawohl*, never to ask questions, always to pretend to understand' (p. 39). What you have to learn is obedience; inequality created and recreated through intimidation. If the sign on the tap is an answer there is no need for a question. The joke is the last-ditch explanation before the questions begin. Levi cannot even pretend to understand what is happening to him: 'I have stopped trying to understand for a long time now' (p. 43); and clearly, by the same token, 'they' are not trying to understand him:

> Some more hours pass before all the inmates are seen, are given a shirt and their details taken. I, as usual, am the last. Someone in a brand new striped suit askes me where I was born, what profession I practised 'as a civilian', if I had children, what diseases I had had, a whole series of questions. What use could they be? Is this a complicated rehearsal to make fools of us? (p. 55)

They are asked questions, but cannot ask them — except, as Levi does here, in their minds. And once again, out of his general bewilderment he wonders, and it is another question, whether what they are really doing is making fools of them. 'For many weeks', he writes of the signs around the camp, 'I considered these warnings about hygiene as pure examples of the Teutonic sense of humour' (p. 46), as though this may just be a matter of translation. Shaved — 'What comic faces we have without hair,' Levi remarks — there is another shower ordeal; and Levi asks one of the officials what has happened to the women, will they see their wives and daughters again. 'Certainly we will never see them again,' the man replies, 'but by now', Levi writes, 'my belief is that all this is a game to mock and sneer at us' (p. 30). Levi keeps coming to the conclusion that the only way of explaining this deranged and brutal world he has found himself in is that it is someone's joke; that they are all there being laughed at. And the reason that this is at once grotesque and intelligible as an assumption and an explanation is that *when one is being laughed at one is giving someone pleasure*. Someone is, as we say, getting pleasure at our expense. The only reason people could possibly do all this to other people is because it gives them pleasure; and the specific pleasure is that these people get to laugh at people. They keep playing jokes on them. As though the Nazis were like a particularly nasty pantheon of hedonistic pagan gods. People could only have devised this otherwise unintelligible regime if it gave them the kind of pleasure jokes give them. And mocking people is so compelling as a form of satisfaction that people will clearly do literally anything to achieve it.

The preconditions for the concentration-camp model of mockery, as inferred by

Levi, are first that there is no equality between the jokers and their victims (they don't share a sense of humour); secondly, that they must be kept in a state of total ignorance about what is really going on, and about the mentality of the jokers; thirdly, that they should feel sufficiently intimidated to submit to the joke in question; and fourthly, at least in Levi's version, they must be unsure whether it is a joke they are in, whether or not they are actually being laughed at. After all, if they are not, if they are not giving anyone pleasure by their utter abjection, then the so-called human world is even less intelligible than was previously assumed (imagine a world in which pleasure was dead rather than God). So there is being laughed at, and the wondering what else might be going on if one is not, in fact, being ridiculed. But basically, as long as someone is giving someone pleasure, the world, any of our worlds, seem to make sense. The thing about being laughed at — the true horror of it — is that it makes perfect sense. When someone says, in that frantic way, 'what's so funny?', they know that there is something that is so funny.

When Levi assumes at Auschwitz that he must be being laughed at, he assumes that he is giving someone pleasure; but whether he wants to or not. When the child asks in the playground, 'what's so funny?', he resents that he is giving someone a pleasure that he has not chosen to give them. Or indeed that something about him provides someone else with a pleasure that diminishes him. When we laugh at someone else, we violate, or simply disregard, their preferred image of themselves. To be mocked, in other words, is the narcissist's nightmare (which is why narcissists like us can be so good at it) and why all children go through at least a period of dreading it. Adolescence is, as it were, the high noon of ridicule, when what is continually on show, what is continually being exposed, is the unpredictable sexually and emotionally developing bodily self. So I want to ask, as a kind of utopian thought experiment: what would have to happen for someone to grow out of the fear of being laughed at? And so, by the same token, what is the fear of being laughed at a fear of? Why, in other words, would it be a good thing to not fear being laughed at?

II

The subtlest punishment he had suffered was to think his own order came from others.

NORMAN MAILER, *Ancient Evenings*

Ridicule is clearly the enemy of what psychoanalysts and democrats call free association — and what other people might just call sociability. In circulation with others — and in the circulation with ourselves that is called psychoanalysis — it becomes extremely difficult to sustain, to hold in place our preferred images of ourselves, of who we would rather be. One keeps being translated, redescribed. And it is this perhaps that makes comedy at once the most reassuring and the most scarifying of genres. Sustaining because, at its best, as in say *Tristram Shandy* or *Waiting for Godot*, it generously diminishes us; it lowers us down gently from our own ideals. It exposes our wish for exposure. 'Comedy', John Carey writes in the Preface to his book on Dickens, *The Violent Effigy*, is felt to be artificial and escapist; tragedy toughly real. The opposite view seems more accurate. Tragedy is tender to man's dignity and self-importance, and preserves the illusion that he is a noble creature. Comedy uncovers the absurd truth, which is why people are so afraid of being laughed at in real life.[2]

I want to pursue the idea that this is a terrible fear and a terrible wish.

The absurd truth that comedy uncovers, to use Carey's words, is not merely that, really, we are undignified and far from important (let alone self-important) in the larger scheme of things. It is simply that we are always other than what we want to be; that we don't want to look the same as we look to ourselves. Primo Levi wanted to be what he thought of as a man, but his experience in Auschwitz was that there were other people who didn't share his own description of himself, or indeed of what a person is. For mockery to work, something about a person has to be exposed, usually something they would prefer to conceal from themselves and others because it is at odds with the person they would rather be. And what is exposed has to be described in such a way as to render it amusing. What was exposed in Auschwitz was how absolute people's vulnerability can be, how utterly dependent people are on fellow feeling. What Levi realized in Auschwitz was that his body, his bodily self, could be nothing else than the instrument of another's desire. The concentration camp, one could say, as an object of cultural horror and fascination, exposes everyone's fears about dependence, about one's life in other people's hands. This is the nightmare version, this is the other side that shadows our perpetual need for others. This is what happens when sociability becomes unbearable, when people start keeping fellow feeling at a distance.

And yet, of course, what the playground version of ridicule reveals so starkly is that children's groups, when they don't cohere around pleasurable shared activities, share a version of fellow feeling constituted around a chosen object of mockery. That children can be extremely cruel is a cliché worth remembering; and when they are together in groups or gangs, mockery is often the form their cruelty takes. Children take easily to ridicule; it is a currency, a language that they, as it were, understand. A childhood without teasing is inconceivable to us. If it was, as we are so often told, strangely easy for people in the nineteenth century to deny or to ignore the sexuality of children, the violence of children, at least to each other, has never been a secret. Clearly it didn't need Freud to show us, for example, that children have, to put it mildly, mixed feelings about their siblings; that feeling displaced — feeling that they have lost their place, and therefore their life, to a new baby — doesn't tend to make children kind. Children are only instinctively good at sharing in so far as they have to be. Whether or not children are innately cruel, deprivation often makes them so. Children, like adults, have a radar for scarcity, for what we might call the unequal distribution of (emotional) wealth. Ridicule, I want to suggest, is a fantasy of restoration of status; and mockery is always performed from a position of wished-for privilege. It is, whatever else it is, the revenge of the displaced. And whether or not one has siblings, to be a child, to 'grow up' as it is called, is to be displaced. To grow up is to discover what it is one is unequal to.

'As soon as responsibility for founding society came to rest on human shoulders,' Pierre Saint-Amand writes in *The Laws of Hostility* — that is to say, after the collapse of all forms of transcendence (God, the King), as soon as it was possible to conceive man's future in terms of horizontal, egalitarian relations [...] in the perspective of social autonomy the eighteenth century found itself confronted with a new social economy. And hence it boasted of optimism and good faith, by endowing man, its philosophical creature, with ideal qualities.

The philosophers needed a being who was up to the demands of a future both glorious and realisable. The violence of relations, the bewildering antagonism between human beings could only be relegated to a long ago past. Exit hostility ... natural human goodness will provide the cornerstone for a new concept of justice.[3]

It is as though the idea of equality is a cover story; or that equality between people is only conceivable if we forget what Saint-Amand calls 'the violence of relations, the bewildering antagonism between human beings' that one has only to go to one's local playground to observe. It is as though, he suggests, this new concept of justice, based on an ennobled and ennobling version of human benevolence, makes a mockery of who we really are. That modern societies, like the modern individuals that constitute them, are the site of competing claims makes conflict inevitable, cruelly necessary. What it does not in and of itself explain is how we can get such pleasure from cruelty. If cruelty is the worst thing we do, what then is enjoying our cruelty? To be able to laugh at another person, to learn to do this, would seem to be a remarkable cultural artefact (if not necessarily an impressive cultural achievement). Sociability without mockery and teasing and taunting would be both dreary and verging on the pointless. And this suggests that the ordinary version of what Levi experienced *in extremis* in Auschwitz is, so to speak, an important pleasure for us.

We may, unless we are consensual or compulsive sadomasochists, deplore humiliation, or claim to; but we cannot help but enjoy what we cheerfully call making fun of people. We are always reassured when people can, as we say, laugh at themselves. There is a violence we do to ourselves and others that is both enlivening and strangely consoling. There is the good mockery of everyday life that regulates our self-importance, and so relieves us of too much responsibility for the world. And there is the bad mockery that foists something upon us that we would rather, if we could choose, protect ourselves from.

For Freud, jokes are forms of disinhibition; what he calls the 'joke-work' 'protects (the) original yield of pleasure from the attacks of critical reason'.[4] What Freud calls critical reason, in other words, could be called moral reason. The joke, like a dream or a symptom, gives us (regulated) access to otherwise forbidden pleasures. And yet, or so, 'we scarcely ever know what we are laughing at in a joke'. That we laugh makes it appear self-evident that we know what has amused us. But the joke, Freud suggests ominously, only works because it conceals this piece of knowledge from us (Freud characteristically assumes that it is knowledge that is hidden here). A joke is a translation from a secret language. So when we laugh at others — when the joke is on them — we can infer that at least three things are going on. First, that we have found a way of using them for our forbidden pleasure; secondly, by the same token, our knowledge of what it is about them that is giving us pleasure is opaque to us, is hidden or disguised in what we have chosen to laugh at; and thirdly, where we are amused is where we desire (tell me what makes you laugh, tell me what or whom you laugh at, and I could tell you what you want). What Freud calls my 'attacks of critical reason' are there to protect me from too much knowledge of what I desire (clearly this version of critical reason has no sense of humour). And a sense of humour acknowledges the apparent senselessness of humour; we mustn't know what we are laughing at. We can know that we are getting pleasure, but not what is giving it to us. Laughing at someone is — like all real pleasures — a stolen pleasure. But when we laugh at someone, they feel stolen from.

So what is this daylight robbery that at its best is simple teasing, and at its worst is degrading humiliation? As ever, it must be impossible to speak for every case; generalization makes a mockery of differences. And yet to describe laughing at someone as stealing is also to say that it takes from them their protection from being stolen from. As though somebody were to take photographs of you that you couldn't stand, and then circulated them. What has been stolen is your freedom to supervise, to control the representations of yourself. The other person or people no longer care to protect, or wholly disregard, the images of yourself that you believe you need to sustain you. Humiliation strips the self of its safeguards; ordinary teasing frees the self of its safeguards.

But it is the nature of the pleasure, the quality of the pleasures involved that is, as ever, the more difficult thing to describe. There is the pleasure of yielding, of abrogating one's self-protective images; and then there is the mortification, the shame of one's destitution, of being rendered abject. And there is the doing of these things and the being done to (however complicit they can be, through unconscious processes of identification; the sadist being the masochist in unconscious fantasy, and vice versa). To laugh at someone, one must enjoy their hatred of being laughed at. But there is also something else that one must not let oneself feel.

It is worth describing what we do in terms of what we are wanting to feel, and what we are wanting not to feel. If the pursuit of pleasure is also the avoidance of pain, we might ask ourselves at any given moment, or in retrospect, 'what was I doing to stop myself feeling?' Clearly, in any successful act of mockery I am not feeling (consciously) what I inflict on the other person. At that moment it is the other, not me, that is mortified. It is, like all cruelty, a calculated not-me experience. I have apparently created a boundary, a distance, between myself and my victim. Indeed, it may be the separateness — the belief that I can instate such a distance — that is the important thing. It is not me who feels this, it is him. So one thing that is so funny at the moment is just how different we are; there is a gulf between us in terms of feeling. My pleasure is as much in your suffering as in my lack of it. What's so funny is that we are both the same kind of creature, and yet I can make you worlds apart from me; almost another species, an utterly abject untriumphant one. The shame is now elsewhere, projected or evacuated, as certain psychoanalysts would say. I have rid myself of something unbearable, but I am, as it were, still in touch with it through the medium of pleasure, my sadistic pleasure in your desolation.

It is one thing to acknowledge — if one is psychologically minded to — that we are likely to project whatever it is we find unbearable about ourselves into others. It is quite another to ridicule or mock this unbearable something once it has been so projected. We have to imagine a kind of cartoon; I ascribe to someone else something about myself — my shameful love of money, say, my racism — and then I have to do something else; I have to persecute them, through mockery, for being the bearers of it. So the question becomes not only 'what's so funny?' but 'why and how is this made to seem funny?' Being able to be amused is being able to get the pleasure of seeing the funny side of things. Mockery, in other words, can be the cruellest part of cruelty.

When Freud wrote in his joke book that 'laughing at the same joke is evidence of far-reaching psychical conformity',[5] he implied that those who share a sense of humour share far more than a sense of humour. But if the shared joke is the sign of pervasive recognitions, of a profounder unity between people, then not sharing a joke — which is what laughing at someone and being laughed at necessarily involves — is disunity in action. The triumphalism, the inner superiority of being in a position to ridicule someone, is the grand illusion of disunity, of apparently having nothing in common with one's victim. What Freud calls 'far-reaching psychological conformity' and what we might call some sense of equality or in-commonness, has, at least in fantasy, been ablated. We only laugh at those with whom we feel we have an affinity that we must repudiate, that we feel threatened by. Ridicule, in other words, is a terror of sociability. We laugh at to sabotage our feeling of being at one with; but the feeling of at-oneness has already happened.

It is a question, as it often is, of anticipated catastrophe; what, we must ask, is the imagined devastation that will occur if the mocker doesn't mock? If he isn't laughing at his victim, if he stops arranging his humiliation, what does he fear might happen? What might they do together? The so-called psychological answer might be, he will see too much of himself, too much of something about himself, in his chosen victim. He might, for example, see his chosen victim as an object of forbidden desire. He might see how vulnerability always makes us yield or punish. The political answer would be, he would turn democratic. What mockery reveals, in other words, is the emotional terror of democracy. That what is always being ridiculed is our wish to be together, our secret affinity for each other.

Notes to Chapter 13

1. Primo Levi, *If This is a Man*, trans. by Stuart Woolf (London: Abacus, 1979), p. 28. Further references are given after quotations in the text.
2. John Carey, *The Violent Effigy: A Study of Dickens' Imagination*, 2nd edn (London: Faber, 1991), p. 7.
3. Pierre Saint-Amand, *The Laws of Hostility*, trans. by Jennifer Curtiss Gage (Minneapolis and London: University of Minnesota Press, 1996), pp. 3–4.
4. Sigmund Freud, *Jokes and their Relation to the Unconscious*, in *The Standard Edition of the Complete Psychological Works of Sigmund Freud*, trans. by James Strachey and others, VIII (London: The Hogarth Press and the Institute of Psycho-Analysis, 1960): section IV: 'The Mechanism of Pleasure, and the Psychoanalysis of Jokes', pp. 117–39.
5. Freud, section V: 'The Motives of Jokes — Jokes as a Social Process', pp. 140–58.

CHAPTER 14

Laughing and Talking

Sukanta Chaudhuri

Nonsense, by definition, is what is not sense. But not-sense can achieve that gratifying state in various ways. One might simply be the reversal of sense. Take this rhyme by Rabindranath Tagore:

> Old Mother Khanto's Grandma-in-law
> Has the strangest sisters you ever saw.
> Their saris on the stove they keep,
> And saucepans on the clothes-horse heap.
> From carping tongues to be at rest,
> They hide inside an iron chest,
> But at the window air their cash
> Without a jot of worry.
> They put salt in their betel-leaves,
> And quicklime in their curry.[1]

This is the programmed inversion of logic. The eccentric ladies simply exchange the rightful locations of two classes of articles: clothes on the kitchen stove, pots and pans on the clothes-rack, and so on. It is all profoundly logical. There is patent method in the madness.

Contrast the following account by Tagore's contemporary and, by common consent, his superior in the field of Bengali nonsense verse, Sukumar Ray:

> Have you heard of the monarch of Bombagarh's orders
> To fry mango jelly and frame it with borders?
> And why does his queen wear a pouffe on her head?
> Or the queen's eldest brother knock nails into bread?
> There people turn cartwheels to cure their catarrhs,
> Rub rouge in their eyes by the light of the stars,
> Musicians walk muffled in blankets of state,
> And bald-headed scholars stick stamps on their pate.[2]

Bombagarh is an imaginary kingdom. Going a stage further, here is a warning against an imaginary creature, the Pumpkin-Puff. His features seem to have been suggested by Lewis Carroll's Mock Turtle, but he is a more aggressive creature altogether.

> *If Pumpkin-Puff should dance —*
> Beware! Beware! You mustn't dare beyond the stalls advance.
> You mustn't glance to fore or aft, or cast your eyes aslant,
> But grapple close with tips and toes the Rancid Radish Plant.

FIG. 1. Pumpkin-Puff, from *Abol Tabol*, written and illustrated by Sukumar Ray
(Calcutta: U. Ray and Sons, 1923 [Bengali year 1330]).

If Pumpkin-Puff should cry —
You simply mustn't mount the roof to contemplate the sky.
But stretched upon a pumpkin-frame and muffled in a quilt,
Sing hymns to Radha-Krishna with a slily solemn lilt.
If Pumpkin-Puff should roar —
You perch upon a single leg beside the kitchen door;
Then whisper Persian verses with an eloquence forlorn,
And slink entirely supperless to lie upon the lawn.[3]

Now these are truly irrational dispensations. We cannot begin to imagine why the
denizens of Bombagarh should behave as they do, or the Pumpkin-Puff demand such
responses to his antics and be incensed by any departure. Every one of the advised
actions is physically possible, provided one can find a Rancid Radish Plant. But they
do not conform to what we may call the syntax of event, the functions assumed
by actions in the accustomed pattern of our lives. In other words, the actions are
meaningless — just as we may question whether words remain words if they resemble
the headwords in a dictionary but serve no recognized grammatical function.

Sukumar Ray also wrote a somewhat Carrollean fantasy, *A Topsy-Turvy Tale.* There a
strange old man with a green beard, who has popped out from inside a tree, tells the
boy narrator the following delectable story:

Meanwhile the Head Vizier had swallowed the Princess's spool of thread. Nobody
knew about it. And just at this moment along came the man-eating giant, roaring

as he rolled off the bed in his sleep. At once there was a hideous din of drums and bugles and cymbals and bassoons and guards and gunners and dragoons and cavalry, clash, clash, bang, bang, boom, boom, rattle, rattle — when suddenly the king cried out: 'What's this magic horse doing without a tail?' And the pastors and masters and doctors and proctors began telling each other, 'A very good question. What's happened to its tail?' Nobody knew the answer: they all tried to slink away.[4]

This rigmarole evokes Alice's bewilderment at the Mad Tea-Party: 'The Hatter's remark seemed to her to have no sort of meaning in it, and yet it was certainly English'.[5] Going further, we may question whether it *is* English. Can a superficial adherence to the forms of disparate words qualify as language if there is no sequential meaning? Is language meant solely to convey meaning? These are the questions I wish to address.

In the simple cases I have cited so far, the words used are familiar ones, and the syntax of language is not radically disturbed, unlike what I have called the syntax of event. In that superficial sense, the words do 'mean' something. Yet not only is the subject matter fictitious, it corresponds to nothing in external reality. We have encountered the Pumpkin-Puff. Here is the Blighty Cow:

> No words can paint the curious creature:
> This portrait limns each noble feature.[6]

He is clearly a composite being compounded of many species — like another of Sukumar's creations, the Super-Beast who wished for the good points of all animals

FIG. 2. The Blighty Cow, from *Abol Tabol*.

FIG. 3. The Super-Beast, from *Abol Tabol*.

and acquired them in the above rather disconcerting way.[7] We may recall that Carroll's Mock Turtle, as drawn by Tenniel, had the head, hooves and tail of a cow, no doubt because mock turtle soup is usually made from veal. There is a logic behind such visualizations. Leonardo da Vinci, in his notebooks, describes how a dragon is to be composed:

> Take for its head that of a mastiff or hound, with the eyes of a cat, the ears of a porcupine, the nose of a greyhound, the brow of a lion, the temples of an old cock, the neck of a water-tortoise.[8]

If these are fantasies, they are fantasies of an intellect that has not cast aside its basic fealty to reason and reality.

But the *conception*, as against the visualization, of the Mock Turtle is in a different mental category. A mock turtle is an entirely notional creature, conjured out of sheer verbal space by syntactical legerdemain. Carroll has made a noun (or let us use the full-bodied term, a substantive) out of a compound adjective, *mock-turtle*. In fact, I have derived the compound adjective — questionably enough — by reconstituting the combination (simple adjective + compound noun), *mock turtle-soup*. The word has brought the creature into being. Its visualization is a secondary matter.

By a comparable process, various original insects are presented in *Through the Looking-Glass*:

> 'Look on the branch above your head,' said the Gnat, 'and there you'll find a Snapdragon-fly. Its body is made of plum-pudding, its wings of holly leaves, and its head is a raisin burning in brandy.'[9]

This is less arbitrary than it sounds, for 'snapdragon' was a Victorian Christmas game where raisins had to be picked up from flaming brandy. Given the name, the visualization follows a certain logic — like that of the Rocking-horse-fly, made of wood and swinging from branch to branch, or the Bread-and-butter-fly, chiefly constituted of that repast. But it is a *post facto* visualization. The idea of such creations is derived from their names, and the names are derived by conflating the name of an actual insect with another word. Carroll himself famously termed such coinages portmanteau words.

Sukumar Ray has a zoo-full of such animals:

> A pochard and a porcupine, defying the grammarians,
> Combined to form a porcochard, unmindful of their variance.
> A stork upon a tortoise grew, exclaiming 'What a hoot!
> A very handsome storkoise, now, we jointly constitute'.
> A parakeet its features lent unto the lowly lizard,
> In puzzle whether flies or fruit would better suit its gizzard.
> The very goat began to feel impatient of its state:
> It leapt upon a scorpion's back, and grew incorporate.
> The tall giraffe refused to roam its ancestral savannah,
> But tried to don a locust's wings, and glide in graceful manner.
> The cow was led to view itself, and staggered from the shock:
> Its noble limbs had been usurped by some designing cock.
> And rent by schizophrenia the whalephant we view:
> The open seas, the forest trees are tearing it in two.
> The lion longed for antlers, and was doomed to dwell in care
> Until a stag supplied it with a truly splendid pair.[10]

The illustrations are simpler versions of the composite animals we saw earlier; but the notable thing about them is that each has been conjured into being by a portmanteau word in Bengali, of which I have been able to render only one or two rather roughly in English. In each combination, the last letter in the first animal's name is the first letter in the second one's, providing a link or overlap between the two. In other words, these are creatures of language: they have evolved by a process of verbal selection. The pochard could not have combined with the lizard, nor the giraffe with the parakeet, simply because their Bengali names have no letters in common.

To illustrate this principle to perfection, I would crave the reader's indulgence to present in the original a very short Bengali rhyme by Amitabha Chaudhuri:

> *Hate niye dictionary*
> *Charichhen ricksha nari.*
> *Chharakhani kalpanik*
> *Jake bale 'fictionary'!*[11]

This can be rendered as:

> A woman rides by in a rickshaw
> Clutching at a dictionary.
> The scene's entirely fanciful —
> Or, as you might say, fictionary.

In Bengali, the lines rhyme *aaba*, like Omar Khayyám's rubais. The word *dictionary* occurs at the end of the first line. The Bengali word for 'woman' is *nari*, so that, following the Bengali word order, *ricksha nari* provides a rhyme to *dictionary* and *fictionary*.

My point is this. Once the dictionary was brought on at the outset, its possessor had to be a *nari* or woman, and she had to ride in a rickshaw, not a car, bus, or train, in

FIG. 4. Hotch-Potch, from *Abol Tabol*.

order to create the verbal pattern. It is like the party game where you have to draw a full picture around a single given object. In this case, the scene is dictated not by the visual but by the verbal or rhyming compulsions of the starting object, the dictionary. This creates a special kind of 'fictionary' exercise. A scene, a potential story, is woven directly and literally out of words by tapping their non-referential, intrinsic, phonic properties.

Think of that best-known instance of a narrative built out of the purely intrinsic attributes of words, *Jabberwocky*. It requires a novel hermeneutics:

'It seems very pretty,' [Alice] said when she had finished it, 'but it's rather hard
to understand! [...] Somehow it seems to fill my head with ideas — only I don't
know exactly what they are! However, *somebody* killed *something*: that's clear, at
any rate.'[12]

Portmanteau words are only part of the puzzle. *Gyre* and *wabe* are back-formations
(from *gyroscope* or *gyrate* and *way before/way behind*), and *gimble* something like one
(from *gimlet*). These coinages from identifiable sememes lead us into a terrain of
utterly free creation. *Tove, borogove*, and *rath* are entirely fanciful names of no obvious
provenance, of the sort we associate with Lear more than Carroll. *Outgrabe* is similarly
formed. In these cases, Carroll is using disjunct phonemes (can we then still call them
phonemes?) as his building-blocks to create new 'words'. He thereby both affirms and
subverts the Saussurean concept of linguistic structure. 'The science of sound,' writes
Saussure, 'becomes invaluable only when two or more elements are involved in a
relationship based upon their inner dependence [...] (T)he single fact that there are
two elements calls for a relationship and a rule.'[13] In *tove, rath*, or *borogove*, the amassed
phonemes (or in Saussure's more careful phrase, sound-images) are not related by any
known rule; but Carroll is setting up a new rule whereby such potential phonemes
can acquire the status of real ones — in other words, he is creating new words. He
does not defy the legislature of language, but rather admits its authority by getting it
to pass a new law.

Above all, Carroll buttresses his specific coinages by conforming to the standard
English word order and thereby establishing a narrative design. That is why Alice
can readily deduce that '*somebody* killed *something*'. Even if we set out to describe
the activities of Martians, we can only do so in our own language. They may have
special words for activities peculiar to themselves, but we must deploy our own terms
to describe them as best we can. If their syntax involves mental processes we cannot
articulate, we shall willy-nilly reformulate them, as we do when translating out of
another language family. Through the meshes of our verbal perception, we glimpse a
world of different categories. To name them, we must generate new terms shadowing
the identity and function of existing ones, but with a different relation to accustomed
reality. Toves are 'something like badgers [...] something like lizards — and [...]
something like corkscrews',[14] and yet none of these. They are toves.

To describe unfamiliar things, we have no alternative but to redeploy the familiar
resources of language. So, too, we must make up new visual images out of components
that derive, however fragmentarily and obliquely, from known or 'real' forms. In
the passage quoted previously, Leonardo says 'You know that you cannot invent
animals without limbs, each of which, in itself, must resemble those of some other
animal'.[15] But there is a possible path out of this visual confinement: to take the
verbal articulation of the imagined form or structure — the name we give to it (*rath*)
or to its attributes or actions (*mome, outgrabe*) — and stress its pure or 'disembodied'
verbal values. Needless to say, this free, verbally guided conceptualization extends to
actions, events, processes, and attributes as well as to creatures and objects. That is to
say, we need not conjure up imaginary beasts, but can conceive of 'real' ones as being
or doing things they normally are not or do not, or things that we do not normally
conceptualize at all.

This fictive autonomy of word-form is especially prominent in nonsense writing; but ultimately, it reflects the defining and concept-generating process of all language. 'The Imagination,' said Keats, 'may be compared to Adam's dream — he awoke and found it truth.'[16] This may strike us today as a very Foucauldian statement. What we conceive is what we see: the sememe is the ultimate episteme. But if I may be pardoned a riot of jargon, the sememe is sibling to the phoneme, the morpheme and the syntagma. From this cluster of overlapping linguistic functions, it is possible to isolate a combination, seizing on the phatic rather than the referential functions of language (to borrow Jakobson's terms)[17] to signify an autochthonous verbal world.

Think of e. e. cummings's poem:

> anyone lived in a pretty how town
> (with up so floating many bells down)
> spring summer autumn winter
> he sang his didn't he danced his did.

And then, when no one came to love anyone 'more by more',

> when by now and joy by leaf
> she laughed his joy she cried his grief
> bird by snow and stir by still
> anyone's any was all to her.[18]

The poem sticks to orthodox word order and sentence structure. Its unusual quality lies in the unorthodox syntax of particular words, especially their use as new parts of speech: *which* as a descriptive adjective, *didn't* or *did* as substantives, *still* as a substantive in tandem with *stir*, most basically *anyone* and *noone* as specific, virtually proper nouns. We may compare Rabindranath Tagore's elaborate fantasy about a man called simply *se*, 'He': 'a Man built wholly out of words, a Man named after a pronoun [...] That's why I can make up any stories I like around him and no questions asked'.[19] The imaginary man becomes the most universally real and valid man simply because 'He' can stand for anyone at all, embrace all experience — and yet, because he is no one specific or real, also be credited with experiences that no real man can have.

The creations dreamt up by and around this universal Adam include both fantasy of event and fantasy of word. A whole chapter of 'That Man' is devoted to these contrastive fantasies. The poet-narrator himself is credited only with the 'cheap chutney' of inventing fantastic events:[20]

> While keeping goal for Mohan Bagan Club in a football fixture against Calcutta Club, Smritiratna Mashai let in five goals, one after another. Swallowing so many goals didn't spoil his appetite; on the contrary, he grew ravenously hungry. The Ochterloney Monument was near at hand; our goalkeeper started to lick it from the bottom up, all the way to the top. Badaruddin Mian, who was mending shoes in the Senate Hall, rushed up at full speed and cried, 'You're such a learned man, so well versed in the scriptures! How could you defile this huge thing with your licks? Shameful, shameful,' he uttered, spat three times on the Monument, and headed for the office of *The Statesman* newspaper to report the matter.
>
> It suddenly struck Smritiratna Mashai that he had polluted his tongue. He walked across to the watchman at the Museum.

'Pandey Ji,' he said to the watchman, 'you're a brahman, so am I. You must help me'.

Pandey Ji saluted him and said, fingering his beard, '*Comment vous portez-vous, s'il vous plaît?*'

Our scholar pondered for a while and said, 'A very baffling conundrum. I need to look into the books of Sankhya philosophy'.

By contrast, the style favoured by the 'Man built wholly out of words' weaves a story out of invented words and their fantastic *signifiés*:

I was invited to Cardiff for a game of cards.[21] The head of the family there was a gentleman named Kojumachuku. His wife was Mrs Hachiendani Korunkuna. Their elder daughter, Pamkuni Devi by name, cooked with her own hands their celebrated dish, meriunathu of kintinabu, whose aroma wafts across seven districts. Its fragrance is so strong that it tempts even wild jackals to come out during the day and howl [...] and the crows desperately flap their wings for three hours with their beaks stuck in the ground [...] The pudding was victimai of iktikuti.

[Before this could be eaten, it needed to be crushed underfoot by elephants, then licked by the sharp spiky tongues of 'the largest of their beasts, a cross between a man, a cow and a lion which they call gandisangdung' (composite animal again!), and finally pounded with pestle and mortar.]

Many lose their teeth while eating this food, and then they make a gift of their broken teeth to their host. The hosts deposit these teeth in the bank and bequeath them to their children. The more teeth a person collects, the higher is his standing. Many people secretly buy other people's collections and pass them off as their own. This has been a cause of many great lawsuits. Lords of a thousand teeth are so high and mighty that they won't marry their daughters to families with only fifty teeth. A man with no more than fifteen teeth choked to death while eating a ketku sweet, and not a soul could be found in that quarter of the thousand-tooth tycoons who'd agree to take the body to be cremated.

The nonsense words and nonsense names are not superficial or dispensable items. They activate the total fantasy. Even here, nonetheless, what I have called the fantasy of event surpasses the fantasy of words and acquires independent being.

To illustrate the most radical symbiosis of imaginary and real, individual and universal, embodied in the synthesis of the verbal and the substantial, let me continue from where I left off with e. e. cummings, to the most decisive example of all: the language of *Finnegans Wake*.

I shall confine myself to a single two-tier passage. A schoolmaster addresses his pupils, and then reads out to them a story from their reader:

As my explanations here are probably above your understandings, lattlebrattons, though as augmentatively uncomparisoned as Cadwan, Cadwallon and Cadwalloner, I shall revert to a more expletive method which I frequently use when I have to sermo with muddlecrass pupils. Imagine for my purpose that you are a squad of urchins, snifflynosed, goslingnecked, clothyheaded, tangled in your lacings, tingled in your pants, etsitaraw etcicero. And you, Bruno Nowlan, take your tongue out of your inkpot! As none of you knows javanese I will give all my easyfree translation of the old fabulist's parable. Allaboy Minor, take your head out of your satchel! *Audi*, Joe Peters! *Exaudi* facts!

The Mookse and the Gripes.

Gentes and laitymen, fullstoppers and semicolonials, hybreds and lubberds!

> Eins within a space and a wearywide space it wast ere wohned a Mookse. The onesomeness was alltolonely, archunsitslike, broady oval, and a Mookse he would a walking go (My hood! cries Antony Romeo), so one grandsumer evening, after a great morning and his good supper of gammon and spittish, having flabelled his eyes, pilleoled his nostrils, vacticanated his ears and palliumed his throats, he put on his impermeable, seized his impugnable, harped on his crown and stepped out of his immobile *De Ruro Albo* (socolled becauld it was chalkfull of masterplasters and had borgeously letout gardens strown with cascadas, pintacostecas, horthoducts and currycombs) and set off from Ludstown *a spasso* to see how badness was badness in the weirdest of all pensible ways.[22]

It would take a lifetime to trace each coinage, allusion, and echo to its source and work out its combination with the rest, sometimes within the ambit of the same word. The framing schoolroom scene at least retains the contours and components of reality, going beyond it chiefly in the verbally extravagant style of description and address. In the story-lesson, we have moved further into the terrain of self-sustaining verbal fantasy. Following Alice's method, we might say '*Somebody* leaves home and goes *somewhere*, that's clear at any rate'. It may be the start of a quest romance or a picaresque novel. The structures of Aesop and the rhyming nursery-tale hover in the background. Shapes of familiar objects lurk behind the adjectives-turned-nouns ('he put on his impermeable, seized his impugnable'), famous people behind the imaginary names (Bruno No(w)lan: Giordano Bruno came from Nola), and familiar places behind the fantasy sites (Ludstown/London, or the 'chalkfull' *De Ruro Albo* like the white cliffs of Dover). It is a world made out of words, suggesting the familiar world only to the extent that words, word components, and verbal structures cannot disavow a referential function. This world exists in the interspace between the signifier and the signified.

Finnegans Wake opens up the world of the subconscious, which is also the world of myth. This makes it appropriate to end with a notion out of Ernst Cassirer's acutely speculative book, *Language and Myth*.[23] Cassirer posits myth making as a pristine function of language, from which it progresses to rational discourse and factual knowledge. Yet to conceive of these two functions as opposite or inimical is to foster a 'self-dissolution of the spirit'. The remedy lies in seeing in each intellectual form or mode

> a spontaneous law of generation [...] From this point of view, myth, art, language *and science* appear as symbols [...] in the sense of forces each of which produces and posits a world of its own. [...] Thus the special symbolic forms are not imitations, but organs of reality, since it is solely by their agency that anything real becomes an object for intellectual apprehension, and as such is made visible to us. (p. 8; my emphasis)

Cassirer goes further. As science develops — that is to say, as the rational, recording, explicitly referential function of language develops — its myth-making function declines and becomes an isolated, increasingly discredited entity. Henceforth the 'original creative power' of language can be preserved, in fact renewed, only in art by 'a sort of constant palingenesis' (p. 98). We may link up with this (although Cassirer does not do so explicitly) the development of the concept of imagination in the modern sense, as a way of mediating reality through mental perception and, in particular, artistic form.

I have tried to show how, in nonsense literature, the autonomous creative power of language is specially and exclusively stressed. It is no accident that nonsense literature is a creation of the modern world, where myth is marginalized and the autonomous symbolic function of language specially recognized in all spheres of discourse: it *becomes* itself a sphere of discourse as never before.

One can hardly claim for nonsense more than a marginal presence in the corpus of the world's literature. But margins are equally frontiers. Nonsense writing marks some of the profoundest explorations of the conceptual possibilities inherent in the process of language.

Notes to Chapter 14

1. Translation by Sukanta Chaudhuri of a rhyme in Rabindranath Tagore's *Khapchhara* [At Sixes and Sevens], in *Selected Writings for Children* (Delhi: Oxford University Press, 2002). The betel leaf is smeared with quicklime paste before spices are placed on it.
2. 'The Customs of Bombagarh', from *The Select Nonsense of Sukumar Ray*, trans. by Sukanta Chaudhuri (Kolkata: Oxford University Press, 1987), p. 22.
3. 'Pumpkin-Puff', *The Select Nonsense of Sukumar Ray*, p. 10.
4. 'A Topsy-Turvy Tale', *The Select Nonsense of Sukumar Ray*, p. 51.
5. Lewis Carroll, *Alice in Wonderland*, in *The Annotated Alice*, rev. edn, with intro. and notes by Martin Gardner (Harmondsworth: Penguin, 1970), p. 97.
6. *The Select Nonsense of Sukumar Ray*, p. 41.
7. See *The Select Nonsense of Sukumar Ray*, p. 17.
8. *The Literary Works of Leonardo da Vinci*, ed. by Jean Paul Richter, 3rd edn (New York: Phaidon, 1970), I, 342.
9. Lewis Carroll, *Through the Looking-Glass*, in *The Annotated Alice*, rev. edn, with intro. and notes by Martin Gardner (Harmondsworth: Penguin, 1970), p. 223.
10. *The Select Nonsense of Sukumar Ray*, p. 1.
11. Amitabha Chaudhuri, *Ikri Mikri* (Kolkata: Ananda, 1971), p. 22.
12. Carroll, *Through the Looking-Glass*, p. 191.
13. Ferdinand de Saussure, *Course in General Linguistics*, trans. by Wade Buskin, rev. edn (London: Fontana, 1974), p. 50.
14. Carroll, *Through the Looking-Glass*, p. 271.
15. *The Literary Works of Leonardo da Vinci*, I, 342.
16. Letter to Benjamin Bailey, 22 Nov. 1817, in *Letters of John Keats: A New Selection*, ed. by Robert Gittings (London: Oxford University Press, 1970), p. 37.
17. Roman Jakobson, 'Linguistics and Poetics', in *Style in Language*, ed. by Thomas Sebeok (Cambridge, MA: Technology Press of Massachusetts Institute of Technology, 1960); repr. in *Modern Criticism and Theory*, ed. by David Lodge (London: Longman, 1988), pp. 35–38.
18. e. e. cummings, *selected poems 1923–1958* (London: Faber & Faber, 1960; repr. 1972), p. 44.
19. This and the following extracts are from Tagore's *Selected Writings for Children* (see note 1 above). The translations from *Se* [That Man] are by Sukhendu Roy.
20. Smritiratna Mashai is a Hindu pundit learned in Sanskrit, and thus presumably expected to be orthodox. Pandey Ji is also a Hindu brahman, but Badaruddin Mian is a Muslim. The Ochterlony Monument (now called Shahid Minar) is a prominent landmark of Kolkata (Calcutta), as the Senate Hall (now pulled down) of Calcutta University once was. The other references are, I hope, self-explanatory.
21. Needless to say, this pun is possible only in English. In the Bengali, the narrator went to Tashkent for a game of cards (*tas* in Bengali).
22. James Joyce, *Finnegans Wake* (London: Faber & Faber, 1950; repr. 1960), p. 152.
23. Ernst Cassirer, *Language and Myth*, trans. by Susanne K. Langer (New York: Dover, 1953); page references in text.

CHAPTER 15

Le Rire comme accident en peinture

Georges Roque

Pourquoi y a-t-il si peu de représentations du rire en peinture et en sculpture? Telle est la question à laquelle j'aimerais pouvoir apporter quelques éléments de réponse. Je partirai pour ce faire d'un texte de Charles Blanc. Bien oublié de nos jours, Blanc fut sans doute le critique et l'historien d'art le plus influent en France dans la seconde moitié du XIXe siècle. Fondateur de la *Gazette des Beaux-Arts*, directeur à deux reprises de l'Ecole des Beaux-Arts de Paris, académicien et professeur au Collège de France, il exerça une influence déterminante sur nombre d'artistes, et non des moindres, parmi lesquels figurent notamment Van Gogh et Seurat.[1] Son principal livre est la *Grammaire des arts du dessin,* qui connaîtra de nombreuses éditions après sa première publication en 1867. C'est dans cet ouvrage qu'il se livre aux commentaires suivants:

> On a remarqué avant nous qu'il était malséant de prendre le portrait d'un homme riant aux éclats. La raison en est sensible: le rire est accidentel, le fou rire surtout, et s'il peut trouver place dans une composition qui le motive, où il ne remplit pas le tableau tout entier, il nous répugne de voir un accident aussi fugitif caractériser pour toujours une physionomie, et, en s'éternisant sur la toile, nous imposer à jamais sa grimace stéréotypée et invariable. Au contraire, le portrait sérieux d'une femme attristée ou d'un poète mélancolique n'a rien qui nous déplaise, parce que la tristesse est moins passagère dans la vie que l'éclat de rire, et que l'une, plus conforme à l'état permanent de notre âme, nous y ramène doucement et sans efforts, tandis que l'autre nous en tire brusquement et quelquefois avec violence. Est-il rien, d'ailleurs, de plus triste au fond que d'avoir sans cesse présente l'image d'une gaieté folle, imprimée sur le portrait de ceux qui ont vécu, ou qui seront bientôt des ancêtres?[2]

Ce texte est remarquable à plusieurs égards. Il affirme avec force sur un exemple particulier l'idéalisme qui caractérise la profession de foi artistique de Blanc. Or l'un des principaux concepts qui lui servent à articuler sa doctrine est celui d'"accident" utilisé tout à la fois pour qualifier le rire et le condamner. Le terme, emprunté au vocabulaire philosophique, est opposé à celui de substance, ou de propre. Aristote qualifie ainsi la couleur d'accidentelle à l'homme, puisque le fait qu'un homme soit blanc ou noir ne change rien à sa qualité d'homme; la couleur est donc une propriété accidentelle et non substantielle des choses.[3] C'est d'ailleurs en ce sens également que le terme d'accident en est venu à faire partie du vocabulaire artistique, pour qualifier des accidents de lumière, voire la couleur elle-même, dans son opposition au dessin.[4] Ainsi, suivant de Piles, "l'accident en peinture est une interruption qui se fait de la lumière du soleil par l'interposition des nuages, en sorte qu'il y ait des endroits éclairés sur la terre et d'autres ombrés".[5] Par extension, on considère que "la lumière accidentelle est celle qui est accessoire au tableau, et qui s'y trouve par accident, comme la lumière de quelque fenêtre, ou d'un flambeau".[6] Il y a évidemment ici un paradoxe, ou une ironie du sort, à savoir que la catégorie aristotélicienne d'accident soit mobilisée par Blanc pour qualifier le rire, alors que le rire est justement caractérisé, au moins depuis Rabelais, comme une qualité essentielle, et non accidentelle, de l'homme.

En réalité, le paradoxe s'estompe si l'on prend en compte le fait que Blanc ne s'en prend nullement au rire comme tel et souscrivait sûrement à l'idée selon laquelle le rire est le propre de l'homme, lui qui mettait la figure humaine par-dessus tout et considérait que l'homme, en s'élevant par-dessus l'instinct animal, se différenciait ainsi des animaux et venait couronner l'accomplissement de la création, de la beauté et de l'harmonie.[7] Ce n'est donc pas le rire qui est en question, mais sa représentation, ou mieux, sa traduction en peinture. C'est là en effet que réside le problème: en représentant le rire en peinture, on fige pour l'éternité un moment transitoire, passager. Peindre le rire, c'est donner à voir à tout jamais une caractéristique qui n'est pas essentielle à l'être mais précisément accidentelle.[8] "Il nous répugne, écrit Blanc, de voir un accident aussi fugitif caractériser pour toujours une physionomie."

En ce sens, le rire occupe une place importante en apparaissant comme le paradigme des accidents que le peintre se doit non de représenter, mais au contraire d'éliminer. En effet, toute la doctrine dont Blanc se revendique consiste à idéaliser les objets pour n'en retenir que l'essentiel. A ses yeux, comme il l'affirme au début de son ouvrage, l'artiste "purifie la réalité des accidents qui la défiguraient, des alliages qui l'avaient altérée, il en dégage l'or pur de la beauté primitive; il y retrouve l'idéal".[9] Le culte du beau idéal qu'exalte Blanc explique donc le rejet brutal du rire en peinture, sa condamnation ferme et sans appel.[10]

On pourrait cependant objecter qu'une telle condamnation resterait limitée à l'idéalisme néo-classique du XIXe (Ingres était l'un des peintres préférés de Blanc), avec lequel elle cadre d'ailleurs très bien, mais qu'elle n'aurait de ce fait guère de valeur en dehors de cette période. En fait, il n'en est rien, car Blanc n'a en l'occurrence rien inventé. Il s'appuie, comme souvent dans son livre, sur Diderot. Celui-ci notait en effet, dans ses *Essais sur la peinture*, rédigés un siècle avant la publication du livre de Blanc:

> Un portrait peut avoir l'air triste, sombre, mélancolique, serein, parce que ces états sont permanents; mais un portrait qui rit est sans noblesse, sans caractère, souvent même sans vérité et par conséquent une sottise. Le ris est passager. On rit par occasion; mais on n'est pas rieur par état.[11]

Tout était déjà dit: non seulement l'opposition de la tristesse et de la mélancolie au rire, qu'exaltera Blanc, mais aussi et surtout la nature accidentelle du rire, que résume si bien le philosophe des Lumières lorsqu'il souligne le caractère occasionnel, circonstanciel du rire: "[o]n rit par occasion, mais on n'est pas rieur par état".

Diderot affirmait donc déjà de façon percutante la nature accidentelle du rire, que Blanc n'a fait que replacer dans sa théorie idéaliste. Il y a cependant quelque chose de plus dans le texte de Diderot: l'indication suivant laquelle "un portrait qui rit est sans noblesse". Cette affirmation n'implique cependant pas une stricte hiérarchie des passions car, comme le note par ailleurs Diderot, "il y a des boudeuses charmantes et des ris déplaisants".[12] Mais qu'est-ce qui rend un rire déplaisant? Une réponse avait été apportée par Félibien dans son *Sixième Entretien* (1679), en prenant en compte la différence sociale: "A la vue des spectacles, les hommes graves & de qualité s'empêchent mieux de rire que le vulgaire." Cette réflexion donne lieu à une remarque ironique dans la suite du dialogue:

> Selon vous, interrompit Pymanthe en souriant, il y a donc des ris de condition?
> — Assurément, répartis-je: & si vous avez jamais considéré de quelle manière un Paysan exprime sa joye, je m'assure que sa façon de le faire a été capable de vous faire rire vous-même, mais d'une manière différente.[13]

Ceci, cependant, ne disqualifie pas toutes les formes de rire, mais appelle à différencier l'expression des passions suivant les classes sociales, ce que de Piles, entre autres, avait déjà noté: "la joie d'un roi ne doit pas être comme celle d'un valet, et la fierté d'un soldat ne doit pas ressembler à celle d'un capitaine; c'est dans ces différences que consiste le vrai discernement des passions".[14]

Je n'entrerai pas dans la question, largement débattue dans l'esthétique classique,[15] de savoir s'il est préférable pour un peintre d'exprimer les passions du paysan, parce qu'elles seraient plus "vraies" ou s'il faut au contraire les tempérer, ainsi que l'énonçait Watelet dans son *Art de peindre*:

> Ce qui caractérise principalement une Nation civilisée, c'est cette gêne utile que les hommes imposent à la plus grande partie des expressions subites et inconsidérées tant de l'âme que du corps. Ces mouvements libres et naturels troubleraient en effet la société et entraîneraient le blâme: on a donc soin de les modérer.[16]

Pour comprendre ce que veut dire Diderot lorsqu'il estime qu'un portrait qui rit est sans noblesse et sans caractère, il peut être utile de rappeler que pour lui, à la suite, notamment, de l'abbé Du Bos, la peinture a une fonction morale et c'est ce qu'il apprécie chez Greuze, qu'il oppose souvent à Boucher. Dans son *Salon de 1763,* il l'apostrophe ainsi: "Courage, mon ami Greuze ! Fais de la morale en peinture, et fais-en toujours comme cela", c'est-à-dire une peinture qui vise "à nous toucher, à nous instruire, à nous corriger et à nous inviter à la vertu".[17] Or comment faire de la peinture une leçon de morale si l'on représente une passion comme le rire?[18] La tâche paraît bien difficile, voire impossible.

A l'époque classique, il existe en effet une hiérarchie des sujets, implicite ou explicite, en fonction de laquelle sont jugées les œuvres, et dans cette perspective, celles qui réussissent à "élever l'âme", suivant une expression qui revient sous toutes les plumes, sont celles qui montrent un sujet lui-même élevé. D'où le débat qui fera rage entre partisans de la peinture de genre et partisans de la peinture d'histoire, cette dernière étant seule à même, suivant ses défenseurs, de remplir cette fonction d'élever l'âme par la représentation de sujets élevés.[19] Il n'est d'ailleurs pas indifférent pour mon propos que les remarques de Diderot sur la représentation du rire en peinture prennent place à la fin du chapitre des *Essais sur la peinture* précisément consacré à discuter des mérites respectifs de la peinture de genre et de la peinture d'histoire. Or la position de Diderot est à cet égard plus nuancée qu'on ne le dit d'ordinaire. Il a certes pris parti, passionnément même, pour des peintres de genre comme Greuze, mais cela ne signifie pas pour autant qu'il nie la pertinence de la hiérarchie des genres. A ses yeux, en effet, "la division de la peinture en peinture de genre et peinture d'histoire est sensée".[20] Partisan, en effet, d'une peinture morale visant à élever l'âme, Diderot ne pouvait s'inscrire que dans la lignée de ceux qui, de Du Bos à La Font de Saint-Yenne, considéraient la peinture d'histoire comme la seule à même de remplir cette fonction éthique. Aussi ce qu'il défend chez Greuze, ce n'est pas le peintre de genre contre le peintre d'histoire, mais le fait qu'à ses yeux Greuze *est* un peintre d'histoire, étant donné la vertu morale qui se dégage de ses tableaux.[21] Dans le même esprit, le reproche qu'il adresse à la peinture d'histoire est de ne pas être suffisamment élevée.[22]

C'est donc dans ce contexte que s'insère la note sur le rire, présentée comme une remarque concernant les peintres de portrait. Or dans la hiérarchie des genres en peinture, telle que l'a établie Félibien dans sa préface au premier recueil des Conférences de l'Académie, le portrait occupe un lieu intermédiaire entre la peinture de genre (qui ne portait pas encore ce nom) et la peinture d'histoire.[23] Et d'une certaine façon ce partage se retrouve dans la manière dont Diderot présente les différents types de portraits, opposant au rire la mélancolie, sujet "noble" qui a depuis longtemps droit de cité parmi les sujets artistiques, d'autant plus aisément que depuis Aristote, elle a été très souvent assimilée à l'état d'âme par excellence de l'artiste.[24] Diderot fait donc fond sur une opposition entre sujet élevé et bas qui reste cependant implicite car il ne la revendiquerait pas de manière aussi tranchée. Il n'a au reste nul besoin de l'expliciter, puisqu'il joue plus clairement sur l'opposition entre état permanent (tristesse, mélancolie) et accident (le rire).

Si la position de Diderot est nuancée, il n'en va pas de même pour Charles Blanc qui souscrit entièrement, quant à lui, à la hiérarchie établie par Félibien deux siècles plus tôt et s'y réfère explicitement cette fois. A ses yeux, il existe en effet dans l'art du peintre "une hiérarchie fondée sur la signification relative ou absolue, locale ou universelle de ses œuvres".[25] D'où sa critique de la représentation du rire, disqualifié comme accident, par rapport aux valeurs essentielles et universelles que la peinture devrait transmettre. Et, de même que Diderot parlait du rire à propos du portrait, Blanc reviendra à la charge en fustigeant les portraitistes modernes qui "depuis un siècle, ont en ce genre quelquefois enchéri sur leurs devanciers, par le besoin d'exagérer l'exception, d'outrer l'accident, pour exprimer certains types étranges".[26] Le propos, ici encore, cadre parfaitement bien avec la condamnation de la représentation du rire.

Sémiologie des expressions faciales

Il y a donc, entre Diderot et Blanc, une continuité dans le blâme. Ceci, pourtant, ne laisse pas d'étonner. Car, depuis le XVIIe siècle, il existait une tout autre tradition pour laquelle le rire avait pignon sur rue. Dans sa fameuse conférence sur l'expression générale et particulière, Charles Le Brun lui avait donné ses lettres de noblesse en l'incluant au nombre des passions que le peintre se doit de représenter. Il la décrit après la haine, la tristesse, la douleur corporelle et la joie, et avant les pleurs, la colère,

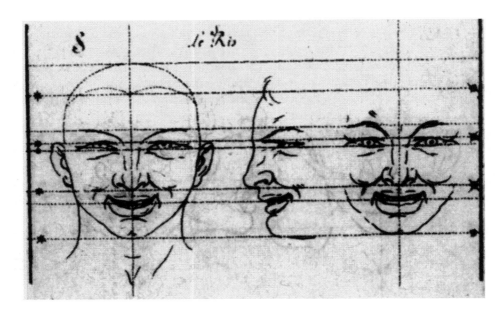

FIG. 1. Charles Le Brun, "Le Ris", dessin, illustration de la conférence
"Sur l'expression des passions", 1668. Photo: Archivo fotográfico Manuel Toussaint,
IIE, Universidad nacional autónoma de México.

l'extrême désespoir et la rage. La description nosographique, ou mieux, sémiologique,
au sens médical, qu'il en donne montre d'ailleurs qu'il n'établit aucune distinction
hiérarchique entre le rire et la tristesse:

> Et si à la joie succède le rire, le mouvement s'exprime par les sourcils élevés
> vers le milieu de l'œil et abaissés du côté du nez, les yeux presque fermés, la
> bouche paraîtra ouverte, et fera voir les dents. Les coins seront tirés en arrière,
> et s'élèveront en haut, ce qui fera faire un pli aux joues qui paraîtront enflées et
> surmonter les yeux, le visage sera rouge, les narines ouvertes, et les yeux peuvent
> paraître mouillés et jeter des larmes, qui étant bien différentes de celles de la
> tristesse, ne changeront rien au mouvement du visage, mais [bien] quand elles sont
> excitées par la douleur.[27]

Aux yeux de Le Brun, mais aussi de Testelin à sa suite, quelques années plus tard, le
rire n'est donc pas moins noble que la tristesse. La position de Le Brun concernant les
passions et leur expression en peinture ne faisait certes pas l'unanimité; dès l'époque,
des voix s'étaient élevées contre l'autorité du Premier Peintre du Roi, notamment
celle de Roger de Piles, se plaignant du fait que le caractère trop codifié des passions
constituait une entrave excessive à la liberté des peintres.[28] Il ne semble cependant pas
que l'on ait critiqué Le Brun pour le statut égal qu'il conférait aux passions.

En effet, la conception du rire comme accidentel repose sur son opposition à
la tristesse: les deux passions évoquent non seulement des valeurs diamétralement

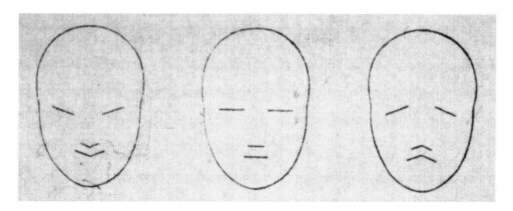

FIG. 2. Schéma des signes esthétiques du visage, Humbert de Superville,
Essai sur les signes inconditionnels dans l'art (La Haye, 1827). Photo de l'auteur.

opposées, mais elles sont en outre associées respectivement à un état passager et permanent. Or pour Le Brun, si le rire et la tristesse sont également opposés, ce n'est plus au sens d'une hiérarchie des valeurs. Pour lui, les passions sont envisagées d'un point de vue sémiologique, comme l'a fait remarquer Hubert Damisch, à qui l'on doit en outre d'avoir attiré l'attention sur les dessins originaux de Le Brun qu'il a, semble-t-il, reproduits pour la première fois.[29] Le Brun, en effet, avait bien noté que dans le rire les traits "s'élèvent", tandis qu'ils "s'abattent" dans le cas de la tristesse, opposition dont témoignent ses remarquables dessins. De plus, le tout premier d'entre eux est la tranquillité; dans la mesure où les horizontales y dominent, on peut le considérer comme le degré zéro des passions.

L'aspect pour ainsi dire structural de cette opposition a été brillamment synthétisé par Humbert de Superville dans son *Essai sur les signes inconditionnels dans l'art* (1827). Dans son fameux schéma, les horizontales du calme, que Le Brun avait mises en tête des passions, servent ici très astucieusement de milieu entre les obliques montantes et descendantes, respectivement associées au rire et aux pleurs. Humbert précise à cet égard que "la *valeur* [est] attachée, non point aux organes de la face comme tels, mais à leurs *directions* comme *signes esthétiques*, c'est-à-dire comme éléments visibles et constants de tout le jeu non convulsif de la physionomie".[30] Cette approche sémiologique des traits élémentaires du visage n'introduit donc en principe aucune hiérarchie de valeur entre rire et pleurs. L'un n'est pas plus noble que l'autre. Aussi le premier exemple que donne Humbert des trois types d'expression faciale est celui de trois déesses grecques, Pallas, associée aux horizontales, Vénus et Junon, liées respectivement aux obliques ascendantes et descendantes, et qui sont les "symboles de la vertu, des plaisirs et des grandeurs".[31]

Or Blanc connaissait bien le texte d'Humbert, auquel il accordait une grande importance. Il est d'ailleurs le premier à avoir attiré l'attention sur ce livre rare, et il a reproduit le fameux schéma des trois visages dès l'introduction de sa *Grammaire des arts du dessin*.[32] D'où la question qui ne manque pas de se poser: si la source de Blanc, Humbert, part d'une approche sémiologique qui ne privilégie pas les pleurs ou la tristesse au détriment du rire, pourquoi donc Blanc a-t-il choisi de disqualifier ce dernier en l'assimilant à un accident? D'une façon générale, je crois avoir déjà répondu en insistant sur la hiérarchie des genres qui primait dans l'esprit de Blanc. De plus, s'il pouvait y avoir contradiction entre l'approche sémiotique de l'opposition entre rire et tristesse et la condamnation du rire comme accident, cette contradiction n'est qu'apparente, car en liant les trois directions (horizontale, lignes ascendantes et descendantes) à des valeurs morales, Humbert fournissait à Blanc les raisons lui permettant de condamner le rire. Les attributs de Vénus, associée aux obliques du rire, sont en effet "les passions vives, le mouvement, l'agitation, l'inconstance et le changement", tandis que les valeurs morales liées aux obliques de la tristesse, et par extension à Junon, sont "la réflexion, la profondeur de la pensée, l'élévation d'âme, la solennité, le sublime".[33] Or ces dernières qualités sont justement celles que Blanc attend de la peinture, et en particulier de la peinture d'histoire, alors que les premières caractérisent fort bien l'accident. Mais il y a plus, car en liant les lignes caractéristiques du rire au mouvement, à l'agitation, à l'inconstance et au changement, Humbert fournissait malgré lui d'autres raisons à Blanc pour récuser la représentation du rire en peinture.

Aspects narratologiques

En effet, je n'ai insisté jusqu'à présent que sur un seul aspect, statique, si l'on peut dire, de la représentation du rire en peinture, l'accident opposé à la substance, ou sa nature contingente face à des caractéristiques essentielles, comme le seraient la tristesse ou la mélancolie. Or le rire en peinture a pu être également disqualifié, comme accident, dans une perspective dynamique, en prenant en compte le mouvement et le changement, car les passions présentent cette caractéristique capitale qu'elles se déploient dans le temps, ce qui constituait pour le peintre une grande difficulté dont l'époque classique était très consciente et dont elle a longuement discuté. On trouve par exemple à l'article "Expression (peinture)" de l'*Encyclopédie* les commentaires suivants:

> Les passions ont des degrés, comme les couleurs ont des nuances; elles naissent, s'accroissent, parviennent à la plus grande force qu'elles puissent avoir, diminuent ensuite et s'évanouissent. Les leviers que ces forces font mouvoir, suivent la progression de ces états différents; et l'artiste qui ne peut représenter qu'un moment d'une passion, doit connaître ces rapports, s'il veut que la vérité fasse le mérite de son imitation.

Diderot aborde lui aussi ce problème difficile du choix du moment à représenter, déjà largement discuté par Du Bos,[34] lorsqu'il observe que "le peintre n'a qu'un instant, et il ne lui est pas plus permis d'embrasser deux instants que deux actions".[35] Cependant il ne lie pas directement ce problème à la question de la représentation du rire. En revanche, ce lien est très clairement posé par Charles Blanc dans le texte qui nous a servi de point de départ et auquel je souhaite à présent revenir. Ce texte, en effet, s'inscrit dans un court chapitre consacré aux "limites" de la peinture. Or l'une des principales limites de la peinture classique est justement celle de ne pouvoir représenter qu'un moment d'une action. Juste avant le passage concernant le rire, Blanc écrivait en effet:

> Réduit à ne présenter qu'une seule action de la vie, et dans cette action qu'un seul moment, le peintre a la faculté de choisir, il est vrai; mais sa faculté n'est pas sans bornes, son choix n'est pas sans restriction. Si les limites du mouvement sont infiniment plus reculées pour la peinture que pour la statuaire, il n'en est pas moins à craindre que les mouvements excessifs, convulsifs, ne soient gênants pour le spectateur dans un spectacle qui doit durer toujours. Il en est de même de certains accidents dont la durée est offensante.

Et Blanc enchaîne avec le début de ma citation de départ: "On a remarqué avant nous qu'il était malséant de prendre le portrait d'un homme riant aux éclats..."[36]

On comprend mieux à présent le caractère doublement accidentel du rire en peinture et en sculpture: synchronique et diachronique. De ce dernier point de vue, il est non seulement difficile de choisir un moment dans la séquence de mouvements et d'actions qui caractérisent le rire, mais ce moment apparaîtra d'autant plus accidentel qu'il est fixé à tout jamais. Blanc insiste beaucoup dans son commentaire sur cet aspect diachronique, ou narratologique, si l'on veut, de l'accident que constitue le portrait du rire, lorsqu'il souligne que sa "durée est offensante" ou qu'il lui "répugne de voir un accident aussi fugitif caractériser pour toujours une physionomie [...] en s'éternisant sur la toile". Ceci nous aide à mieux comprendre pourquoi Blanc, tout en étant fasciné par la sémiologie des traits élémentaires dégagée par Humbert, ne pouvait le suivre dans l'expression fixe et rigide du rire.

Si son ton est à l'évidence exagéré, Blanc n'en met pas moins l'accent sur une difficulté réelle, qui constitue en effet une des "limites" de la peinture, soit la nécessité de rendre par une seule image fixe la séquence d'un mouvement qui a en outre un début, un acmé et une fin. L'oublier peut conduire à de graves erreurs méthodologiques. C'est ainsi que Meyer Schapiro a raconté qu'un de ses collègues de Columbia, Carney Landis, professeur au Département de Psychologie, avait fait une série d'expériences tendant à prouver que les différentes formes d'expression faciale étaient conventionnelles, de sorte qu'il n'y avait aucun sens à prétendre qu'un visage avec "les coins de la bouche élevés et tirés en arrière",[37] comme l'écrivait Testelin, signifierait nécessairement le rire ou même une idée expansive. En présentant une série de photos de différentes expressions faciales et en demandant aux étudiants quel en était le sens, il n'avait eu aucune difficulté à réunir des interprétations si différentes qu'elles jetaient le doute sur l'idée qu'il y aurait des traits expressifs dont la valeur serait immédiatement et universellement reconnaissable. Ses détracteurs ont eu encore moins de difficulté à disqualifier ces expériences, en faisant remarquer que, par exemple, notre expérience du sourire est un changement qui s'opère dans le visage lorsqu'il passe d'un état à un autre, de sorte qu'isoler un moment de cette séquence, c'est nécessairement la déformer et lui enlever un des traits principaux — le changement dynamique qui s'opère dans le visage — qui en permettent la lecture.[38]

Dans les pages qui précèdent, j'ai tenté d'expliquer pourquoi la représentation du rire en peinture et en sculpture est si rare, en particulier dans la peinture académique de l'âge classique: elle est non seulement difficile puisqu'elle doit synthétiser en une image fixe une séquence dynamique d'expressions faciales; elle a en outre été sévèrement critiquée par certains des principaux porte-parole de l'esthétique classique. Il va cependant sans dire que je ne souscris pas aux propos sévères que j'ai rapportés. Aussi aimerais-je terminer en évoquant un remarquable exemple de représentation du rire, non en peinture, mais en sculpture, où il est encore plus rare, car la plupart des bustes étant des commandes, on a eu encore plus tendance, pendant longtemps, à figer dans la pierre une expression solennelle du visage, plutôt que le rire, en conformité avec les canons de l'esthétique classique. Le thème a pourtant intéressé Georges Vantongerloo avant qu'il ne devienne le sculpteur et un des principaux peintres du mouvement hollandais De Stijl. Il réalisera d'abord en 1909 un premier buste d'une jeune fille riant, pas très réussi, au sens où le modèle a plutôt l'air de sourire; c'est du moins ce que l'on aurait tendance à interpréter, sans le titre qui nous indique qu'il s'agit d'une *Fille qui rit*. Le fait que l'accent soit mis sur le portrait d'une personne particulière (Mademoiselle X) explique sans doute pourquoi l'expression du rire reste discrète. En revanche, dans un buste de 1910, *Eclat de rire*, le modèle qui a sans doute servi à l'artiste n'est plus directement reconnaissable.[39] Quelque chose ici a basculé, et sans doute pour toujours. Car la représentation du rire n'apparaît comme accidentelle que tant que l'art a pour but la représentation fidèle du modèle, c'est-à-dire tant que l'accent est mis sur les traits reconnaissables du visage, qui sont les traits permanents, et au regard desquels une expression comme le rire est nécessairement secondaire et passagère. Mais lorsque, avec l'avènement de la modernité, cette finalité de l'art s'estompe, le rire peut alors enfin entrer en scène. Non plus le rire comme caractéristique accidentelle et expression passagère sur le visage d'une personne qui doit rester identifiable,[40] mais le rire comme tel, le rire comme motif et sujet unique de l'œuvre. Et lorsque le rire devient sujet, il n'y a plus ni accident ni essence, ces catégories perdant leur raison d'être. *Eclat de rire* est en ce sens une des plus belles icônes de la modernité, qui se rit du portrait pour montrer, souverain, l'éclat de rire, le rire comme tel, c'est-à-dire le propre de l'homme.

Notes

Je tiens à remercier Ana-Laura Nettel, dont les commentaires m'ont aidé à améliorer une première version de ce texte.

1. Je me permets de renvoyer sur ce point à mon livre *Art et science de la couleur. Chevreul et les peintres, de Delacroix à l'abstraction* (Nîmes: Jacqueline Chambon, 1997), p. 225 sq.
2. Ch. Blanc, *Grammaire des arts du dessin* (1867; Paris: Renouard, 1880), p. 486–87.
3. Aristote, *Métaphysique*, v. 30, 1025a13–20.
4. Sur la catégorie de l'accidentel dans l'art du XIXe siècle, cf. mon article "Lo accidental en el arte occidental del siglo XIX", dans *Arte y violencia. XVIII coloquio internacional de historia del arte* (Mexico: Universidad nacional autónoma de México, 1995), en particulier p. 23 sq.
5. R. de Piles, *Cours de peinture par principes* (1708; Nîmes: Jacqueline Chambon, 1990), p. 104; c'est la définition qui sera reprise dans l'article "Accident, en peinture" de l'Encyclopédie: "On dit des *accidents de lumière*, lorsque les nuages interposés entre le soleil et la terre produisent sur la terre des ombres qui l'obscurcissent par espace; l'effet que produit le soleil sur ces espaces qui en restent éclairés, s'appelle *accident de lumière*".
6. De Piles, p. 169.
7. Cf. par exemple, "La figure humaine est encore l'objet le plus noble de ses études [du peintre],

puisque, les animaux n'ayant que du caractère, l'homme est le seul être capable d'atteindre à la beauté": Blanc, p. 596.

8. On notera que dans une perspective très différente, Bergson assimile lui aussi le rire à l'accident: aux yeux du philosophe, le rire est souvent provoqué par une cause accidentelle (un passant qui tombe dans la rue, par exemple); d'où l'idée suivant laquelle "le comique est donc accidentel": *Le Rire. Essai sur la signification du comique* (Paris: Presses universitaires de France, 1941; édition de 1970), p. 391.

9. Blanc, p. 9.

10. Je n'insisterai pas ici sur les relents théologiques d'une telle conception que Baudelaire, pour sa part, avait bien vus dans son analyse de l'adage "le Sage ne rit qu'en tremblant": "Il est certain, si l'on veut se placer du point de vue de l'esprit orthodoxe, que le rire humain est intimement lié à l'accident d'une chute ancienne, d'une dégradation physique et morale", "De l'essence du rire et généralement du comique dans les arts plastiques", in Ch. Baudelaire, *Œuvres complètes*, éd. par Cl. Pichois, II (Paris: Gallimard, 1976), p. 527–28.

11. D. Diderot, *Essais sur la peinture* [texte rédigé en 1766], Salons de 1759, 1761, 1763 (Paris: Hermann, 1984), p. 68.

12. Diderot, p. 53.

13. Félibien, *Entretiens...* (Paris: Trévoux, 1725), II, 345; cité par R. Démoris, "Le Langage du corps et l'expression des passions de Félibien à Diderot", in *Des mots et des couleurs*, II, éd. J.-P. Guillerm (Lille: Presses universitaires de Lille, 1986), p. 54. On notera que la permanence de cette attitude est remarquable: dans l'édition revue (en 1964) du *Penguin Dictionary of Psychology* de Drever, le rire est encore défini comme "an emotional response, expressive normally of joy, in the child and the unsophisticated adult".

14. De Piles, p. 99.

15. Cf. sur ce point l'étude de Démoris, "Le Langage du corps".

16. C.-H. Watelet, *Art de peindre* (Amsterdam, 1761), p. 137; cité par Démoris, "Le Langage du corps", p. 39.

17. Diderot, p. 234.

18. Dans une perspective très différente de celle abordée ici, R. de Sousa s'est interrogé sur la valeur éthique du rire; cf. le chapitre 11: "When Is It Wrong to Laugh?", de son livre *The Rationality of Emotion* (Cambridge, MA., et Londres: MIT Press, 1987), p. 275–99.

19. Cf. sur ce point R. Démoris, "La Hiérarchie des genres en peinture de Félibien aux Lumières" in *Majeur ou mineur? Les Hiérarchies en art*, éd. par G. Roque (Nîmes: Jacqueline Chambon, 2000), p. 59–60.

20. Diderot, p. 66.

21. Diderot, p. 66–67.

22. Diderot, p. 68.

23. A. Félibien, "Préface aux Conférences de l'Académie royale de peinture et de sculpture pendant l'année 1667" [1668], in *Les Conférences de l'Académie royale de peinture et de sculpture au XVIIᵉ siècle*, éd. par A. Mérot (Paris: Ecole nationale supérieure des beaux-arts, 1996), p. 50. Sur le portrait dans la hiérarchie des genres, cf. R. Wrigley, *The Origins of French Art Criticism from the Ancien Regime to the Restoration* (Oxford: Clarendon Press, 1993), p. 301–05.

24. Cf. R. et M. Wittkower, *Les Enfants de Saturne: psychologie et comportement des artistes de l'Antiquité à la Révolution française*, trad. de D. Arasse. (Paris: Macula, 1985), p. 128.

25. Blanc, p. 595.

26. Blanc, p. 611.

27. Ch. Le Brun, "Sur l'expression des passions" [1668], in *Les Conférences de l'Académie royale de peinture*, p. 160.

28. "Une même passion peut être exprimée de plusieurs façons toutes belles et qui feront plus ou moins de plaisir à voir, selon le plus ou moins d'esprit des peintres qui les ont exprimées et des spectateurs qui les sentent": de Piles, p. 95.

29. Ch. Le Brun, "Conférence sur l'expression des passions", suivie de H. Damisch, "L'alphabet des masques", *Nouvelle revue de psychanalyse*, 21: *La passion* (printemps 1980), p. 93–131.

30. D. P. G. Humbert de Superville, *Essai sur les signes inconditionnels dans l'art* (Leyde: C. C. van der Hoek, 1827), p. 7; souligné par lui.

31. Humbert de Superville, *Essai sur les signes inconditionnels dans l'art*.

32. Blanc, p. 33.

33. Humbert de Superville, p. 7. Plus loin dans le texte (p. 61), il creusera encore l'écart en associant une bacchante aux lignes montantes, et … une Madeleine pénitente aux lignes descendantes.

34. Cf. Abbé Du Bos, *Réflexions critiques sur la poésie et sur la peinture* (1719; Paris: Ecole nationale supérieure des beaux-arts, 1993), p. 28 sq.

35. Diderot, p. 54.

36. Blanc, p. 486.

37. H. Testelin, "Sur l'expression générale et particulière" [1675], in *Les Conférences de l'Académie royale de peinture*, p. 322 (voir n. 23, *supra*).

38. Cf. M. Schapiro, "Color as Expressive", in *Meyer Schapiro: His Painting, Drawing and Sculpture* (New York: H. N. Abrams, 2000), p. 28.

39. Ces deux bustes ont été reproduits dans les planches qui figurent à la fin du livre théorique que Georges Vantongerloo a publié sous le titre *L'Art et son avenir* (Anvers: De Sikkel, 1924).

40. Il est intéressant de noter à ce sujet que l'étude des techniques de reconnaissance automatique des formes par ordinateur a conduit au concept de "propriété non accidentelle" pour qualifier les aspects d'un objet qui restent relativement constants et facilitent donc sa reconnaissance; cf. S. M. Kosslyn, *Image and Brain: The Resolution of the Imagery Debate* (Cambridge, MA, et Londres: MIT Press, 1994), p. 108 sq.

CHAPTER 16

La Couleur du rire: peinture et traduction

Laurent Bazin

La peinture n'est pas faite pour rire
BERNARD BUFFET

Y'a pas que la rigolade, y'a l'art
RAYMOND QUENEAU

Si le sourire en peinture a depuis longtemps conquis ses titres de noblesse (jusqu'à valoir universalité sinon immortalité au plus célèbre d'entre eux), le rire en comparaison fait figure de parent pauvre sinon d'exception. A cette absence qui pose problème — serait-ce que l'art, modalité privilégiée d'expression de l'humain, peut se passer de ce qui passe pour le propre de l'homme? — on pourra sans doute trouver des raisons, au gré de l'histoire des formes et des idées. Il en est une, plus structurelle, qui est la raison d'être du traducteur en ce qu'elle met en scène le paradoxe de la transposition: comment visualiser du sonore, comment rendre de la temporalité avec de l'espace? D'aucuns pourtant s'y sont essayés, quitte à risquer cet impossible pari visant à projeter du bruit sur la toile et à faire de durée couleur (après tout on rit bien jaune). La tentation est grande alors de relever à son tour le gant: peut-on, en retour, dresser l'histoire d'un tel pari?

C'est à tenter semblable gageure qu'on s'attachera ici, à deux réserves près qui permettront de fixer les limites de l'exercice. En termes d'objectif, d'abord, puisqu'il ne s'agira pas de parler de la couleur, *stricto sensu*, du rire. On aura pu bien sûr se divertir à identifier, outre l'inévitable rire jaune, un rire pourpre (mais dans les *Voyelles* de Rimbaud), un rire rouge (soit le nom de guerre pris par le journal satirique *Le Rire*) et un bien intrigant *Rire bleu* du nom d'une galerie française d'art contemporain; mais c'est dans un sens un peu différent qu'on se risquera ici à évoquer du rire la *couleur*, c'est-à-dire l'aspect ou la spécificité — bref son idiosyncrasie. En termes d'objet, ensuite, dans la mesure où l'on privilégiera une approche générique: nous dirons "du rire", bien conscient qu'eu égard à l'histoire des mentalités on aurait pu tout autant parler des rires. Du rire inextinguible de la civilisation hellénistique à l'apocalypse joyeuse du tournant du siècle en passant par le rire carnavalesque ou les éclats du siècle des lumières, innombrables sont ainsi les études à avoir mis en évidence, avec toujours plus de finesse analytique, la place particulière du rire pour un temps et un espace donnés.[1]

Notre perspective sera plus cavalière — mais c'est bien le moins en peinture. Elle procède d'un choix délibéré, privilégiant une perspective an-historique en forme de promenade à travers les œuvres. C'est donc un parcours placé sous le signe de l'analogie qu'on revendiquera ici: parcours certes conscient des propriétés de l'Histoire ou de l'histoire de l'art, mais s'efforçant de dépasser la spécificité des genres et la diversité des époques. Bref il s'agira de chercher des constantes, thématiques et structurelles, pour tenter de lire, par delà la variation des contextes, les modalités d'une même aventure.

Or il n'est pas indifférent, bien au contraire, que cette aventure se caractérise par sa singularité, au point de faire souvent figure d'anomalie. Difficile bien sûr de quantifier ce déficit, mais un regard même rapide sur l'histoire de la peinture (on se bornera à la peinture occidentale du Moyen-Age à nos jours) mettrait vite en évidence une indéniable rareté des occurrences qui fait du rire le parent pauvre des postures physionomiques. Les raisons en sont diverses (religieuses, morales, psychologiques...) et les lectures plus multiples encore au gré des approches choisies (anthropologie, esthétique, psychanalyse...); il en est une, structurelle sinon structurale, qu'on retiendra ici pour la relation analogique privilégiée qu'elle entretient avec l'activité de traduction. La représentation du rire se heurte en effet à une difficulté fondamentale qui frappe toute tentative en ce sens d'une carence décisive: pour qu'il y ait rire il faut qu'il y ait bruit et durée; or à l'espace plan de la toile il manque, entre autres, ces deux dimensions que sont profondeur sonore et profondeur temporelle. Est-ce à dire que rire et peinture sont par nature irréductibles? Bernard Buffet prétendait pour sa part que "*la peinture n'est pas faite pour rire*"; peut-être faut-il entendre par là qu'elle n'est pas faite pour *le* rire.

Il se trouve que cette problématique, plus formelle que thématique, est la raison d'être du traducteur confronté à la tâche délicate de passer d'un code à l'autre: l'acte de peindre, tout autant que le travail de traduction, exigent la mise en place d'un principe de translation. L'un comme l'autre sont des modalités de la transposition; dans les deux cas il s'agit de dépasser la barrières des codes en s'efforçant de projeter, dans un autre langage, le contenu du premier. En ce sens on peut légitimement arguer, et pas seulement de façon analogique, que la peinture partage avec la traduction la même problématique première: peut-on *prolonger* le visible, ou le lisible, sachant qu'on n'a aucune garantie de continuité entre les plans et qu'on dispose en tout et pour tout de l'attirail des formes?

Et donc en traduction comme en peinture, tous les coups seront permis: atténuation, surenchère, du moment que perdure le sens de l'original. En peinture cela prendra la forme de procédés divers, qui sont moins des subterfuges que des *figures* — au sens rhétorique du terme — chargées de lever l'ambiguïté de la figuration: l'opposition (la complexité d'un visage tenant à la fois du rire, de la grimace et du grincement de dents est précisée par sa confrontation avec des attitudes distinctes: larmes, sourire, etc.),[2] la gradation (avec la multiplication de postures qui finissent par se nuancer l'une par l'autre par proximité)[3] ou encore l'explicitation (une attitude qui paraît tenir du sourire est élevée au rang de rire par le titre à valeur performative).[4]

On remarque avec ce dernier exemple qu'à la limite n'importe quel élément est susceptible de représenter le rire du moment que telle est la volonté de l'artiste. Contraint dans son appréhension du tableau, le spectateur se voit imposer un code de lecture au titre des pouvoirs du langage: dire, c'est rire. En poussant la logique à fond, on obtiendrait telle composition de Magritte[5] où une forme vide entre en figuration par le biais de l'inscription qui s'y superpose (*"Personnage éclatant de rire"*). D'où un premier constat: le rire en peinture, plus sans doute que les autres traits physionomiques, rappelle ce qui en lui procède du signe, au sens linguistique du terme. Signifiant au signifié flottant, sa valeur est une valence dépendant de sa *contextualisation* (au double sens paradigmatique et syntaxique). On se laissera plus volontiers abuser par le sourire, enclin soi-même à prolonger dans son propre sourire de spectateur la connivence d'une illusion partagée; bien moins par le rire qui dérange sinon inquiète, et ce d'autant plus qu'il déjoue la trop facile complicité des regards. On en voudra pour preuve telle composition de Bacon, dont les *Trois études pour des figures au pied d'une crucifixion*[6] reprennent le dispositif de Bosch en détachant chaque figure de tout contexte; il en résulte une ambiguïté profonde de la représentation qui n'est pas sans rejaillir sur le climat de l'œuvre: ça rit, ou ça crie?

Ainsi l'entreprise n'est pas sans risque, puisqu'en quittant le confort de la ressemblance on bascule dans l'incertitude de la composition, où le *sens* peut changer de direction au gré des interactions entre les éléments en jeu. Peindre le rire, ce n'est pas seulement quitter la sécurité de la mimesis pour entrer dans l'ambivalence de la semiosis; c'est encore et simultanément renoncer à la transparence de la motivation pour l'opacité de l'arbitraire. Au fond peindre le rire est délicat, difficile sinon dangereux, et tenter l'aventure n'est pas innocent; bien au contraire, il s'agit d'un moment décisif qui engage l'acte même de peindre, dans ses orientations comme dans ses prérequis.

Quel sens faudra-t-il alors donner à une représentation plus complexe qu'il n'y paraissait de prime abord? On s'arrêtera, pour ce faire, sur quelques occurrences privilégiées pour le degré de lucidité dont elles semblent faire preuve, à commencer par un premier exemple emprunté à Vermeer, *Chez l'entremetteuse*.[7] Le rire, ici, participe de la scène qu'il semble légitimer, à la façon d'un signe de connivence cautionnant le spectacle de la débauche jusqu'à porter un toast au triomphe des sens. On voit pourtant que la composition complexifie la thématique, puisque le personnage qui rit occupe un statut paradoxal: sur le côté, à la fois valorisé par le fond lumineux sur lequel il s'enlève et détaché du groupe par une ligne d'angle qui semble le repousser aux marges du tableau. Cette position ambiguë — à la fois dedans et dehors — se retrouve exacerbée dans le regard qui semble dirigé vers un hypothétique témoin hors champ sinon hors cadre, et qui ce faisant frappe soudain le reste de la scène d'un soupçon de faux-semblant. Les choses s'aggravent dès lors qu'on prend garde que le rieur est un autoportrait; et que le groupe montré renvoie à un tableau de Dirck van Baburen,[8] qui représente un groupe similaire mais cette fois sans témoin. Possédé par la belle-mère de l'artiste, le tableau est bien connu du peintre qui n'hésite d'ailleurs pas à le reproduire dans deux de ses propres œuvres.[9] Dès lors l'ensemble s'éclaire de profondeurs nouvelles, puisque dans cette conflagration des niveaux qui bouleverse l'ordonnancement de la mimesis tout se passe comme si l'artiste lui-même prenait directement à témoin le spectateur de l'ambiguïté profonde de la scène représentée. Vous croyiez que j'étais en train de vous montrer le monde? En aucune façon, ceci n'était jamais qu'un tableau, pire encore, une citation de tableau. Cette leçon vaut bien que j'en rie, sans doute: moins un rire franc toutefois qu'un rire grinçant, entre ironie et désillusion; peut-être après tout un rire *jaune*, de distanciation bien plus que de complicité.

On voit ainsi que le tableau de Vermeer ne s'inscrit pas seulement dans une tradition de peinture flamande d'autant plus complaisante à l'égard des scènes d'hilarité que trouve à s'y exercer le mécanisme de compensation symbolique évoqué par Bakhtine. Il correspond aussi au moment où la fonction carnavalesque du rire se double d'une valeur conceptiste voire conceptuelle où la farce ne se contente plus de rire du monde mais aussi d'elle-même — quitte à faire les frais de sa propre lucidité. En somme le risque inhérent à toute représentation du rire est, sinon conscientisé, du moins exposé sur la toile; et cette exposition, qui tout à la fois sanctionne et sanctifie, prend alors la forme d'une composition aux allures de mise en scène: de l'ambivalence du monde, bien sûr, mais plus encore et surtout de l'ambiguïté de la représentation. De façon générale on dira que la représentation du rire peut bien prendre ici et là des allures de méditation (sur la complexité du monde, le comique des êtres, la vanité des choses), sa dimension métaphysique se double d'une interrogation d'ordre esthétique qui porte sur le statut même de la figuration. L'œuvre ne renvoie plus au monde mais au monde des œuvres; et rire devient synonyme de réfléchir, si par là on entend la dimension spéculative tout autant que spéculaire du processus.

Rien d'étonnant alors que le rire en peinture prenne volontiers la forme de l'auto-portrait dont il cristallise les mises en question. Ainsi dans tel tableau de Rembrandt au titre explicite (*Rembrandt et Saskia dans la scène du fils prodigue*);[10] en choisissant de se peindre en flagrant délit de citation l'artiste s'expose sans vergogne dans une posture résolument dialectique: montreur montré, figurant figuré, interprète interprété. Dans ce jeu de dupes où le clin d'œil tourne à l'auto-dérision, c'est au fond la foi dans une hypothétique transparence des signes qui se perd. Dès lors la peinture du rire n'est pas seulement une *représentation* au sens théâtral du terme, c'est-à-dire une mise en scène chargée d'interpeller le spectateur; c'est aussi une *exposition* au sens rhétorique, autrement dit une mise en évidence (sinon une mise en abyme) où le peintre énonce ses stratégies au risque de les désamorcer. Bref et pour le dire plus crûment au gré d'un chiasme attendu: représenter le rire, c'est rire de la représentation.

Les exemples en sont multiples, qui prennent des modalités diverses non sans les plus pervers raffinements: ainsi chez Aert de Gelder[11] qui transpose dans le cadre de son atelier le mythe de Zeuxis (lequel, à la fin de sa vie, se serait mis à rire au moment où, lancé dans le portrait d'une vieille femme, il aurait compris la vanité de son art) et, ce faisant, propose une mise en abyme particulièrement retorse puisque le mythe transposé est lui-même un mythe de l'échec de la transposition. Mais l'on aurait pu pareillement penser aux œuvres de Judith Leyster,[12] qui pastiche le tableau de Aert de Gelder avec une double inversion du dispositif (une femme au lieu d'un homme, le rire sur la toile et non plus chez le modèle); ou encore de Picasso, dans l'une ou l'autre de ses séries sur la peinture à mi-chemin de la citation et de la parodie (on pense à ce *Peintre et son modèle*,[13] lui aussi démarqué de l'œuvre de Aert de Gelder mais avec extériorisation du rire sur une figure extérieure, ou à telle variation des

Ménines[14] où le rire est dissimulé dans le petit miroir en lieu et place des figures royales attendues).

On s'arrêtera enfin sur un autoportrait de Böcklin,[15] au dispositif doublement inquiétant: d'une part parce que l'invisible modèle se confond avec la position du spectateur; d'autre part parce que la figure chargée de cristalliser le rire est la non-figure par excellence, à savoir la Mort. Les deux motifs ne sont pas liés pour rien, bien au contraire: le crâne, comme chacun sait, est rieur presque par définition, par une sorte de raccourci morbide qui rappelle à l'homme sa condition; et de même que le sourire est un sous-rire, c'est-à-dire un rire en puissance, de même le rire n'est-il lui-même à son tour qu'un seuil ouvert sur sa négation. On peut mourir de rire, rappellent non sans cynisme le tableau de Böcklin ou les masques de Ensor — à condition toutefois de ne pas s'arrêter à la portée morale de ce *Memento mori*.

Il semble en effet que la référence à la mort soit moins thématique que structurelle, et doive se lire ici encore dans la relation dialectique qu'elle entretient avec les fondements même de l'acte de représenter. De fait le rire a ceci de commun avec la mort que, comme elle, il ne se laisse pas si aisément transposer; d'où la nécessité de substituer au principe de ressemblance un principe de projection, celui-là même que les géographes utilisent pour contourner les résistances du réel à se laisser reproduire. Remarquons que dans cette perspective le projet de traduire (les mots tout autant que les choses) est moins une création qu'une projection, dont le rire sera alors comme une cristallisation au second degré. C'est ce que rappellent, chacun à leur façon, Velasquez[16] (chez qui le rire porte moins sur le monde, lieu de dérision, que sur le globe, lieu de déformation) et Vermeer[17] (puisque le même principe de projection construit le rire de la jeune fille et la carte de géographie juste au dessus d'elle). Dans les deux cas on assiste à un insoupçonné glissement des niveaux: du rire comme métaphysique au rire comme métalangage.

Traduire le rire en peinture, ce sera donc d'une certaine façon tenter de dire l'indicible ou de penser l'impensable, en pariant contre la déformation du sens au nom du postulat de traductibilité — mais avec la prise de conscience simultanée que l'entreprise pourrait bien n'être qu'un leurre: après tout qui dit projeter dit aussi déformer. Par quoi le rire en peinture tient un rôle identique à celui du crâne dans les Vanités, à commencer par le tableau des *Ambassadeurs* de Holbein où l'on peut légitimement penser qu'il se dissimule au terme de l'exégèse. C'était déjà au fond la leçon du tableau de Böcklin: d'une part parce qu'il est puissamment surdéterminé autour de deux séries symboliques opposées (l'artiste et la Mort); d'autre part parce que, portant sur la question de la traduction (peut-on transcrire le visible, peut-on transposer l'invisible), il élève à un degré supérieur cette interrogation en *exposant* l'ambiguïté de la figuration — entre création et destruction, sens et absence. Le rire fonctionne alors très exactement comme une anamorphose à qui le lient d'insoupçonnables affinités: une projection du regard qui distend la perception aux dimensions de la réflexion et, ce faisant, révèle subrepticement la *vanité* de tout projet de traduction.

Le phénomène est plus sensible encore dans l'œuvre de Bacon où la représentation du rire, jamais immédiate, paraît sanctionner le risque extrême qu'encourt toute représentation. Car chez Bacon aussi on peut mourir de rire, quitte à passer par toutes les étapes de la dégradation: du sérieux au sourire, du rire au cri, et ainsi de suite jusqu'à la déliquescence. C'est que le rire montre et déforme simultanément; dès lors les grimaces du sujet riant seront-elles autant de fissures où se brise le bel ordonnancement de l'œuvre et par où s'engouffre le désordre du monde. Aux masques ricanants de Ensor, figurants en attente de contenus, Bacon oppose, ou superpose, des signes *décomposés* — signifiants de la disparition des signifiés. On touche ici aux limites mêmes de la représentation: quelque part à l'intersection de la figuration et de la défiguration, de la composition et de la décomposition.

Ainsi le rire, comme la mort, tendent à la peinture le miroir de ce qui lui résiste, en lui rappelant le principe de déformation qui sous-tend toute transposition. Miroirs déformants, reflets irréfléchis, c'est toute la belle assurance de la vision qui se délite dans ce qui prend les allures d'un authentique *travail du négatif,* y compris au sens photographique du terme. C'est le cas par exemple chez Picasso, avec une *Femme au miroir*[18] dont le rire est trahi par un reflet des plus infidèles ou encore telle *Composition avec tête de mort*[19] (mais cette fois c'est le crâne qui se dédouble à travers le rire de l'étrange figure dans un cadre qui tient à la fois du miroir et du tableau). Le phénomène n'est pas moins explicite chez Goya, dont l'*Enterrement de la sardine*[20] est très exactement construit sur le mode d'un négatif photographique: dans son sujet (une fête populaire aux allures de danse macabre) comme dans sa forme (avec le dédoublement de la figure de la Mort défigurée en reflet inversé, blanc pour noir et noir pour blanc, sur une toile en abyme du tableau tout entier).

C'est peut-être là d'ailleurs qu'on pourrait trouver cette très hypothétique couleur du rire annoncée: la couleur du rire, c'est l'absence de couleur, ou plus exactement les non couleurs que sont le noir et le blanc. Blanc du spectre et noir de la mort, sans doute; mais aussi blanc de la toile ou du papier, noir du pinceau ou de l'encre. A la limite on pourrait soutenir que décrire le rire, c'est écrire, si tant est qu'il suffit de quelques traits sur une surface vierge pour tout à la fois dire le rire et le dédire. C'est en tout cas la leçon du tableau de Magritte déjà évoqué où la peinture se voit ramenée non sans sarcasme aux fondamentaux de Maurice Denis: "Se rappeler qu'un tableau, avant d'être un cheval de bataille, une femme nue ou une quelconque anecdote, est essentiellement une surface plane recouverte de couleurs en un certain ordre assemblées".[21]

J'écris, donc je ris; et je ris, précisément, du bon tour que je suis en train de jouer à tous ceux qui attendaient une armoire, un oiseau "ou une quelconque anecdote". C'est qu'ici le *Miroir vivant,* titre du tableau de Magritte, est de ceux dont Cocteau disait qu'ils "feraient bien de réfléchir avant de nous renvoyer notre image": de réflexion en déflexion, de rires en cris ou d'au-delà (l'horizon) en ici-bas (l'armoire), la figure finit par se perdre et la figuration avec. Ceci n'est pas un rire, ni même un personnage éclatant de rire; tout juste la preuve par l'absurde de l'erreur de la pensée identifiant bon gré mal gré les mots et les choses.

L'argument n'est pas de trop: Dieu — l'horizon de toute œuvre — sait combien nous sacrifions à la tentation de ce leurre. Car nous communions tous bon gré mal gré dans cette illusion qui nous conduit à hypostasier les analogies entre les plans: du réel aux représentations mentales, elles-mêmes dédoublées dans l'image et/ou redoublée dans l'écrit. C'est que nous croyons aux miroirs, et plus encore à ce qui se trouve de l'autre côté; nous n'avons jamais complètement renoncé au pays des merveilles ni à transfigurer la réalité.

Ira-t-on jusqu'à avancer que l'activité du traducteur se nourrit d'une similaire espérance à laquelle il ne saurait jamais vraiment se soustraire? A l'origine de tout projet de traduction il semble bien qu'on retrouve l'horizon biblique et le pari de transparence: derrière chaque forme un sens, derrière le sens une essence, et c'est ce postulat de continuité qui garantit la traductibilité (des œuvres, du sujet, du monde). Traduire, à cette aune, participe du projet divin; de même que l'artiste, pour sa part, émarge à l'entreprise de création.

A l'inverse le rire n'est pas pour rien le propre de l'homme, lui qui rappelle précisément à l'homme qu'il est humain, trop humain, rien qu'humain. Le rire correspond au moment où les points de vue ne coïncident plus et où les perspectives se renversent: le créateur n'est jamais qu'un faiseur. Et si rire c'est installer une distance décisive (entre les mots et les choses, entre le sujet et le monde, entre soi et soi), traduire le rire revient à approfondir cette distance; spéculer, en la réfléchissant, sur la menace qui guette toute entreprise prétendant remonter par delà la différence des codes jusqu'à un hypothétique Sens premier. Ainsi le rire appartient-il de droit au monde d'après-Babel dont il cristallise la dispersion: des éclats de rire pour des éclats de langage.

Confirmée désormais l'hypothèse initiale; la représentation du rire en peinture a partie liée avec la question même de la traduction dont elle met en scène, par delà le domaine réservé des beaux-arts, quelques paradoxes constitutifs: dialectiques de la lettre et de l'esprit, de la forme et de la signification, de l'identité et de l'altérité — bref de la translation et de la trahison. Sans doute est-ce cette dichotomie constitutive qui fait la richesse de ce qui pourra passer non sans raison pour un signe, et même un signe de signe. Il est d'autres dispositifs qui, dans l'histoire des formes picturales, auront su cristalliser à leur façon les paradoxes de la représentation (le miroir, le tableau abymé, le nuage, la flamme d'une chandelle...); aucun pourtant dont la leçon ne soit un tel concentré d'ironie lucide et de tension larvée. En peinture comme en traduction le rire fait figure de *révélateur*, plus que de révélation: un instant éminemment clivé où le sujet tout à la fois se libère et s'aliène; un lieu de liesse et de schize qui jubile des pouvoirs de la représentation et dénonce la transparence des signes. On choisira de s'arrêter sur le constat de cette tension irréductible, à mi-chemin du mystère et de la mystification; comme aurait dit Wittgenstein, "ce dont on ne peut parler il faut le taire".[22] Quant à ce qu'on ne peut traduire, le dernier mot reste à l'artiste: *il faut en rire*.[23]

Notes

1. Cf. par exemple et entre autres: Antoine de Baecque, *Les Eclats du rire. La culture des rieurs au XVIIIe siècle* (Paris: Calmann-Lévy, 2000); Dominique Bertrand, *Dire le rire à l'âge classique* (Aix-en-Provence: Publications de l'Université de Provence, 1995); *Le Rire au Moyen-Age dans la littérature et les arts*, éd. par Thérèse Bouché et Hélène Charpentier (Bordeaux: Presses universitaires, 1990); Georges Minois, *Histoire du rire et de la dérision* (Paris: Fayard, 2000); ou encore *Le Rire des anciens*, éd. par Monique Trédé (Paris: Presses de l'Ecole normale supérieure, 1998).

2. Georges de La Tour, *Rixe de musiciens*, vers 1620, huile sur toile, 85,7 × 141 cm, Paul Getty Museum, Malibu.

3. Hieronymus Bosch, *Le Portement de croix avec Sainte-Véronique*, vers 1515, huile sur bois, 76,5 × 83,5 cm, Musée des beaux-arts, Gand.

4. Frans Hals, *Cavalier riant*, 1624, huile sur toile, 86 × 69 cm, Wallace Collection, Londres.

5. René Magritte, *Le Miroir vivant*, 1928, huile sur toile, 54 × 73 cm, collection particulière.

6. Francis Bacon, *Trois études pour des figures au pied d'une crucifixion*, 1944, huile et pastel sur panneau, 3 panneaux 145 × 128 cm, Tate Gallery, Londres.

7. Jan Vermeer, *Chez l'entremetteuse*, 1656, huile sur toile, 143 × 130 cm, Gemäldegalerie Alte Meister, Dresden.

8. Dirck van Baburen, *L'entremetteuse*, 1622, huile sur toile, 101,5 × 107,6 cm, Museum of Fine Arts, Boston.

9. Vermeer, *La Jeune Fille au virginal*, vers 1674–75, huile sur toile, 51,5 × 45,5 cm, National Gallery, Londres; et *Le Concert*, vers 1664, huile sur toile, 69,2 × 62,8 cm, Isabella Stewart Gardner Museum, Boston.

10. Rembrandt, *Rembrandt et Saskia dans la scène du fils prodigue*, vers 1635, huile sur toile, 161 × 131 cm, Gemäldegalerie, Dresden.

11. Aert de Gelder, *Autoportrait du peintre à son chevalet*, 1685, huile sur toile, Städelsches Kunstinstitut, Frankfurt.

12. Judith Leyster, *Autoportrait*, vers 1635, huile sur toile, 72,3 × 65,3 cm, National Gallery of Art, Washington.

13. Pablo Picasso, *Le Peintre et son modèle*, 1963, huile sur toile, 89 × 116,5 cm, Hakone Museum, Japon.

14. Picasso, *Les Ménines, d'après Velasquez*, 1957, huile sur toile, 194 × 260 cm, Musée Picasso, Barcelone.

15. Arnold Böcklin, *Autoportrait avec la Mort jouant du violon*, 1872, huile sur toile, Preussischer Kulturbesitz, Berlin.

16. Diego Velasquez, *Démocrite*, 1628, huile sur toile, Musée des beaux-arts, Rouen.

17. Vermeer, *Cavalier et jeune fille riant*, vers 1655, huile sur toile, 50,5 × 46 cm, Frick Collection, New York.

18. Picasso, *Femme au miroir*, 1929, huile sur toile, 71 × 60,5 cm, Collection particulière.

19. Picasso, *Nature morte avec crâne*, 1907, huile sur toile, 116 × 89 cm, Ermitage, Leningrad.

20. Francisco José de Goya, *Enterrement de la sardine*, 1816, huile sur toile, 82,5 × 62 cm, Académie Royale de San Fernando, Madrid.

21. Maurice Denis, "Définition du Néo-traditionnisme", *Art et critique* (août 1890; repris dans son livre *Théories, 1890–1910*, Paris: Bibliothèque de l'Occident, 1912, pp. 1–13 [p. 1]).

22. Ludwig Wittgenstein, *Tractatus logico-philosophicus* (1921); tr. par Pierre Klossowski (Paris: Gallimard, 1961).

23. Ben [Benjamin Vautier], *Il faut en rire*, in "*Nice carnaval, roi du rire*", s. d., gravure, 78 × 58 cm, signée, numéro 162/350, n° d'inventaire 580, Collection particulière.

CHAPTER 17

Views on the Physics and Metaphysics of Laughter

Gérard Toulouse

My own scientific background has been in physics, with interests in biology and cognition studies, and latterly in the ethics of science. Obviously the choice of issues raised in this paper is influenced by my professional experience. But I prefer to relinquish any claim to disciplinary expertise at the outset, in exchange for a permit for free navigation. Despite the daunting immensity of past literature, personal experience seems to entitle any newcomer to compose poems about love, or to submit reports about laughter.

Laughter and smiling (rire et sous-rire)

A comparison of two contrasting dictionary definitions of 'laugh' and 'smile' helps to point up their specific attributes:

> Laugh: To manifest the spasmodic utterance, facial distortion, shaking of the sides, etc., which form the instinctive expression of mirth, amusement, sense of the ludicrous, scorn, etc.

> Smile: To give to the features or face a look expressive of pleasure or amusement, or of amused disdain, scorn, incredulity, etc. (the characteristic features are a brightening of the eyes and an upward curving of the corners of the mouth).[1]

The act of laughter is a type of *behaviour*, the manifest bodily expression of an *emotion*, whose private, conscious component is a *feeling*. In its full generality, including causes and effects, laughter appears as a complex phenomenon with individual and social dimensions, and a wide diversity of potential inducer stimuli (from tickling, or laughing drugs, to higher reaches of humour, *cognition*, and creativity).

From smile to laugh there is continuity and a sort of phase transition: a smile is seen, but laughter is both seen and heard. As a noisy act, laughter belongs to a large class of instinctive types of behaviour, with which it shares similarities in one or more aspects: sneezing, coughing, yawning, hiccupping, screaming, speaking, stammering, singing, etc. In mammal child-rearing, laughing/smiling and crying are the two basic modes of expression, indicating contentment and discontent respectively.

Laughter pervades the world of entertainment (obviously) and many of the arts (laughter has inspired music, smiling has done the same for the plastic arts; both have been important in the theatre), and enters into other cultural domains such as religion, philosophy, science, ethics, and politics. It may equally well be considered as a sport or as a therapy. Surveys (presumably culture-specific) have indicated that 'we are ten times more likely to be seen sharing a moment of laughter than any other form of strong emotion'.[2] Laughter can be considered in terms of both quantity and quality: it is a common, shared experience, and is also, like art and sport, amenable to the search for perfection. Furthermore, it can reveal personality: show me what you laugh at, and I can tell who you are.

Laughter as a (supreme) challenge for science

Laughter as a challenge for science may be apprehended in two stages: the general challenge of emotions as objects of study for the natural sciences; and within the category of emotions, the special challenge of laughter.

The scientific study of emotions runs against a persistent, profound trend. Scientific objectivity has been encapsulated in one injunction: Avoid emotions![3] Distrust of human unreliability (in observations, measurements, computation) has led to an ever more mechanical conception of objectivity, with photographs, for instance, replacing artistic drawings. In academic circles, scientific rationality is recurrently and systematically opposed to the emotionality of the general public. Moreover, the suspicion of emotion has been so deeply felt that it also extends into a suspicion of the study of emotions, as if the topic were somehow infectious, and compromising.

During the last twenty years, however, a number of scholarly studies have undertaken a rehabilitation of the subject, under the general theme of 'the rationality of emotion'.[4] Emotions have been vindicated as adequate mechanisms for the preservation of the self, and the maintenance of its vital equilibria. They allow for the expression of valuable past experience, either innate (stored in memory through phylogenetic legacy) or acquired during life. It is true that emotional reactions may be ambiguous or misleading (for instance, panic in crowds) or foolish (fits of the giggles), but the point is that a weakening of the capacity to react emotionally may also be the cause of irrational behaviour. Emotions are depositories of much life-saving wisdom. Indeed, emotions have strong special links with memory acquisition: a recent popular survey article was aptly entitled (in translation): 'Deprived of emotions, memory fails'.[5]

Behind the obstacle of prejudices (which are now at least partly overcome thanks to the emergence of the 'affective sciences' alongside the older-established cognitive sciences) there subsist deep and lasting difficulties.

Emotions, at least in humans, may be described as involving three levels: instinctive reflexes, unconscious mental processes, and conscious feelings. Emotional feelings are an essential constitutive core of consciousness, and conscious feelings are an important dimension of our emotional experiences. Between emotions and consciousness the links are thus reciprocal and strong. But consciousness implies subjectivity. To what extent is an objective study of subjectivity possible? Is the scientific study of emotions intrinsically hampered and limited by their subjective dimensions?

The repertoire of emotions is vast, and a bit fuzzy. The classification and precise definition of distinct emotions, and their grouping into subcategories, are still under discussion. As an example, some authors would identify six primary emotions — happiness, sadness, fear, anger, surprise, disgust — and distinguish them from other (secondary, or social) emotions such as embarrassment, jealousy, guilt, or pride.[6]

For several reasons, the emotion of fear figures as a prominent one, and it has been selected as a choice target for study.[7] Its function (survival value) is easily identified: mobilization against danger. In contrast, the function of laughter is not so evident, a priori. Arthur Koestler went so far as to call it the 'luxury reflex', 'unique in that it serves no apparent purpose'.[8] That statement seems excessive, if only because of the variety of trades where professionals do make a direct, profitable living out of being funny: comedians, clowns, satirists, cartoonists, etc. But why and under what circumstances does this funniness elicit bursts of laughter as opposed to the more subdued response of smiling?

For many emotions, such as fear or anger, analogous behaviour is found in a large number of animal species, but this is less obviously so for laughter. It has been said that laughter, like speech, is uniquely human: *risus proprium hominis*. This statement also seems excessive. Actually, a coherent and plausible scheme can be traced to show the evolutionary origins of laughter: from universal mechanisms of non–self–detection (which serve to defend the body surface) to reciprocal tickling and rough–and–tumble play (in mammals), to vocalization and panting (in chimpanzees). This helps to explain the odd mixture of components (touching and tickling, vocal communication, social play, appeasement) whose vestiges continue to be observable in our own behaviour. What remains unaccounted for, however, is the huge gap between the instinctive act of laughing and the higher (cognitive, ethical) forms of humour.

The mind/body mix of laughter is challenging because of its amplitude, ranging from strongly physical to highly mental, from orgasmic to spiritual. In this regard, a comparison between laughter and love commends itself. 'It is infinitely less simple to love than Nature would pretend when it entrusts its tools to the first hamfisted newcomer'; 'the moment of love may be a feather fallen from the wing of an angel, or of a goose'.[9] There is a similar ambivalence in the case of laughter.

Incidentally, this analogy may be pursued to generate intriguing hypotheses. In recent millennia, the reproductive function of sex within the human species has been well understood. But this function was not recognized by our earlier ancestors, before they discovered the relationship between sex and pregnancy. Could there similarly be a yet unperceived function of laughter? An inverse conjecture may also be contemplated. If the current phase of dissociation between sex and reproduction continues, it may happen that our offspring will eventually consider the act of love as an evolutionary fossil — as awkward perhaps as the act of laughter today, when it takes us by surprise.

The evolutionary origins of laughter

A recent work by Robert Provine offers a plausible solution to the puzzle, where each step of the evolutionary story makes sense:

> The basic mechanism of tickle is the nonself detector that operates by subtracting out stimuli produced by our own movements, leaving only those having an external, unpredictable origin that we interpret as tickle.

The detection and removal of nonself moving objects on our body surface (parasites, predators, and aggressors) are crucial, and the tickle response is part of this process. Vulnerable body areas are the most ticklish and are the most vigorously defended.

The evolutionary history of tickle, physical play, and laughter are intertwined, with tickle and play predating laughter. Laughter began as a ritualization of the panting sound of rowdy play of which tickle was a trigger and central component. In the great apes, laughter was emancipated from its original context in the labored breathing of play, the heavy panting now signaling playful intent or anticipation, even when the ongoing level of activity does not demand labored breathing. The laughter of chimpanzees and other nonhuman great apes maintains its ancient pantlike character and association with physical play. Human laughter is a further ritualization (second-order ritualization) in which 'ha-ha' is one step removed from the ape pant-laugh and is elicited by a wider range of stimuli, including conversation and the consciously produced and task-oriented cognitive contrivance of humor. Whether the 'pant-pant' of apes or the more abstract 'ha-ha' of humans, the acoustic structure of laughter is rooted in the respiratory sounds of physical play. *There is nothing arbitrary about the sound of laughter in humans and other great apes.*

The path between tickle and humor is more tortuous and uncertain.[10]

Note that the dictionaries contain a rich set of suggestive animal names containing the element 'laughing' (laughing hyena, jackass, bird, crow, goose, thrush, etc.), which is likely to be a mock anthropomorphic qualification.

Laughter and the brain

What are the neural correlates of laughter? What is happening in the brain of someone who laughs? What are the areas and pathways involved?

Over a decade ago, in a general review article aimed at physicists, I presented the challenge of a neuronal theory of humour in these terms:

> One of the charms of biology is that its objects of study have a meaning; they are here because they have been preserved by evolution, because they fulfil a function; they have been sorted and selected. Whereas the materials of physics and chemistry often owe their existence to sheer inertia, if not to the arbitrary and artificial creation of the scientist.
>
> When moreover these biological objects subserve thought, and the higher functions of the brain, our interest is further enhanced. However, attempts to explain the mind by starting from the brain meet with limited success. In fact we have an intuitive, immediate knowledge of our consciousness, compared to which neuro-psychological explanations often appear as heavy and cumbersome as the jargon of Molière's doctors. A neuronal theory of humour would no doubt be monumentally ludicrous. A contemporary mathematician has summed it up well: 'It happens that nature lacks wit. This is the ground which physics exploits.'[11]

In the mid-1990s, a tool-driven revolution occurred in the study of the brain, with the advent of functional magnetic resonance imaging (fMRI). For the study of emotions, this new technique has been a fruitful addition to previous experimental tools such as EEG (electro-encephalography), PET (positron-electron tomography), or skin conductivity measurements. Functional MRI has a convenient space and time resolution for monitoring relevant changes of activity in various areas of the brain during dynamic events such as reacting to the telling of jokes.[12] The method is non-invasive, and is best suited to large brains, such as those of humans. Limitations still exist, however, because the set-up is such that the head of the experimental subject must stay motionless inside the scanning apparatus. As a consequence, the act of laughter remains muted because it is prevented from developing fully: the essence of laughter proves wild and hard to capture!

In 1998 a curious discovery was reported in the correspondence section of *Nature* by a team of Californian surgeons. While applying electrodes to the left frontal lobe of an epileptic girl in order to locate the focus of her seizures, they found an unexpected result:

> Although there is considerable information on the neuronal representation of speech, little is known about brain mechanisms of laughter. Here we report that electrical stimulation in the anterior part of the human supplementary motor area (SMA) can elicit laughter. This area is also involved in the initiation of speech and has been shown to have increased activity in people who stutter.
> The duration and intensity of laughter increased with the level of stimulation current. At low currents only a smile was present, while at higher currents a robust contagious laughter was induced.[13]

Stimulation studies in the surrounding vicinity suggest that the investigated brain area accommodates specialized functions for speech, manual dexterity, and laughter. This chance observation is to be compared with findings obtained from other, more standard modes of investigation (such as lesion studies, functional imaging, etc.), which report the activation of several distinct areas elsewhere in the brain.

What is surprising? What remains mysterious?

Embodiment and infectiousness

More than a century ago, William James drew attention to the embodiment of emotions with his famous question: Do we run from the bear because we are afraid, or are we afraid because we run?[14] In our case the question might be rendered as: Do we laugh because we feel merry, or do we feel merry because we laugh? Or more bluntly: Do we start laughing before we are aware of what it is about?

The compelling contagiousness of laughter provides test cases where James's theory is clearly validated. In a 'fit of the giggles' we do begin laughing before knowing what it is about, and indeed in the absence of any mental motivation whatever.

Yawning and coughing are two other instinctive acts where contagion is commonly observed. One hypothesis that attempts to explain such automatic behaviour is that the human brain contains two dedicated neural circuits, serving respectively as (perceptual) laugh-detector and (motor) laugh-generator. Perceptual stimulation of the laugh-detector would facilitate (and under favourable circumstances, actually trigger) arousal of the laugh-generator, and therefore (re-)production of the act. This hypothesis is potentially testable for laughter (though not easily), and also for other similar stereotypes of instinctive behaviour.

The act and its aftermath

Observation shows a whole continuum of behavioural modes associated with laughter and smiling. In this section I attempt to focus on the ideal essence of laughter: its limit form, so to speak, in contradistinction to smiling. Analysis will be restricted to the individual person engaged in the act of laughing. I distinguish two phases: the act itself, and its aftermath.

The first (motor) phase may be described as a sudden spasm: 'a nervous convulsion, an involuntary spasm comparable to sneezing', as Baudelaire described it.[15] It is 'sudden' in that the act is (ideally) surprising, unexpected, unintended, involuntary. It is a 'spasm' or seizure, because it is an explosive shaking, an exuberant burst, an uncontrolled jolt. In these respects, laughter may be compared to some extent with sneezing and hiccupping (note that while these two are not contagious, they do tend to elicit laughter or at least a smile among observers).

The motor phase is followed by an uplifting aftermath, and leaves a memory trace. 'Uplifting', because a mood of high spirits is reached, involving feelings of liberation, domination, elevation, exaltation. The stronger the act, the higher the mood, and the deeper the mnesic trace. The height of the mood and the depth of the trace may be considered as medium-term and long-term internal rewards, and therefore as inner measures of the success of the act of laughter.

What? How? Why?

Many of the natural and social sciences, and indeed the arts, are involved in this cluster of questions about mental causes, processes, and functions. A few insights are presented here for the benefit of further discussion.

• What makes us laugh?

Apart from straight stimuli (tickle, drugs, contagion, etc.), three classes of causes have received special attention:

1. Relief of tension, détente: 'Laughter comes from an expectation which suddenly resolves into nothing' (Kant); 'In laughter there is above all a movement of release of tension, often remarked upon, of which we must seek the cause'; laughter 'provides rest from the fatigue of thinking' (Bergson).[16] 'Comic relief' has become an idiom in English.

2. A sudden connection: A sudden connection or juxtaposition may be established between two previously distant domains. This causal process is methodically used in verbal jokes, where the role of the punch-line is to introduce a new way of seeing things, associated with another mental set. Laughter may also be called forth by the sheer incongruity of a chain of absurd, grotesque, delirious ramblings. Humour then appears as a form of creativity, analogous to artistic inventions, strokes of genius, and scientific breakthroughs. Laughter can be seen as a mind/body shortcut that echoes some perceived or imagined shortcut in the outside world. About mental juxtapositions in aesthetics, Kundera had this remark: 'The idea came to him that beauty is the spark that flies when, suddenly, across the years, two different ages meet. Beauty sweeps away chronological time; it is a revolt against time.'[17]

3. A manifesto of domination, of the exaltation of the self: 'A sudden glory arising from some sudden conception of some eminency in ourselves, by comparison with the infirmity of others, or with our own previously' (Hobbes).[18] For the better (for example, ultimate resistance to an adverse destiny) or for the worse (scorn, disdain).

Note that these three schemes all invoke similar feelings of ascendancy, either because an obstacle has suddenly collapsed, or because we have managed to contemplate a scene from above.

- How do we laugh?

Laughter, in humans, is a vocal and noisy act that interferes with verbal communication. 'Laughter is not serious' because it tends to disrupt serial trains of thought and especially the linear flow of linguistic emission and reception. To this extent, the disruptive character of human laughter appears as a novel dimension, compared to animal behaviour.

In situations of play or appeasement, animal laughter serves as a form of sustained communication, and in occasional situations (for instance, between two people who do not share a common language) human laughter may revert to a similar use, as a substitute for dialogue, in association with gesture.

- Why do we laugh?

The general function of emotions has already been mentioned. Laughter is a pleasurable emotion. Its purported medical virtues and curative functions have been discussed and commented for centuries, with a revival of both theory and practice during recent decades.

- Is there a reproductive value of laughter, linked to gender differences and the observation that 'boys make girls laugh'?[19] (Note that the Bible associates laughter and unusual fecundity, in the story of Isaac, the son of laughing centenarians, in Genesis.)

Bergson emphasised the social, corrective function of laughter:

Laughter is above all a corrective [for unacceptable behaviour]. [...] Society thereby gets its revenge for liberties that have been taken with it. [...] We laugh each time that a person gives us the impression of being a thing.[20]

Laughter is conformist for Bergson, but rebellious for Freud, who traced its links with childhood, dreams, and repressed impulses, seeing it in terms of relaxation of constraints, dream displacements, and removal of inhibitions.

An interlude, about mysteries

At this stage we may note that several features of laughter still remain puzzling, even when hints and arguments have been produced. Fortunately, science is unlikely ever to explain laughter away!

Many questions remain open: gender differences; the hypothesis of dedicated neural circuits; the connections between laughter and speech, laughter and music, laughter and health, etc.

The deepest mysteries of laughter seem to be related to the boundaries unconscious/conscious, passive/voluntary. Baudelaire, in his considerations on the essence of laughter, evokes its strange attributes:

> [In caricature, certain works] contain a mysterious, durable, eternal element, which recommends them to the attention of artists. What a curious and noteworthy thing it is, this introduction of the intangible element of beauty into works designed to show man his own moral and physical ugliness! And what is no less mysterious is that this lamentable spectacle arouses in him an immortal and incorrigible hilarity.
>
> [...] the comic is one of the clearest satanic marks of man, and one of the numerous pips in the symbolic apple.
>
> [...] as laughter is essentially human, it is essentially contradictory, that is to say that it is the sign both of an infinite greatness and of an infinite wretchedness: the latter is infinite in relation to the absolute Being of which he has the conception, the former is infinite in relation to the animals. It is from the perpetual clash of these two infinites that laughter is born.[21]

The novelist Milan Kundera, heir to the Czech tradition of humour, in bringing to bear his experience of the challenge of survival under a totalitarian regime, has traced new ways of approaching the intricate ambiguities (tragi–comic, angel–devil, memory–oblivion, etc.) of love and laughter.[22] Many of his short stories are lucid illustrations of the potential wisdom of these two emotions, as disruptive antidotes to a madly serious doctrine.

The genuinely liberating capacity of laughter deserves further mention. Any attempt at explaining laughter (that is, making it plain), or at circumscribing it within closed limits will provide the motivation for a new salvo of humour. An illustrative allegory for this indomitable property has been given by Umberto Eco in his medieval detective novel *The Name of the Rose*. Fearful of the subversive, satanic power of laughter, the blind librarian monk, Jorge, has tried to keep secret in his monastery the only surviving copy of Aristotle's lost treatise on comedy. Professional respect for books has prevented him from destroying the manuscript; however, as a measure of additional safety against dissemination, he has poisoned its pages. When the book is about to be discovered by an erudite and inventive fellow monk, Jorge resolves on a supreme move, in order to eradicate the pagan treatise that threatens to provide scholarly support for laughter: he eats the accursed manuscript and, in his triumph, punctuates his definitive victory ... with a burst of laughter.

In addition to their shared property of suspending speech, the mysteries of laughter have some affinities with those of music. In a vibrant sentence, the anthropologist Claude Lévi-Strauss stressed the mysteries and paradoxes of music, which, he claimed, 'hold the key to progress' for the human sciences:

> That music should be a language for elaborating messages, some of which are understood by the immense majority, while only a tiny minority are capable of producing them; and that out of all languages, this one alone should possess the contradictory characteristics of being intelligible and yet untranslatable at the same time; makes of the music maker a god-like being, and of music itself the supreme mystery of the human sciences, against which they stumble, and which holds the key to their progress.[23]

Music has been defined by Stendhal as a memory of the happiness of youth, and by Adorno as a promise of reconciliation. Remarkably, these two definitions seem to be equally applicable to laughter. At a symbolic level, the word 'amusement' suggests a link between mirth and music.

Furthermore, the ancient saying 'la musique adoucit les mœurs' ('music tempers manners') recalls Bergson's 'nothing disarms like laughter'. A disarming power reminiscent of the might of the trumpets in the Bible: 'and the walls of Jericho came tumbling down'.

Laughter at its best

On 30 December 1941 Winston Churchill addressed the Canadian Parliament. As he retraced the harsh beginnings of the war, he reached this point:

> On top of all this, came the great French catastrophe. The French army collapsed, and the French nation was dashed into utter — and it has proved so far, irretrievable — confusion. When I warned them that Britain would fight on alone, whatever they did, their generals told their Prime Minister and his divided cabinet: 'In three weeks England will have her neck wrung like a chicken!'
> 'Some chicken!' (cheers)
> 'Some neck!' (roars of bursting laughter)[24]

The generalities of the previous sections may be tested on this special example, in order to probe its ingredients (preparation, release; the genie encapsulated in the bottle). It is more than a decade since I first stumbled on this example. Since then, the perfect condensation of the last two syllables ('some neck!') has been an inexhaustible source of wonder.

Emboldened by the previous example, let us enlarge the scope and dare to propose a description of laughter at its best. In the absence of the act of laughter, what would have been missing? What does laughter signal and provoke?

Successful laughter signals a powerful invocation of past experience in a new situation; and it imprints a deep mnesic trace. At such a pitch, laughter is a manifestation of vivacity, associated with reinforcement of the self (through affirmation and expansion).

Conversely, the loss of the sense of humour is an ominous symptom. One's mood falls prey to being invaded by enduring pathological affects (depression, irritability, etc.). Observation of the dire effects of such a loss and fall shows that laughter is indeed a vital affair. Laughter shakes out of traps.

With the critical distance and fresh vision that it implies, humour appears as a guardian against obsessions and mental confinements.

An attempt to circumscribe the reducible and the irreducible

Emil Du Bois-Reymond contrasted the provisional 'ignoramus' (we do not (yet) know) of the physical scientist and the definitive 'ignorabimus' (we shall never know) of the metaphysician.[25]

Concerning life and the mind, there is a 'fundamentalist' attitude, widespread among scientists, that holds firstly that the only valid knowledge is science, and secondly that science means the reduction of a phenomenon to the properties of its material elements. Anything that resists such reduction is called 'metaphysical'. The temptation is then to consider that metaphysics, so defined, is altogether futile, and that our ideas about 'irreducible' entities can only be myths or illusions.

The psychologist Donald Hebb defined such a doctrine of eliminative reductionism as the 'nothing-but' fallacy:

> What has given reductionism a bad name is the conclusion, after a theoretical analysis of a mental variable has been made and it is 'reduced' to some pattern of neural activity, that the mental process in effect no longer exists. This is the nothing-but fallacy: Mental activity is a myth, what 'really' exists is something in the brain.
>
> When a complex is reduced, theoretically, to its component parts, the whole still exists. Anxiety must be a set of neurons in action in the limbic system, but the whole is as real as the individual neurons. [26]

Is 'life' an illusion, because living matter is 'nothing but' interacting molecules? Over the past two centuries, biology managed to acquire its autonomy as a discipline, despite the reluctance of many physicists, who tried to impose their disciplinary methods and norms (equations of motion, predictions starting from initial conditions, etc.). Other forms of knowledge that did not fit within these schemes, such as Darwin's theory of evolution, were deemed to be unscientific.

Nowadays, this debate is largely superseded because, thanks to the development of ecology and bioethics, it has been acknowledged (in universal declarations) that the present human generation has a responsibility towards future generations, including the duty to preserve life and biodiversity. In the process, life has acquired a dignity of its own.

Attention has shifted from the life–matter debate to the mind–body controversy, which pits neuroscientists and other similar experts against those in the human sciences, arts, and humanities. Transposing the older physical fundamentalism to their own disciplinary level, some neurobiologists have expressed a plain reductionist attitude towards the higher mental faculties. 'Man no longer has anything to do with the "mind", it is enough for him to be a Neuronal Man.'[27]

Is human dignity then an illusion? What about moral conscience? Freewill? Consciousness?

If they are not just arbitrary constructions, myths, or illusions, if they have some real existence, what are the proper ways to study these entities?

Laughter is clearly a domain in which many approaches converge. My claim here is that laughter, taken as an object of study, offers an attractive field for observing the boundaries between scientific disciplines, the limits of science, the interplay between science and other forms of knowledge, and the dialogue of cultures. This field opens up important issues of epistemology and ethics.

Studies of laughter, in its manifold dimensions, raise the most basic questions. What can I know? What should I do? What may I hope?

My approach will now focus on the triangle of science, laughter and ethics.

Laughter and science

Science and society

Here are two examples of laughter from ancient Greece:

> Thales was observing the stars, and while he was gazing at the sky, he fell into a hole. A witty servant-girl from Thrace laughed at him, saying that he was so concerned to know what happened in the sky, that he did not care about what was in front of his feet.[28]

The absent-minded professor has become a classic comic character in popular imagery: 'le savant Cosinus' (by 'Christophe', 1890s), Hergé's Professor Calculus (originally 'Tournesol'), and so on. Abstraction, distraction.

In contrast stands the attitude of Democritus, the 'laughing philosopher', who was provoked to hilarity by observing the activities of his countrymen. In a recent book about science and public opinion, Bernadette Bensaude-Vincent brings together these two examples which, whether apocryphal or not, may be viewed as early manifestations of the famous gap between science and society.[29]

An outsider (a dissident) versus an established society: laughter can flow both ways. Thales and Democritus have a long progeny: Don Quixote, Molière's Misanthrope, etc.

Inside the scientific community itself, a situation of tension recurs between non-conformist individuals (precursors, innovators, whistleblowers, etc.) and established hierarchies (entrenched disciplines or castes, fossilized institutions, etc.). Proper status and adequate treatment for non-conformity is a permanent issue in science. 'Every true scientist should undoubtedly muster sufficient courage and integrity to resist the temptation and the habit of conformity' (Sakharov).[30]

Scientific breakthroughs and shortcuts

'Thought is only a flash of lightning in the middle of a long night, but the flash is everything': this striking description of the creative process, by the mathematician Henri Poincaré, is reproduced on the medals awarded by the French Centre national de la recherche scientifique (CNRS).

In a smart, polemical article about the hierarchical structure of science, the physicist P. W. Anderson criticized an earlier statement that each scientist should 'cultivate [his] own valley, and not attempt to build roads over the mountain ranges [...] between the sciences': 'Rather,' he said, 'we should recognize that such roads, while often the quickest shortcut to another part of our own science, are not visible from the viewpoint of one science alone'.[31] The words used (quick, shortcut, viewpoint) make evident an affinity between such processes of scientific breakthrough and the cognitive forms of laughter. Indeed, science and humour at their best are intelligent activites, in the etymological sense (intelligere = interligere = interlink). It has even been suggested that laughter blocks other emotions and thereby 'speaks to pure intelligence' (Bergson). Moreover, as an avenue to knowledge, laughter 'has the advantage of always seeking fresh perspectives'.[32]

The DNA double helix: a ludicrously simple trick?

Scientific investigations lead to occasional surprises. Sometimes because of the discovery of radically new phenomena, which require counter-intuitive concepts: quantum theory is an excellent illustration of this kind of surprise. Sometimes because the solution to the problem turns out to be much simpler than expected: in this case, the sudden vanishing of a mystery may induce reactions of laughter among researchers.

A posthumous book by Max Delbrück, a physicist turned biologist, contains a neat description of what is probably the most remarkable experience in this second category. Niels Bohr, the physicist, had been one of the most imaginative theoreticians of quantum theory. He came to expect that new and revolutionary concepts might also prove necessary in the study of biology and psychology.

> With respect to biology, Bohr proposed in his 1932 lecture 'Light and Life' that life might not be reducible to atomic physics. He suggested that there might be a complementarity relation between the physiological and physical aspects of life analogous to that obtaining for the wave and particle aspects of the electron. In that case there would exist a sort of uncertainty principle of biology. [...]
>
> Bohr thus suggests another conspiracy of nature. This suggestion made many biologists, especially biochemists, as uneasy as the uncertainty principle of quantum mechanics had made many physicists. In fact Bohr's suggestion turned out to be wrong. [...]
>
> It might be said that Watson and Crick's discovery of the DNA double helix in 1953 did for biology what many physicists had hoped in vain could be done for atomic physics: it solved all the mysteries in terms of classical models and theories, without forcing us to abandon our intuitive notions about truth and reality. Upon the discovery of the DNA double helix, the mystery of gene replication was revealed as a ludicrously simple trick. In people who had expected a deep solution to the deep problem of how in the living world like begets like it raised a feeling similar to the embarrassment one feels when shown a simple solution to a chess problem with which one has struggled in vain for a long time.[33]

Science is (potentially) a playful game, a competitive sport where goal-scoring triggers cheers.

Opening jokes and concise formulae

Communication is a key component of scientific activity. For an oral presentation, it is important to capture the attention and goodwill of an impatient and sceptical audience from the outset. From my collection of souvenirs, here is one opening joke which approached optimal efficiency in its context (the talk was scheduled in the middle of a long and tiring session): 'As the sultan said to his fourth wife: I'll be brief'.

Such an opening sentence establishes a moral contract: the audience will grant its attention in return for the speaker's promise of brevity. In science, the principle of parsimony has been explicitly praised since Occam's razor in the fourteenth century, perhaps particularly among theoreticians, for whom it often becomes a driving incentive in their search for perfection.

A formula is, etymologically, a little form. Mathematical formulae often consist of equations of the type $x = 0$, where x may be a complex expression. If x is particularly cumbersome and incomprehensible, the appearance of the final zero may trigger laughter. Cartoonists have imagined many variations on this theme. The relief of laughter conforms here ideally to the Kantian definition in terms of the sudden annihilation of an expectation.

Wit is also summoned to grace the end of scientific talks, and to aid the recall of their main thrust. 'There always comes a moment when the essence of a theory that seemed very abstruse is explained in three words by a man of wit' (Valéry).[34]

In brief, laughter serves to punctuate scientific talks. Initial laughter clears and resets the hearers' minds, dispels apprehensions, and establishes trust. Final laughter makes recall easy and pleasurable.

The saving friend of science

Abstraction and reduction are instruments of science that become dangerous when wielded as tools of radical elimination. Emotion-free and value-free science is thus a potential source of peril. In this context, it is worth recognizing that among the emotions, laughter appears again as the best friend of science. It may even help to reconcile science and ethics.

Ethics and laughter

There has been a long philosophical tradition stressing the evil, nasty practices of laughter. Ronald de Sousa, in his 1991 book *The Rationality of Emotion*, chose to address the question 'When is it wrong to laugh?' as a first step towards a general theory of ethics and the emotions. The basic potential ambivalence of laughter is here taken as admitted, and we attempt to explore further some aspects of its relationship to ethics.

'Castigat ridendo mores'

Because of its double-edged potency, laughter may serve either as a corrective to non-conformity (literally: eccentricity, enormity), or as an irreverent rebellion against the establishment with its vanities and abuses. For both insiders and outsiders, getting the laughs on your side is a consideration in any public debate about forms of society, changes in social norms, and so on.

Charlie Chaplin's films are masterpieces in this respect, and in Churchill's speech quoted earlier, laughter was used as a moral weapon.

My personal experience as a member of the newly created ethics committee (Comité d'éthique pour les sciences) of the CNRS has made me aware that humour is a necessary antidote to the perversion of ethics. The main risk for such a committee is hypocrisy, which may take two forms: the Charybdis of excess (over-zealous puritanism), or the Scylla of uselessness (ineffectual sham). When I decided to write an introductory book on the ethics of science, it soon became clear that it would have to include humorous drawings in order to keep a proper balance: the chosen artist was the famous American cartoonist Sidney Harris, a satirical observer of the scientific community. [35]

Juxtaposition, conflict, clash

Since it is concerned with arbitration between conflicting logics, values, interests, and allegiances, ethical reflection requires a capacity for comparative examination from different viewpoints. In real life, ethics often demands rapid choices, when decisions about action cannot wait.

In these two respects (the juxtaposition of widely separated domains, and the need for rapid resolution), deep connections appear between ethics and laughter. The quotation from Baudelaire pointed to the contradictory essence of laughter and the clash which gives rise to it. With equal relevance, similar comments might be made about the contradictory essence of ethics, and the tension from which decisions emerge.

Moral indignation

According to Paul Ricœur, ethics is the concern for a good life, with and for others, within just institutions. He also points to the existence of an 'essential and mysterious thing', namely moral indignation.[36]

Moral indignation is an emotion. It may be strongly expressed, although I have never seen it listed alongside anger or disgust. As the etymology indicates, moral indignation is closely associated with the concept of human dignity, which is now universally acknowledged as the foundation of human rights. Like any other emotion, moral indignation may occasionally be misguided and irrational. But in a person who never shows any moral indignation, as in one who is totally devoid of laughter, something essential is missing. This analogy may be pursued further.

Expressions of moral emotion, like expressions of mirth, may cover a wide range, including muted and covert forms of dissidence (aloofness; withdrawal; conscientious objection; silent resistance, as for example in Vercors's wartime story *Le Silence de la mer*) which may be compared with smiling. In its strongest form, that of the 'sursaut', moral indignation becomes a sudden spasm, akin to laughter.

Laughter preceded speech, but then evolved to become a major punctuating element and control tool of verbal communication. Moral indignation may have developed a similar relationship to ethical deliberation and decision making.

There are several respects in which moral indignation appears as even more human and more mysterious than laughter. Our intuition that there are deep affinities between these two major qualities of the human mind is supported by Molière's masterpiece *Le Misanthrope*. This play holds a unique position in his repertoire, on the border between comedy and tragedy. The delicate and flexible interplay between these two similar yet conflicting emotions allows for a wide range of interpretations on the stage.

Effects and causes

'God laughs at those creatures who deplore the effects when they continue to cherish the causes' (Bossuet).[37] Rationality attempts to relate effects to their true causes. A concern for causality in the realm of the natural sciences translates, quite reasonably, into a concern for responsibility in the realm of ethics. Bossuet's maxim dates from an age when the modern, Western divorces between science and religion, science, and ethics had not yet been both promulgated.

From another perspective, this sentence might be construed as an attempt to define several attributes of divinity: acumen, exaltation–jubilation, serenity.

Closing remarks

In his recent works which emphasize the role of 'body and emotion in the making of consciousness', the neurobiologist Antonio Damasio quotes a remarkable maxim of Spinoza: 'The effort to preserve the self is the prime and sole foundation of virtue'.[38]

At first glance, this statement appears paradoxical, because virtue and ethics are associated not with egoism but with altruism. Yet the evolutionary story of laughter, from detection of non-self, to tickling, social play and so on, tentative as it is, does offer a plausible solution to the conundrum of how virtue might have emerged from selfishness.

Laughter has been a key helper and adjuvant in the scientific enterprise. One subtle reason for this may be that laughter is the emotion that allows an escape from the hold of other emotions, and thereby opens up the way to 'pure intelligence'.

Laughter enhances vitality in two main ways. It acts as a control on emotive and cognitive tensions, in such areas as speech and thought, mental effort, moral questioning, and affective deadlock, and thus provides comfort and relief. And when fully enfolding, laughter brings reconciliation (or the promise thereof) between mind and body, cognition and emotion, self and non-self.

Notes to Chapter 17

Unattributed translations from French originals are by the editors.

1. *The Shorter Oxford English Dictionary* (Oxford: Clarendon Press, 1973).
2. See J. McCrone, 'Comic Relief', *New Scientist*, 27 May 2000, 32–36.
3. M. Midgley, 'Being Objective', *Nature*, 12 Apr. 2001, 753.
4. R. de Sousa, *The Rationality of Emotion* (Cambridge, MA, and London: MIT Press, 1991).
5. M. Meunier, 'Privée d'émotions, la mémoire flanche', *La Recherche*, no. 344 (July–Aug. 2001), 82–84.
6. See A. Damasio, *Descartes' Error: Emotion, Reason and the Human Brain* (New York: Putnam, 1994).
7. See J. LeDoux, *The Emotional Brain: The Mysterious Underpinnings of Emotional Life* (London: Weidenfeld and Nicolson, 1998).
8. Arthur Koestler, *The Act of Creation* (New York: Macmillan, 1984).
9. Robert Musil, *The Man without Qualities* (1930–43), Eng. trans. by E. Wilkins and E. Kaiser (London: Secker & Warburg, 1953–60); Musil quotes a poem by Lichtenberg.
10. See R. R. Provine, *Laughter: A Scientific Investigation* (London: Faber, 2000).
11. G. Toulouse, 'Réseaux de neurones et théories du cerveau', *Bulletin de la Société française de physique*, 79 (Jan 1991), 8–11.
12. See V. Goel and R. Dolan, 'The Functional Anatomy of Humor: Segregating Cognitive and Affective Components', *Nature Neuroscience* (Mar. 2001), 237–38.
13. I. Fried and others, 'Electric Current Stimulates Laughter', *Nature*, 12 Feb. 1998, 650.
14. W. James, *The Principles of Psychology* (London: Macmillan, 1890).

15. C. Baudelaire, 'De l'essence du rire' (1852), in *Curiosités esthétiques* (Paris: Michel Lévy, 1868).
16. I. Kant, *Critique of Judgement*, II, E 307, quoted by H. Bergson in *Le Rire. Essai sur la signification du comique* (Paris: Félix Alcan, 1900).
17. M. Kundera, *The Book of Laughter and Forgetting* (1978), Eng. trans. by M. H. Heim (New York: Knopf, 1980); see also *The Joke* (1965; Eng. trans. by Heim, 1982), and *Laughable Loves* (1969; Eng. trans. by S. Rappaport, 1974).
18. T. Hobbes, *The Elements of Law Natural and Politic* (1640), IX.13.
19. Provine, *Laughter*.
20. Bergson, *Le Rire*.
21. Baudelaire, 'De l'essence du rire'.
22. Kundera, *Book of Laughter and Forgetting*.
23. C. Lévi-Strauss, *Le Cru et le cuit* (Paris: Plon, 1964).
24. Speech to Canadian Parliament, Ottawa, 30 Dec. 1941. In *Churchill in his Own Voice*. Audio cassette, Caedman 52018/2c. 1965.
25. E. Du Bois-Reymond, *Über die Grenzen des Naturerkennens* (Leipzig: Veit, 1872).
26. D. O. Hebb, *An Essay on Mind* (Hillsdale, NJ: Lawrence Erlbaum, 1980).
27. J.-P. Changeux, *L'Homme neuronal* (Paris: Fayard, 1983).
28. Plato, *Theaetetus*.
29. B. Bensaude-Vincent, *L'Opinion publique et la science. A chacun son ignorance* (Paris: Institut d'édition Sanofi-Synthélabo, 2000).
30. *Andrei Sakharov from Exile* (New York: International League for Human Rights, 1983).
31. P. W. Anderson, 'More is Different: Broken Symmetry and the Nature of the Hierarchical Structure of Science', *Science*, 177 (1972), 393–96; repr. in *Biology and Computation: A Physicist's Choice*, ed. by H. Gutfreund and G. Toulouse (Singapore: World Scientific, 1994).
32. De Sousa, *Rationality of Emotion*.
33. M. Delbrück, *Mind from Matter? An Essay on Evolutionary Epistemology* (Oxford: Blackwell Scientific Publications, 1986).
34. Paul Valéry. It has not been possible to find the exact source of this quotation.
35. G. Toulouse, *Regards sur l'éthique des sciences* (Paris: Hachette, 1998).
36. See e.g. Paul Ricœur, *Soi-même comme un autre* (Paris: Seuil, 1990).
37. Bossuet, *Sermons et oraisons funèbres*.
38. Damasio, *Descartes' Error*, quoting Spinoza, *Ethics*, IV.xxii (cf. IV.xxiv, v.xli); cf. A. Damasio, *Looking for Spinoza: Joy, Sorrow, and the Feeling Brain* (New York: Harcourt Education, 2003).

INDEX